PRAISE FOR

MW01285253

"Over the course of my career helping large companies identify and develop talent, from the frontlines all the way up to senior executives, I've seen first-hand how often organizations, even the most sophisticated ones, get hiring wrong. Despite the stakes, too many organizations still rely on gut instinct over structured interviews, fall prey to internal biases, and lack consistency in how they evaluate talent. *The Hiring Handbook* is a clear, evidence-based guide that demystifies what great hiring actually looks like. It's a must-read for any leader serious about attracting and selecting the right people—and setting them up to succeed."
Larry Emond, Senior Partner, Modern Executive Solutions, and former Managing Partner, Gallup

"When it comes to hiring, Kasey Harboe Guentert and Mollie Berke really know their stuff, and have the know-how and savviness to guide HR professionals through every possible nuance throughout the hiring supply chain. It's strategy, ops, and real-world examples all in one place. *The Hiring Handbook* is a definitive resource in embedding fair, legal, and inclusive hiring practices into every stage of talent acquisition. As someone who has spent decades working with Global 500 organizations to align DEI with business outcomes, I can affirm that this guide uniquely bridges strategy and execution. For HR leaders seeking to build truly inclusive teams while maintaining rigor, this handbook is a must-have!"
Andrés Tapia, Senior Partner and Global DE&I Strategist, Korn Ferry, and author of *The Inclusion Paradox*

"Hiring is the most important thing your organization will do. This new book takes a comprehensive look at the entire hiring process and translates technical and complex topics into friendly and accessible short chapters. The ideas and approaches shared here are supported by hard evidence and illustrated with stories, samples, and practical tools. This book will be especially helpful for entrepreneurs and small-to-medium-sized business owners looking to level up their hiring game!"
Alexis Fink, former VP, People Analytics, Meta, and author of *Investing in People*

"How and who you hire is vitally important to every company's success, but this mission-critical process often runs on messy autopilot. Thankfully, two thoughtful, seasoned assessment professionals have stepped in to write the book that should be sitting on every hiring manager's desk: *The Hiring Handbook*. Kasey Harboe Guentert and Mollie Berke are the real deal, having helped countless clients choose the talent they need for the future, and they've boiled down the most contemporary people science into digestible insights that anyone who needs to hire can act on.

"Having worked with large, complex organizations myself, I recommend this book wholeheartedly to anyone who sees hiring well as a source of competitive advantage—which should be everyone!"
Melissa Swift, Founder and CEO, Anthrome Insight, and author of *Work Here Now: Think Like a Human and Build a Powerhouse Workplace*

"A practical, well-researched guide that distils decades of consulting and in-house expertise into something hiring managers can actually use. Kasey Harboe Guentert and Mollie Berke bridge the gap between theory and real-world application, bringing deep, in-the-trenches experience to life through concrete guidance, clear frameworks, and thoughtful commentary. Whether you're a seasoned HR leader or first-time manager, this evidence-based toolkit is both insightful and immediately usable."
Christopher Rotolo, Adjunct Professor of Industrial-Organizational Psychology at NYU and Chief Talent Officer at MiTek

"Kasey Harboe Guentert and Mollie Berke have done what is often thought of as impossible: They have written a handbook that fully reflects the psychometric rigor of talent selection and assessment science. But they have packaged that science in a handbook that is engagingly written and provides clear, easy-to-follow, practical help that will equip organizations large and small to do a better job of selecting the talent they need to thrive."
Seymour Adler, Senior Consultant in the Leadership Advisory Solutions Practice, Spencer Stuart, and recipient of the 2019 Distinguished Professional Contributions Award from the Society of Industrial and Organizational Psychology

The Hiring Handbook

A Toolkit for Recruitment, Assessment, and Selection Success

Kasey Harboe Guentert

Mollie Berke

KoganPage

Publisher's note
Every possible effort has been made to ensure that the information contained in this book is accurate at the time of going to press, and the publishers and author cannot accept responsibility for any errors or omissions, however caused. No responsibility for loss or damage occasioned to any person acting, or refraining from action, as a result of the material in this publication can be accepted by the editor, the publisher or the author.

First published in Great Britain and the United States in 2025 by Kogan Page Limited

Kogan Page
Kogan Page Ltd, 2nd Floor, 45 Gee Street, London EC1V 3RS, United Kingdom
Kogan Page Inc, 8 W 38th Street, Suite 902, New York, NY 10018, USA
www.koganpage.com

EU Representative (GPSR)
Authorised Rep Compliance Ltd, Ground Floor, 71 Baggot Street Lower, Dublin D02 P593, Ireland
www.arccompliance.com

Kogan Page books are printed on paper from sustainable forests.

ISBNs

Hardback   978 1 3986 2165 7
Paperback   978 1 3986 2164 0
Ebook   978 1 3986 2166 4

British Library Cataloguing-in-Publication Data

A CIP record for this book is available from the British Library.

Library of Congress Control Number

2025013377

Typeset by Integra Software Services, Pondicherry
Printed and bound by CPI Group (UK) Ltd, Croydon CR0 4YY

CONTENTS

Acknowledgments xi

PART ONE
WHY Structured Assessment

1 Embrace Human Insight 3
What to Expect in This Handbook? 5
Who Is This Book For? 7
A Fresh Start 7
About Us, Your Authors 7
Why This Is So Important 11
Rectifying the Bias Problem 12
Three-Step Assessment Process in Action 13
Notes 14

2 From Frenzy to Fallout: The High Cost of Over-hiring and Its Aftermath 16
An Example of Misaligned Hiring Efforts 16
How Much Interviewer Time in Dollars? 19
More Consequences of Getting Hiring Wrong 21
Notes 24

3 The Funnel 27
Notes 28

4 Your Stakeholders 29
HR Stakeholders 29
What If You Don't Have an HR Team? Advice for Small Business Owners and Entrepreneurs 30
Part 1 Summary: Key Learnings 32
Part 1 Key Terms 34

PART TWO
WHAT to Assess

5   Overview of Job Analysis: About Those Miraculous, Time-Saving Interviews 39

Use Your Time Wisely… 41
Start With the Job 43
Notes 44

6   Job Analysis 45

What Is a Job Analysis? 45
Activities 49
Knowledge, Skills, and Abilities (KSAs) 50
Minimum and Preferred Qualifications (MQ and PQ) 57
Methods for Conducting a Job Analysis 59
Notes 67

7   Job Analysis, Step by Step 69

Preparing to Conduct Your Job Analysis 69
Key Topics and Questions to Include in Your Job Analysis 69
Building Evaluation Criteria for Your Final KSAs 79
How Much Effort Should I Put Into My Job Analysis? 86

8   Building Your Job Profile and Job Description 89

Job Profile 90
Job Description 91

9   Food for Thought 93

To Weight or Not to Weight 93
Where Else Can Job Analysis Be Useful? 94
Point of Diminishing Returns in Data Collection 94
Job Profiles Have Expiration Dates 95
Will My Job Change Due to AI? 95
Documentation 99
Part 2 Summary: Key Learnings 99
Part 2 Key Terms 100
Notes 101

PART THREE
HOW to Assess

10   Out-of-the-Box Questions: Why the Beer Test and Guessing Games Don't Belong in Interviews 105

What Is the "Beer Test?" 105
Notes 107

11   Screen to Focus on the Most Qualified 109

Screening in Action 111
Screening Methodology Without Applicant Tracking Systems 112
Is There a Shortcut? 115
NLP in Action 117
There's the Rub... 117
Final Thoughts 119
Notes 121

12   Structure Focuses on What Matters Most 123

Structured Interviews Are Popular for a Reason... 124
Bias in Action 129
The Interview Sequence 132
Notes 132

13   Building Structured Interviews 134

Interviewing Methods 134
When to Choose Which Interviewing Method and Question Type 141
Importance of Interviewer Trainer 141
Notes 142

14   Other Interviewing Methods and Assessment Types 143

Technical Questions 143
Role Plays 146
Presentation Assessment 149
Considerations 151

15   Let's Write Some Questions! 152

Building the Interview Guide 154
What an Interview Guide Template Could Look Like 156

16   Creating Candidate Trust 163

Prepare Candidates 163
Make it Natural 165

17   Conducting Your Interview 168

Question Framing and Follow-up Probes 168
Standard Probing Questions: STAR framework 169
Probing for Deeper Insight 171
Note 177

18   Including Multiple Interviewers 178

Take Charge 181
Roles and Responsibilities 182
Gather Results and Decide 182
How Many Is Too Many? 183
Make It a Program 186
Part 3 Summary: Key learnings 188
Part 3 Key terms 190
Notes 191

PART FOUR
WHO to Select

19   Taking Outstanding Notes 195

Verbatim or Transcript Notes 196
Summarized Notes 196
How About I Just Record the Interview? 197
Writing Up Evidence 199
Notes 203

20 It's All About Metrics 205

The Scale 207
Using the Data 210
Notes 213

21 Using Evidence to Make Ratings 215

Evaluating the Screen 221
Evaluating a Full Onsite Interview 227
Notes 234

22 Making a Decision 235

Selecting From Multiple Candidates 236
Multiple Qualified Candidates 238
When Too Few Candidates Meet Our Expectations 238
Multiple Interviewers 240
Part 4 Summary: Key Learnings 242
Part 4 Key Terms 244
Notes 245

PART FIVE
Other Considerations

23 Can Human Bias Be Helped? 249

Notes 251

24 Privacy and Employment Best Practices: United States 252

A Little Bit of Legislation... 252
Notes 270

25 Privacy and Employment Best Practices: Europe and the UK 273

General Data Protection Regulation (GDPR) 273
Notes 277

26   Privacy and Employment Best Practices: India and China 278

India 278
China 279
Notes 282

27   Cheating, Leakage, and Lying 283

Stretching and Lying 285

28   Continuous Improvement 287

Ensuring You Gather Relevant Data 287
Not Probing Deeply Enough 289
What Can I Do to Increase Diversity? 291
Notes 291

29   GenAI: General Tips 292

Tips for Using AI Effectively 294
Some Caution 295
Notes 296

30   When the Standard Hiring Process Doesn't Fit 297

Job Profiles Versus Demographics 297
Job Profiles Versus Safety 299
Note 300

31   Concluding Thoughts 301

False Negatives—What Are We Missing? 301
Finding Purpose in Any Job 302
Part 5 Summary: Key Learnings 304
Part 5 Key Terms 305

Index 308

ACKNOWLEDGMENTS

From Both of Us

When we started our journey of "WRITING A BOOK," it felt like standing at the bottom of a huge mountain, looking up at the peak and feeling like… this will be completely impossible to scale! During those vulnerable early months, we had both decided to make a massive career shift back into the craziness of consulting from the cozy, comfortable world of tech company talent management. Somewhere between our deep uncertainty and doubt, we also had a lot of optimism, inspiration, and camaraderie that fueled our first step. In doing so, we were supported by people we admire tremendously and want to express gratitude to. To all of you, we want to say thank you—starting from our earliest conversations in March 2023 to today at the time of publication.

To our current and former teams of Industrial Organizational (I-O) psychologists, and to all the cross-functional partners we've had the privilege of working with—thank you for being part of this journey. The insights we've gained from our collaborations have been invaluable and shaped the very foundation of this book. It's through our shared experiences that we've come to truly understand the need for and application of this work. We hope this book serves as a useful tool and resource in your efforts, both with internal and external clients.

Brooke Barber, our deepest gratitude to you; your dedication and skill as a research assistant made an invaluable impact on this book. The meticulous research and sharp insights were instrumental in bringing this project to life. From sifting through extensive sources to synthesizing complex information, you brought rigor to the research. Thank you, Brooke, for your exceptional contributions—we are incredibly grateful for all you've done.

Chris Clark, you are the shining beacon of wisdom within the field of HR and our role model. Whenever it comes down to "how do you manage something this complicated with real people?" you're the first person we approach for a well-researched and clear answer. Your dedication and respect for your companies, the people you serve, and the leaders who go to you for advice is awe-inspiring. We can only hope that the HR world learns all it can from your experience to further elevate the entire practice.

Paige Munro-Delotto, PhD, it's such a gift to have your insights and thought leadership included in our legal section. Your wisdom has raised this book to a new level. Thank you from the bottom of our hearts.

Dr. John C. Scott, we are deeply grateful to you for your invaluable support in the publication process of our book. Your early review and insightful feedback on our draft helped shape the direction of our work, and your expertise made a significant impact on our journey. Thank you, John, for your guidance and encouragement throughout.

James Bywater, as someone we've worked with for over 20 years across different companies, we are amazed by your research and ways to transform consulting in our field to prepare us for an increasingly changing business world on all fronts. Thank you for taking a moment to weigh in on the importance of law and ethics in our book.

Louis Yang, our heartfelt gratitude to you for your indispensable advice and insights on the laws and ethics of recruiting in China. Your expertise has been instrumental in shaping the content of this book, ensuring it is both accurate and comprehensive. Thank you for your guidance and support.

Ankur Tailang, we are deeply grateful to you for your invaluable assistance with the laws and ethics of recruiting in India. Your expert guidance has been crucial in ensuring the accuracy and depth of this book. Thank you for your unwavering support and insightful contributions.

Jora Stixrud, PhD, Kasey feels incredibly privileged to have a chance to partner with you on research that increases opportunities for all candidates to experience fairness in the hiring process. Your insights on the risks and benefits of AI provide confidence for our readers in treading this ever-changing territory in selection and assessment. Thank you!

David Pennington, your willingness to read and comment on the draft of this book made it possible for us to see it through the eyes of someone we respect. Your prolific career as an I-O psychologist lends us so much credibility. We are so grateful to you.

To those listed below, we could not have gone through this journey without your advice, confidence and encouragement, and we thank you all.

Tacy Byham, PhD

Beth Fisher-Yoshida, PhD

Melissa Swift

Andrés T. Tapia

Joanie Connell, PhD

Richard Landers, PhD

Gary Dumais

Julia Bayless, PhD

Jamie Winter

Bill Westwood

Ruth Cochran

From Kasey

I have to start by thanking you, my awesome husband, Jeff. From diligently reading early drafts of the book to giving me amazing ideas about how managers like yourself embark on the hiring journey in your day-to-day work, you were as important to closing out the drafts as I was. Your experience as a software engineering leader across the various tech firms in Silicon Valley has given me so much food for thought. Thank you from the bottom of my heart and sending you all my love!

My sons, James, Jackson, Carsten, and Drake, all participated in the process of writing this book. We have engaged in countless dinner conversations, debates, and question-and-answer sessions on how to reach our audience with this important information. I appreciate each time you take a moment to ask me a question about something I do, and hope that you see your own wisdom sprinkled throughout here as a result. I love you guys to the moon!

My parents Anna Maria and Karol Berger deserve a huge thank you for paving the way toward publication with your own many books. You always shared and modeled the different pathways being a writer can take. I could not have done any of this without you.

Finally, I want to thank Mollie! Thank you for being the constant voice of logic, reason, ideas, inspiration, and structure that made everything click and come together. I simply would never have had the courage to jump into something like this without your confidence and knowledge. It's been so much fun to partner on this with you.

From Mollie

First and foremost, a huge thank you to my best friend and husband, Jordan. You've been my biggest cheerleader and a constant "reality check" when I got caught up in consulting jargon. Your perspective has been invaluable, always reminding me that not every business has a Fortune 500 budget.

Your support, love, and insistence on asking "How would this actually work in my world?" kept me focused on making this book practical and meaningful. That simple question shaped so much of what's in these pages. You made sure I never lost sight of what truly matters—helping people like you. Thank you for the tough questions, late-night editing sessions, brainstorming marathons, and for being the reason I believe in this work so much. I couldn't have done this without your love, humor, and encouragement. You also took on the role of the book's designer and infographic mastermind—turning our dense bullet lists and tables into something readers will actually want to engage with. Thank you, Jordan, for being the best partner in life and business—and for still loving me despite my endless questions and requests for design tweaks.

To my family—Leslie and Barry, my incredible parents, and Rebecca, my amazing sister—thank you for your unwavering love and support, I'm so lucky to have you in my corner. You've given me the confidence and foundation to chase my dreams, and I appreciate that more than words can say. And to my late grandparents, Marian and Marvin, making you proud has always driven me forward, and I carry your love with me every step of the way.

Kasey, you absolute powerhouse! I owe a tremendous thank you to you for going with me on this incredible journey and for being an exceptional thought partner throughout this experience. I feel deeply inspired by our project. From our early days at Korn Ferry, to navigating the world of big tech, and then returning to consulting, I've always admired your insight and drive. Your ideas, experience, and enthusiasm have been a true inspiration.

PART ONE

WHY Structured Assessment

1

Embrace Human Insight

Hiring is one of the most important decisions you'll ever make—but are you doing it right?

The talent industry offers countless tools to screen and evaluate candidates, but our research proves that nothing beats a well-structured interview for predicting job performance. This book puts you, the interviewer, back at the center of the hiring process. With a straightforward, three-step formula—WHAT you assess, HOW you assess, and WHO you select—we'll show you how to design interviews that reduce bias, improve outcomes, and transform your hiring process into a true competitive advantage. Let's get started and revolutionize the way you hire.

Structured interviewing is a methodical approach to conducting interviews, where all candidates are asked the same predetermined set of questions in the same order, focused on the specific knowledge, skills, and abilities (KSAs) required for success on the job. It involves:

- **Consistency:** Ensuring a uniform process across all interviews to allow for fair comparisons.
- **Job relevance:** Designing questions based on a thorough job analysis to focus only on what is most critical for success in the role.
- **Evaluation criteria:** Using standardized rating scales to objectively assess candidate responses, reducing subjectivity and bias.

Researchers have also been studying structured interviews for a number of years. Renowned I-O psychology researchers Rob Silzer and Richard Jeanerette define structured interviewing as "The process of measuring a person's knowledge, skills, abilities, and personal style to evaluate characteristics and behavior that are relevant to (predictive of) successful job performance."[1,2]

This approach enhances the reliability and validity of the hiring process by linking evaluations directly to the job's requirements, making it one of the most effective ways to predict job performance.[3] In an interview, **you** are the most important tool for evaluation—even in the era of artificial intelligence and automation. While online assessments and automated systems have their place, a human-centered approach remains critical, especially for hiring fewer than 100 roles per year. The additional time invested in a structured, human-led process results in better hires, as evidenced by the stronger job performance of candidates selected using the methodology we'll share with you.

This becomes even more critical for higher-level roles, where the stakes are significantly higher. Poor hiring decisions at any level can lead to noticeable consequences within six months, such as missed deadlines, lack of initiative, inadequate experience, team disruption, or even unethical behavior. Structured interviewing not only improves the likelihood of selecting high performers but also minimizes the costly risks of a bad hire.[4]

Designing your interview like an "oral test" significantly increases your chances of making better hiring decisions. It's a big responsibility that requires careful preparation and thoughtful execution—but we're confident you can excel at it. By following a standardized process rooted in job analysis, you can assess candidates' competence and motivations more accurately than even the most advanced automated systems, despite the inherent challenges of human bias.

Bias often arises when decisions are influenced by preconceived notions rather than objective evaluation of a candidate's data. However, the structured process outlined in this book is designed to minimize the influence of those preconceived ideas, allowing you to make fairer, more informed decisions. Together, let's squash the opportunity for bias and improve the quality of your hiring process!

In *The Hiring Handbook*, we will guide you through the following three-step assessment process:

A WHAT you assess

B HOW you assess

C WHO you select

With our simple methodology, you can make better hiring decisions that launch and elevate your company's success. We've divided our book into parts based on the "order of operations" to create your ideal assessment process. Our assessment process has been proven time and time again to help managers make better hiring decisions, as we demonstrate throughout the handbook, based on our combined almost 40 years of consulting experience and current research studies.

Structured interviewing has been extensively studied and shown to deliver significant benefits in hiring accuracy, fairness, and overall decision-making quality. Here are some compelling findings.

- **Reduction in bias:** Structured interviews reduce adverse impact and bias by focusing on job-relevant criteria and consistent evaluation, resulting in a fairer hiring process for underrepresented groups.

- **Better job performance outcomes:** Employees hired through structured interviews are consistently rated as higher performers compared to those hired through unstructured interviews or informal processes. This is because structured interviews have higher predictive validity (0.63) when compared to unstructured interviews (0.38), indicating they are far more effective at predicting job performance.

- **Improved consistency across interviewers:** Structured interviews produce much higher inter-rater reliability, with coefficients of 0.67–0.74, compared to as low as 0.37 for unstructured formats. Inter-rater reliability means that different interviewers are consistently evaluating candidates in the same way. It's about making sure that no matter who does the interview, they're using the same standards and coming to similar conclusions about a candidate's fit for the role.

- **Enhanced legal defensibility:** Organizations using structured interviews are better protected against discrimination claims. Courts are more likely to rule in favor of employers when hiring decisions are based on structured, job-related assessments.

- **Cost savings through reduced turnover:** Structured interviews improve the likelihood of hiring candidates who are a better fit for the role and organization, leading to lower turnover rates. Estimates suggest that a 5 percent improvement in hiring accuracy can save companies millions annually in replacement costs.[5,6]

What to Expect in This Handbook?

In Part 2, "WHAT to Assess," you'll focus on understanding the job you're hiring for rather than evaluating candidates. This step involves using an analysis process to create a job profile that outlines the key responsibilities and requirements of the position. We'll explain why it's essential to thoroughly understand the job before deciding how to assess potential candidates. You'll develop a detailed job profile that serves as the foundation for your job description and guides your interview process. This profile will help you formulate interview questions and evaluate candidates effectively.

The next section, Part 3, "HOW to Assess," will show you how to use your job profile to create actual interview questions. We'll guide you in developing various types of questions, including "real-life" job simulations. You'll learn effective techniques for asking candidates questions that reveal their knowledge, skills, and abilities, ensuring a consistent process that allows them to demonstrate their qualifications for the role.

Part 4, "WHO You Select," covers the evaluation of your candidate's interview responses, providing process and guidance on how to objectively evaluate and make decisions for your team. Like the process of analyzing a job, this part often gets forgotten or left out. Even more important than what questions you ask is determining how responses align with and compare against what you are looking for, specifically, your evaluation criteria. We'll guide you in building a robust evaluation guide that you can use to ensure each candidate is evaluated in a way that is accurate, precise, fair, and consistent.

We also include information about additional considerations and legal issues ("Other Considerations," Part 5) when conducting interviews in some of the larger economies including the United States, Europe, China, and India. In this part we also cover topics such as cheating and general guidelines for the use of automation or generative artificial intelligence (GenAI), such as chatbots, to build interview tools. We are not employment lawyers and cannot advise on specifics, but we do share our past experiences and learnings from interviews with others who manage recruiting, HR programs, and candidate experience.

Throughout the tips in each part, we may offer guidance for ways that GenAI can help you to generate content more quickly, and how to evaluate the content for accuracy and usefulness. We also let you know when GenAI will not help you. As we write this book, GenAI continues to evolve and grow, but we see clearly how critical this technology is to the recruiting and HR processes.

This handbook addresses ways to assess candidates for a specific role. You won't find us describing facial movements or hand gestures as a way to determine a candidate's integrity, nor will we advise on fascinating questions that get at someone's subconscious motives. We're also not trying to assess liars, stress responses, or psychopathology. Instead, we're going to focus on traditional structured interviewing questions to understand the strengths (not weaknesses) of our candidates against the success profile.

Who Is This Book For?

This book is for anyone involved in interviewing, hiring, or building an organization. Whether you're in HR designing assessment processes, training others to evaluate candidates, an entrepreneur or operator scaling a team, or a manager responsible for hiring, promotions, and feedback—you'll find practical value here.

As a manager, assessing employees is a regular part of your role, and our goal is to provide you with a standardized process to make your evaluations more effective and consistent. Throughout this book, we'll share best practices for assessments and guide you in sharpening your skills as an assessor, so you can build stronger teams and make more confident decisions.

A Fresh Start

Before we dive in, we're asking you to set aside everything you think you know about interviewing and assessing. Forget the training, rules of thumb, or belief systems you've relied on before, and approach our recommendations with an open mind.

Once you've read this book, we challenge you to try the strategies and techniques without preconceived notions—just test them out and see how they shift your perspective. Then, compare your earlier assumptions with what you've learned here.

One of our core messages is this: Human nature often nudges us toward biased decisions. But by learning and applying better techniques for judgment, you'll develop powerful tools to assess others more accurately. The key? Stay mindful and self-aware throughout the process. These tools will only work if you use them intentionally.

About Us, Your Authors

Kasey and Mollie, your friendly authors and virtual consultants, are committed to tackling this issue—one hiring manager at a time. We are both Industrial-Organizational psychologists (or I-Os), bringing research and science to the hiring process. If you've ever heard of a little thing called "Targeted Selection©" or "Structured Interviewing" or "Competency-based Assessment," then you're already familiar with the work of many great people in our field.[7] We leverage psychological principles and research methods to develop and implement tests, interviews, and other assessments to evaluate job candidates' skills, personalities, and abilities. Our goal is to identify those individuals who are best qualified for specific roles within an organization. We've spent a combined 40 years designing and refining hiring processes to make them fairer and more effective.

Kasey became an I-O psychologist because she felt passionate about contributing to a workplace that was consistently motivating and engaging to all employees. She discovered this profession in her second year of college. Her "Introduction to Psychology" professor noted that I-O psychologist was a good career for people who were interested in studying people at work. According to SIOP,[8] "I-O psychologists apply research that improves the well-being and performance of people and the organizations that employ them."

Kasey's mission is to raise the bar on bias-busting and accurate prediction of employee behavior, using clearly structured methods and competencies. Kasey has a track record of 25 years of success increasing the accuracy and legality of the recruiting and selection process for her clients. Her success has been defined by her ability to build fully documented and legal processes that avoided myriad expensive lawsuits and claims. Studying such jobs included job observations, interviews with supervisors, creation of surveys to confirm how often and how important each task was, and writing up the subsequent reports according to US Equal Employment Opportunity Commission Guidelines.

Later, she worked in three separate consulting firms with an eventual focus on leadership and executive roles, during which she had the opportunity to build her internal benchmarks across hundreds of leaders across all industries. With each new leader assessment, Kasey created improved processes to categorize the behaviors, skills, and knowledges that she observed, and then linked those back to the context and jobs.

After this, Kasey spent five years working internally with tech firms. She built Meta's first selection and assessment function. Subsequently, she moved to Airbnb to create measurement and assessment methods across the organization. She found the "late startup" culture in technology a perfect place to build HR excellence, as such firms are often eager to bring in well-researched, solid processes, but early enough in their growth to have avoided building bad habits or becoming too heavily entrenched in bureaucracy. She currently works for APTMetrics, a consulting firm that builds such processes across all industries and for all levels of work.

When Kasey's clients ask whether she calls herself a "ninja" assessor, she says:

> I guess I would say yes and no. At this point, after assessing or building processes to assess thousands of people, I have seen quite a few patterns emerge. It becomes easier to quickly slot someone into a pattern rather than measuring each piece of them one at a time and putting all the pieces together for the summary. But it took me over 20 years. I remember, during my early career, how much I wanted to just skip the "process" and get right to making a decision. Now I know the truth. It will never be possible without a true crystal ball. But one thing my experience has helped me to do is enable our clients to improve the accuracy and the fairness of that assessment with more efficiency, giving them more time to focus on the development of their amazing teams.

Kasey is excited to finally share some of these insights with a broader audience beyond her clients in this handbook.

Mollie's passion for I-O psychology began when she discovered the profound impact of applying psychological and research-based principles to organizational decision-making. She initially studied psychology, focused her research on decision-making, and then worked as a recruiter at a travel nursing agency, always knowing she'd return to graduate school to study I-O psychology. However, she never anticipated how deeply rewarding this path would prove to be.

Her interest in assessment and selection truly blossomed during graduate school at NYU, where she took a course called "Personnel Selection" taught by Dr. Christopher Rotolo, one of her now mentors. Little did Mollie know that this course would significantly shape her career. Dr. Rotolo introduced her to a range of assessment methodologies in the context of personnel selection, such as competency-based and behavioral interviews, psychometrics (including personality and cognitive assessments), and role plays or simulations in assessment centers, where both the assessor and the candidate act out business scenarios and then the assessor evaluates the candidate. Mollie was immediately captivated by the idea of blending evaluation with acting, and thought: "I could be a part-time actress, all while assessing others, providing thoughtful feedback, and helping them grow?" She was hooked. She found this work to be incredibly analytical, yet creative, exciting, and challenging.

Mollie began her assessment career at Korn Ferry, specializing in leadership assessments. She worked with leaders at all levels—from front-line employees to senior executives—using a variety of methods, including 1:1 behavioral interviews, psychometrics, and assessment centers. While she found these tools incredibly valuable, Mollie's husband, Jordan, who is a small business owner, would often remark, "That's cool, I wish we had the budget for something like that," or "I need a general manager—can you assess candidates with these methods?" These conversations made Mollie realize the need to adapt and customize assessment approaches for smaller businesses with fewer resources than large corporations.

After this, Mollie went to Facebook (now Meta) as a Global Talent Selection Partner, where she helped build the company's first global assessment and selection function. She was hired by Kasey (who later moved to Airbnb), and the team's main focus was to build and implement structured interviewing at scale from the ground up. This involved starting small with select teams, securing buy-in, and then scaling the process across the organization. The impacts on hiring, performance, and candidate experience were significant, and Mollie was struck by how simple yet powerful the process could be. Mollie's husband, once again, would ask, "How can I implement something like this in my businesses?"

After a while, Mollie missed consulting and wanted to work with a broader range of clients, getting back to assessing leaders directly rather than simply building processes for others to follow. She now works for a consulting firm that serves clients globally across various industries, where she focuses on leadership assessment and executive coaching. Mollie remains a strong advocate for structured, multi-method assessment approaches, valuing the rigor and depth these methods bring. Yet, Jordan continued to ask, "When are you going to write a book so my peers and I can use these best practices in our businesses?"

Mollie realized there was a gap in resources for HR leaders, hiring managers, and small business owners who needed a simplified guide to building valid and reliable assessment processes. There were plenty of books aimed at experts or academics, but few easy-to-understand resources for non-specialists. Mollie and Kasey recognized this need and decided to create

The Hiring Handbook. This guide is designed to help readers apply best practice principles of assessment and selection to their hiring processes, regardless of industry or company size. With this handbook, managers, HR teams, and entrepreneurs can build stronger, more effective assessment practices in-house, making the process accessible to everyone. Welcome to *The Hiring Handbook*!

Why This Is So Important

The ultimate goal when hiring a candidate is to describe and predict their future performance at work. However, there's a critical caveat: For this prediction to be truly valuable, it must be both accurate and free of bias. By "free of bias," we mean achieving the long-standing aspiration of assessors and psychologists—to measure and forecast performance potential without any interference from preconceived notions or measurement errors.

As we explored this topic, we delved into countless books on assessment and selection, talent acquisition, coaching, and even fringe methodologies like graphology and body language analysis. These resources often promise quick, easy, and almost magical ways to assess future performance—skipping the "tedious" work of defining job requirements, interviewing candidates, and scoring them against a clear rubric. In Part 2, we'll break down why these shortcut methods fail and how they can actually harm your hiring outcomes.

We also noticed a glaring gap in the resources we encountered. Many methodologies either lack research support (meaning they don't work or come with unintended consequences), or they're written for specialists like us. The few books geared toward business managers and small business owners typically focus on technical aspects of the recruiting process, ignoring the actual decision-making, or they narrowly address hiring for leaders and executives. Something essential was missing, and that's where we come in.

In addition, the resources we found failed to address a critical gap: how to retrain our brains to rely on structured data instead of gut judgments. Managers frequently admit to us that they feel lost navigating inconsistent hiring practices. At the same time, HR and recruiting teams are often stretched too thin to provide the tools and guidance needed for sound decision-making. This lack of structure and support doesn't just create confusion—it can cause serious problems for your organization. First, unstructured hiring practices, even if unintentional, often perpetuate systemic biases that reduce workforce diversity. Without diversity, you lose out on the variety of perspectives and experiences that drive innovation, effective teamwork, and better decision-making. Second, in countries like the United States, these practices can leave your organization vulnerable to costly legal claims, with individual managers sometimes being held accountable for biased hiring decisions. Finally, poor hiring decisions can result in higher turnover, decreased performance, and lower employee engagement—all of which are costly and disruptive to your team. Simply put, unstructured hiring isn't just inefficient, it's a liability. Let's explore how structure can mitigate these risks and set you up for success.

In summary, business leaders, HR teams, and hiring managers are trusted to "get it right," but the path to optimal hiring practices can be rocky, and selection mistakes have huge consequences, as revealed through surveys of managers who made hiring mistakes. In the next sections, we outline the Three-Step Assessment Process to offer you a clear, repeatable way to drive consistency and accuracy.

Rectifying the Bias Problem

Perhaps you've attended training courses to "de-bias" yourself. You over-thought the personal characteristics of each non-traditional candidate to better understand systematic oppression against each of them. You may have felt pressured to meet diversity goals in the recruiting process. Although many managers are told that their unconscious bias blocks quality hiring decisions, simply knowing about unconscious bias doesn't make it conscious (or resolved). Instead, our experience has indicated that taking action that shuts down the biased thought and replaces it with a new thought and behavior is the only way to negate the effects of unconscious bias. The Three-Step Assessment Process leverages specific steps when assessing a candidate to help your brain digest information about people in a new way that naturally reduces your bias.

We can't entirely eradicate bias from our human brains. Bias is natural and necessary since humans have evolved to simplify complex information for decision-making. The key is to:

1 understand we all have biases

2 identify what our biases are

3 reduce opportunities for bias to creep into how we recruit, assess, and select candidates into roles

Structured interviewing can reduce bias and the potential for making faulty hiring decisions while helping you hire the best talent to help your organization succeed.[9]

Three-Step Assessment Process in Action

In the sports industry, incredible diligence goes into selecting players. Some team managers, owners, and coaches make outstanding decisions without ever talking to an I-O psychologist. How? Because they apply the same principles that we apply. Some teams even employed academics in the field of I-O psychology to create profiles of players for each team, *Moneyball*-style. *Moneyball*, a 2003 book, and later a movie, explained how Billy Beane, the baseball team Oakland A's general manager, led his team to victory by picking undervalued players who had certain predictive high-performing qualities not previously recognized by the baseball league.[10]

Although sports analogies may be tired in the business world, there is an excellent reason to continue to observe and admire their objectivity and data-driven approach. A client Kasey worked with during the early 2000s used a similar methodology to identify the common traits across high-performing, high-end sales team members. Below is a description of the work from a publication at the time:

> SHL, working with US retailer Neiman Marcus, increased sales per associate by 42 percent and reduced staff turnover by 18 percent by clearly identifying the characteristics needed for the job of sales associate, and designing a test to select employees who showed those traits.[11]

Working closely with Neiman Marcus HR leadership to produce long-term research on sales performance, Kasey and her team found, similar to Billy Beane, that the typical "sales" performance measured was not always the most predictive. In addition, they found that non-intuitive traits were more predictive than expected. Like how Billy Beane identified on-base percentage (OBP) and slugging percentage,[12] they found that managing one's impression of others and willingness to try different approaches predicted higher sales. As a bonus, they found an unexpected population of high performers among retired school teachers, resulting in a recruiting goldmine for the company through the first part of the 2000s. Ultimately, this illustrates how a structured hiring process can help you to find candidates in new places previously not considered.

Did the field of I-O psychology invent how we make hiring and selection decisions? Not at all! Instead, we have been observing and learning from leaders across all types of work, documented as early as the Roman legions. In the case of the Romans, a well-structured process was developed and rigorously followed in selecting each new generation of soldiers. Based on evidence found, prospects went through trial training and interviews before being selected.[13] After our many years of experience in the business world, we have simply found that good predictions are based on data and science—embraced by both the military and various athletic team leaders. I-O psychologists leverage the stories and research from history to build a cohesive framework and methodology.

Notes

1 Silzer, R. and Jeanneret, R. (2011) Individual psychological assessment: A practice and science in search of common ground, *Industrial and Organizational Psychology*, 4(3), pp. 270–96

2 Jeanneret, P. R., D'Egidio, E. L., and Hanson, M. A. (2004) Assessment and development opportunities using the Occupational Information Network (O*NET). In J. C. Thomas (Ed.) *Comprehensive Handbook of Psychological Assessment* (Vol. 4 pp. 192–202), Hoboken, NJ: Wiley

3 Janz, T. (1989) The patterned behavior description interview: The best prophet of the future is the past. In R. W. Eder and G. R. Ferris (Eds.) *The Employment Interview: Theory, research, and practice* (pp. 158–68), Sage Publications Inc

4 Schmidt, F. L. and Hunter, J. E. (1998) The validity and utility of selection methods in personnel psychology: Practical and theoretical implications of 85 years of research findings, *Psychological Bulletin*, 124(2), pp. 262–74, https://doi.org/10.1037/0033-2909.124.2.262 (archived at https://perma.cc/8QMG-5BWL)

5 Sutherland, M. and Wöcke, A. (2011) The symptoms of and consequences to selection errors in recruitment decisions, *South African Journal of Business Management*, 42(4), pp. 23–32, https://www.econstor.eu/bitstream/10419/218468/1/sajbm-v42i4-0502.pdf (archived at https://perma.cc/4A9H-U5SY)

6 Schmidt, F. and Hunter, J. (2003) History, development, evolution, and impact of validity generalization and meta-analysis methods, 1975–2001. In K. R. Murphy (Ed.) *Validity Generalization: A critical review* (pp. 31–65), Lawrence Erlbaum Associates Publishers

7 Development Dimensions International (2020) Targeted Selection®: A comprehensive guide, https://www.ddiworld.com/solutions/targeted-selection (archived at https://perma.cc/M9GK-AN4Q)

8 Society for Industrial and Organizational Psychology (2023) About SIOP, https://www.siop.org/About-SIOP (archived at https://perma.cc/ZES8-FDFB)

9 Bergelson, I., Tracy, C., and Takacs, E. (2022) Best practices for reducing bias in the interview process, *Current Urology Reports*, 23(11), pp. 319–25, https://doi.org/10.1007/s11934-022-01116-7 (archived at https://perma.cc/K5WC-QFNE)

10 Lewis, M. (2003) *Moneyball: The art of winning an unfair game*, New York: W. W. Norton & Company

11 Newsweek (2005) Inside the head of an applicant, https://www.newsweek.com/inside-head-applicant-122389 (archived at https://perma.cc/25R5-BUYV)

12 Wassermann, E., Czech, D. R., Wilson, M. J., and Joyner, A. B. (2015) An examination of the Moneyball theory: A baseball statistical analysis, *The Sport Journal*, 24, https://thesportjournal.org/article/an-examination-of-the-moneyball-theory-a-baseball-statistical-analysis/ (archived at https://perma.cc/9GPM-AH7K)

13 Rangel de Lima, C. (2023) Introduction to Legion: life in the Roman army, The British Museum, https://www.britishmuseum.org/blog/introduction-legion-life-roman-army (archived at https://perma.cc/963B-NU4Y)

2

From Frenzy to Fallout

The High Cost of Over-hiring and Its Aftermath

The ability to understand and document the essential tasks of a given role, the required versus preferred qualifications, critical skills, and abilities is not a formality; it is mission critical and will save you countless hours later, including the worst headache of all—letting your staff go. The sad reality is that most organizations struggle to truly identify their talent needs.

An Example of Misaligned Hiring Efforts

From 2018 to 2022, a hiring frenzy swept through the tech industry. Companies such as Amazon, Walmart, Microsoft, Google (Alphabet), Facebook (now Meta), Apple, Zoom, Instacart, and Salesforce enacted a surge of hiring, driven even further by expanded demand for online services during the pandemic.

The uptick in hiring from 2018–2019 was driven by several key factors, including strong economic growth and historically low unemployment rates, particularly in the United States at 3.5 percent. Companies across industries, especially in tech, finance, and healthcare, were competing for skilled workers due to rapid advancements in technology like AI, cloud computing, and data science. Additionally, a surge in venture capital funding fueled aggressive hiring by startups and tech companies. Many large organizations experienced record profits, which boosted their confidence to expand their workforces. There was also a rise in flexible work models and an increased focus on securing talent amid growing concerns about global talent scarcity. Anticipation of continued economic growth led to over-hiring in some cases, a misstep that became clear when the Covid-19 pandemic disrupted markets and revealed the risks of insufficient workforce planning.[1]

Per an *HR Brew* article from 2022, "With millions sitting at home, isolated, glued to screens, and increasingly dependent on digital goods and services, tech companies such as Stripe, Shopify, and Peloton pounced on a prime opportunity to corner their respective markets by onboarding scores of new recruits."[2] This is a result of a phenomenon called "Blitzscaling," the subject of a 2018 book by the same name, in which rapid growth initially appears justified, but in reality, it results in potential problems that end in layoffs.[3]

Across companies like these, we observed a 10 percent rise in employee count compared to historical year-over-year growth, followed by a plateau. This stagnation in 2022 and 2023 marked a departure from the steady growth patterns that had previously driven their success. For instance, Amazon exemplified consistent growth, expanding from 17,000 employees in 2007 to a staggering 798,000 by 2019.[4,5]

How can a company maintain a thoughtful hiring strategy when it grows to nearly 47 times its original size? During periods of rapid expansion, recruitment planning often becomes an afterthought. This can result in hiring employees based on generic, rapidly evolving job descriptions, while still expecting them to deliver exceptional performance. People we knew who worked at Amazon shared that this was a common challenge, highlighting the strain that rapid growth places on hiring processes.

Despite the allure of abundant opportunities, lavish celebrations, and welcoming open doors, the darker side of the frenzy revealed recruiters eagerly wooing and acquiring talent without clear job descriptions. This was merely a tactic to hoard and thus prevent top talent from joining competitors, leading to a glut of skilled individuals in roles with insufficient work. Sure, employees in the knowledge economy should flex and adapt somewhat, but between 2018 and 2022 we saw far too many employees willingly accept a minimal or generic job description in exchange for high material rewards and status. While appealing on the surface, high material rewards and status can come with an emotional cost, as well as personal time cost. A number of our clients have reported a "golden handcuffs" trade-off, in which their new standards of living make it hard to consider other, more meaningful options of work that they would have normally considered for greater work-life balance and job satisfaction. The "handcuffs" are the promise of increasing material reward that cannot be matched in jobs that are more appealing to them.

The surge in demand for talent, driven by a "war for talent," created artificial talent shortages and raised incomes, but also potentially contributed to global inflation.[6]

For example, a laid-off worker went viral on TikTok explaining that talented new hires at their company felt pressure to create work for themselves and their teams, appear busy, and show their value. This phenomenon resulted in highly inflated workloads through unnecessary meetings and lengthy projects. The situation reached a point where employees felt like commodities, as the TikToker described being "hoarded like Pokemon cards."[7] In late 2022, the company enacted a series of layoffs, prompting the CEO to make a public statement of regret for a systematic policy of over-hiring and damaging candidate trust and experience.[8]

A friend of ours in HR, who works at a smaller tech company and prefers to stay anonymous, shared the lasting damage caused by eroded trust in their organization. When the company over-hired and later had to let people go, candidates felt betrayed, making it difficult for recruiters to attract valuable new talent. This issue wasn't just a one-off—it stemmed from a deeper, systemic problem.

Many companies fail to accurately assess their true talent needs, leading to poorly aligned hiring efforts. The consequences go beyond layoffs: Mismanaged hiring processes undermine trust in the organization, damage leadership credibility, and hurt employee retention. In the end, the ripple effects of these decisions can weigh heavily on a company's future.[9,10] Research in our field has shown that those who survive layoffs are saddened and stressed when their coworkers are asked to leave the company.[11] For many employees, layoffs can feel like a breach of the unwritten "employee contract," even when they're explained as purely "business decisions." It's rare to work in a corporate environment without encountering the ripple effects of layoffs at some point in your career.

Increased workloads are a common result of layoffs as well, which in turn leads to burnout and then poorer performance.[12] A good friend of Kasey's survived a large restaurant layoff. While everyone knew not to take the layoffs personally because they were an obvious and visible result of drops in customer demand, the staff who remained behind felt on edge, fearful, and anxious. Her friend knew that customers could tell the difference, and the percentage of tips actually declined. After all, who wants to be subject to anxiety or stress from the staff when they go out to eat?

David Pennington, Executive Consultant with APTMetrics, explained that not all layoffs, however, are quick or impulsive reactions. Based on his experiences with clients across a variety of industries:

> Under pressure, especially given certain environmental variables, publicly traded institutions more vulnerable to investor and consumer demands are particularly

agile in transitioning talent deemed less appropriate for the current environment with those who may serve the "future" organization better.

How do they decide when this should happen, and what profile of new employee is ideal? David suggests that it depends on "organizational or team goals and the skill sets required to advance the initiatives." Therefore, the circumstances of the layoffs can be complex, not always easy to predict, and very much tied with job performance as it relates to company success in current environments.

How Much Interviewer Time in Dollars?

We often get asked, "How can you prove that this intervention in the assessment process will save us money?" There are a few aspects to estimating value added, or net cost, in a structured interview process—the time to build a new process (or the cost if you're hiring a consultant to do the work), the time spent or saved during the interview process itself, and the long-term performance implications associated with hiring decisions. We walked through examples above of companies over-hiring without clear alignment on talent needs, turnover due to poor performance as well as layoffs, and the costs associated with additional recruiting time. We want to provide another example based on one component: Interviewer time in dollars. So, how much interviewer time in dollars does a company spend to hire a year's worth of Principal Software Engineers?

For one of our clients, we built a selection process for Principal Software Engineers and found that approximately **$1,000** was spent per candidate before our intervention. This could exceed **$10,000** per hire if 10 finalists were involved in the entire hiring process. How was this possible? Each candidate typically went through **six to seven interviews** with highly paid technical leaders.

To calculate the cost of interviewer time, we considered a range of interviewer salaries and estimated the financial impact of each interview. Keep in mind, this calculation doesn't even include the potential loss of productivity—an omission that would only amplify the true cost. While quantifying the cost of interviews might feel abstract, it's a very real expense for the company with measurable consequences.[13]

The key is to find the right balance. Rushing the process could lead to a bad hire, which carries its own significant costs. On the other hand, over-analyzing can waste valuable time and resources. Strive for a sweet spot: Spend enough time to make an informed decision but avoid getting stuck in analysis paralysis.

We helped the team define core job requirements and streamline their process into **five targeted interviews**, reducing total interview time by **195 minutes**—about **3.25 hours**. Throughout the next sections, we'll show you how to achieve similar efficiency while maintaining rigor.

You'll learn how to conduct a job analysis to identify what success looks like in a given role, develop interview questions aligned to the specific knowledge, skills, and abilities uncovered in that analysis, and create evaluation criteria using a clear rating scale. We'll also guide you through conducting structured interviews, capturing detailed notes, evaluating candidate responses against your criteria, and making informed selection decisions. These steps ensure your hiring process is thorough, time-efficient, and aligned with the role's true requirements.

COST CALCULATION

1 **Former cost of interviewer time per candidate:**

o Estimated at **$1,000** per candidate.

2 **New interviewer cost and time per candidate:**

o Total interview time reduced by **195 minutes**, which is **3.25 hours**.

o If the interviewers participating have an average total compensation package of around **$285,000** each and there is an estimated **2,000** working hours in a calendar year:

   – Hourly rate = 285,000/2,000 = 142.50 per hour.

   – Cost for 3.25 hours = 142.50 × 3.25 = 462.25 per candidate.

3 **Total cost savings for 10 candidates:**

o For the reduced process: 462.25 × 10 = 4,622.50 cost savings.

After implementing our improved assessment process, the company now saves approximately **$462.25** of interviewer time per candidate, totaling about **$4,622.50** for 10 candidates. This represents significant savings compared to the original estimate of **$10,000** for 10 hires, demonstrating the financial benefits of a streamlined selection process. If interviewing 200 candidates over the course of a year, the company would save approximately

$92,450 per year with the new vs old assessment process. For an employee making close to $300,000 per year, it seems reasonable to spend 1 percent of that income finding the right person.

You're probably shaking your head at us by this point. No way in the world could we have saved that much money per hire! Note that our calculation is an underestimation since it didn't take into account the lost technical work or the many instances of "follow-up" interviews conducted due to interviewers not gathering "enough signal."

More Consequences of Getting Hiring Wrong

Recruiters, resources, hiring managers, consultants, and even machine learning algorithms leverage endless hours, dollars, and energy to make that perfect hiring decision but continue to get it wrong almost half the time.[14] In the UK, research shows that 24 percent of businesses spend up to 10 hours a week just scheduling interviews.[15] In another study from an HR consultancy, clients indicated that they use up to 30–40 hours over four to eight weeks to hire just one single employee.[16]

After all of this hard work, do we end up with better hires? Not usually! We identified a recent study by Leadership IQ, indicating that out of 20,000 new hires, a whopping 46 percent of them failed within 18 months. Why? Technical skills were to blame for only 19 percent of the failed hires. The other 81 percent failed due to poor interpersonal skills, coachability, motivation, and emotional intelligence.[17] We were *not* surprised, given that this scenario is typical for in-house interview processes, equivalent to employee time. As you can see, specialized professionals in the knowledge economy roles conducting endless interviews can become extremely costly.

David Pennington adds that:

> You can add additional financial impacts of good hiring decisions. For example, if your improved assessment increased the validity of the hiring decision, leading to hiring people who are a better fit for the job and who aren't subsequently fired or quit within 18 months, then you can account for other factors. If a staff member leaves, then the organization pays for another hiring process. Employees are not fully efficient when they start, and the time spent onboarding and training them costs money—resulting in additional costs. Alternatively, if you have an effective assessment predicting job performance and organizational culture alignment and the individual is retained, it results in a greater financial impact.

Robert Half, a recruiting firm, outlines three types of costs resulting from poor hires: Lost productivity/poor performance, lost morale, and replacement cost.[18] The lost confidence of a bad hire becomes increasingly significant with the level and impact of the role. While less noticeable in the short term, it can erode the company significantly over time.

Beyond the cost of lost productivity, the risk of lawsuits in places with strict laws, such as the United States, can cost a lot of money in settlements. In settlements, a company agrees to pay plaintiffs a certain amount of money to avoid having a case brought to trial. In 2022, Sterling Jewelers paid $175 million due to gender pay and promotion inequity across a whopping 70,000 employees.[19] Goldman Sachs, a well-known financial services firm, paid $215 million in 2023 to settle gender pay/promotion equity and performance evaluation across 3,000 employees.[20] Finally, in 2024, Oracle paid $25 million for the same issues across a similar number of employees.[21] The gender pay inequity occurs in the absence of clear standards for what good performance looks like—the starting point in building your assessment and selection process into any job.

Poor Performance Affects Customers Directly

Consider the example of Vioxx Products Liability Litigation. In this case, a multidistrict litigation involving thousands of plaintiffs alleged that they suffered heart attacks, strokes, or other injuries from taking Vioxx, a pain-killer manufactured by Merck. The plaintiffs claimed that Merck was negligent in conducting clinical trials, concealed safety data, misrepresented the benefits and risks of Vioxx, and failed to warn about its dangers. The plaintiffs also claimed that the defendants were negligent in hiring, training, and supervising their sales representatives who promoted the products to doctors and patients. The lawyers and organization eventually settled for $4.85 billion.[22]

According to the Polypropylene Hernia Mesh Products Liability Litigation, a multidistrict litigation involving thousands of plaintiffs who allege that they suffered injuries from defective hernia mesh products manufactured by Davol and C.R. Bard, the plaintiffs claim that the defendants were negligent in designing, testing, marketing, and selling the products and failing to warn about their risks.[23]

In recent news, the Federal Aviation Administration has launched an investigation into Boeing due to concerns over employee negligence in aircraft inspections.[24] Did Boeing staff fail to carry out required inspections and potentially falsify records? Did Boeing adequately hire employees for *vigilance* and *adherence* to safety protocols? Indeed, in the worst case, when poor hiring decisions are made, people's lives are at risk. Other times, poor choices cause gross negligence or incompetence.

Just because a poor hire hasn't caused a massive lawsuit doesn't mean that it isn't hurting your company. Sometimes, mediocre performance doesn't get noticed quickly because the rest of the team works harder to cover for the poor performer. But eventually, other team members become disengaged and may just go work elsewhere. Then you're left with... only your mediocre hires. Unless you're paying close attention or excellent performers are making visible and loud complaints about others' lack of performance, it may be challenging to realize your hiring mistakes. The best remedy is always to avoid making the mistake to begin with.

The literature has cited many impacts from mediocre performance that may not impede results in the short term but erode either the team or the ability of the company as a whole over time. Team dynamics, the ability for a team to collaborate, share ideas, and work in sync with one another, is an immediate impact of poor hiring decisions. The effect is most pronounced when the poor hire is the team leader.

In other cases, productivity is reduced to the detriment of the team and the company. Imagine that a single employee is not well-suited for their role or lacks critical skills and qualifications. As a result, one team member is not likely to perform well, leading to lower output and efficiency. When productivity is reduced by even just one team member, it increases the workload on others. As a result, employees become stressed and in turn reduce their own productivity. A consistently underperforming hire can negatively impact the entire team's morale.[25]

Training and supervision also can cost valuable time or money. Bad hires may require additional training and supervision to reach a highly functioning performance level. Investing time and resources into training and managing underperforming employees can divert valuable effort from other critical areas of the business.[26] When a poor hire interacts with customers, it can result in subpar service, leading to dissatisfaction, lost customers, and a negative impact on both revenue and reputation. Moreover, the costs of a bad hire extend well beyond recruitment and training. Companies may face additional expenses such as severance packages, legal fees, or even lawsuits if the employee's actions or behavior pose a liability. These ripple effects underscore the far-reaching consequences of hiring mistakes.[27,28]

Notes

1   McConnell, M. and Schaninger, B. (2019) Are we long—or short—on talent?, McKinsey, www.mckinsey.com/capabilities/people-and-organizational-performance/our-insights/are-we-long-or-short-on-talent (archived at https://perma.cc/73AA-KE79)

2   Blum, S. (2022) How over-hiring during the pandemic led to the rash of layoffs in 2022, HR Brew, December 6, www.hr-brew.com/stories/2022/12/06/how-over-hiring-during-the-pandemic-led-to-the-rash-of-layoffs-in-2022 (archived at https://perma.cc/P6FR-RVQ4)

3   Hoffman, R. and Yeh, C. (2018) *Blitzscaling: The lightning-fast path to building massively valuable companies*, New York: Crown Currency

4   Statista (2024) Employees of Amazon from 2007 to 2024, www.statista.com/statistics/234488/number-of-amazon-employees/ (archived at https://perma.cc/6V3W-FYE8)

5   Macrotrends (2024) Microsoft: Number of employees 2010-2024, www.macrotrends.net/stocks/charts/MSFT/microsoft/number-of-employees (archived at https://perma.cc/P6JW-7AF8)

6   Michaels, E., Handfield-Jones, H., and Axelrod, B. (2001) *The War for Talent*, Brighton, MA: Harvard Business Press

7   Pringle, E. (2023) Meta "hoarded us like Pokémon cards": Former staffer reveals she had to "fight for work" at company, Fortune, March 16, https://fortune.com/2023/03/16/meta-hoarded-us-like-pokemon-cards-former-staffer-fight-for-work-mark-zuckerberg/ (archived at https://perma.cc/95DL-WB6Z)

8   Zuckerberg, M. (2022) Mark Zuckerberg's message to Meta employees, Facebook Newsroom, November 9, https://about.fb.com/news/2022/11/mark-zuckerberg-layoff-message-to-employees/ (archived at https://perma.cc/B9PQ-29DY)

9   AlignMark (2024) The impact of poor hiring decisions on business performance, www.alignmark.com/2024/07/25/the-impact-of-poor-hiring-decisions-on-business-performance/ (archived at https://perma.cc/TJU2-DBTT)

10 Banerji, G. (2024) Tech shares log worst day of 2024: A selloff in semiconductors and other market stars drives a big market divergence, *Wall Street Journal*, www.wsj.com/finance/stocks/global-stocks-markets-dow-news-07-17-2024-b907e076 (archived at https://perma.cc/Z4MD-QULN)

11 Davisson, A. and Strober, M. H. (2023) You survived a layoff. Here's what to do next, *Harvard Business Review*, https://hbr.org/2023/04/you-survived-a-layoff-heres-what-to-do-next (archived at https://perma.cc/KR5J-JSN6)

12 Morgan, J. (2023) Rebuilding employees' trust in the aftermath of layoffs, *Forbes* Human Resources Council, www.forbes.com/councils/forbeshumanresourcescouncil/2023/06/06/rebuilding-employees-trust-in-the-aftermath-of-layoffs/ (archived at https://perma.cc/3KB7-9TJE)

13 Boskamp, E. (2023) 25+ crucial average cost per hire facts [2023]: All Cost Of Hiring Statistics, February 16, www.zippia.com/advice/cost-of-hiring-statistics-average-cost-per-hire/ (archived at https://perma.cc/6EX2-X9JM)

14 Sutherland, M. and Wöcke, A. (2011) The symptoms of and consequences to selection errors in recruitment decisions, *South African Journal of Business Management*, 42(4), pp. 23–32, www.econstor.eu/bitstream/10419/218468/1/sajbm-v42i4-0502.pdf (archived at https://perma.cc/ZTD9-8LZ4)

15 Agrawal, A. (2024) A quarter of firms spend too long scheduling interviews, *SME Magazine*, www.smeweb.com/a-quarter-of-firms-spend-up-to-10-hours-a-week-scheduling-interviews/ (archived at https://perma.cc/9TB7-XCZT)

16 Shields, S. (2022) Estimated time on HR: Recruiting tasks, Stratus HR, September 29, https://stratus.hr/resources/estimated-time-on-hr-recruiting-tasks (archived at https://perma.cc/SJ7F-SRFM)

17 Murphy, M. (2011) *Hiring for Attitude: A revolutionary approach to recruiting and selecting people with both tremendous skills and superb attitude*, McGraw Hill LLC

18 Half, R. (2022) 3 serious consequences of a bad hire, March 22, www.roberthalf.com/gb/en/insights/hiring-tips/3-serious-consequences-bad-hire (archived at https://perma.cc/E56Q-8EV7)

19 Stempel, J. (2022) Signet Jewelers unit reaches $175 million settlement of gender bias lawsuit, Yahoo Finance, June 9, https://finance.yahoo.com/news/1-signet-jewelers-unit-reaches-163624407.html (archived at https://perma.cc/Z256-H89P)

20 Chapman, M. (2023) Goldman Sachs settles gender discrimination suit for $215 million, AP News, May 9, https://apnews.com/article/goldman-sachs-settlement-gender-equity-b9373d369cb70165565ec83abe03b8c3 (archived at https://perma.cc/4GMU-BVY2)

21 Steinberg, E. M. (2024) Oracle women fought 7 years for equity, only to win just an extra paycheck or two, Yahoo Finance, February 15, https://finance.yahoo.com/news/oracle-women-fought-7-years-130000230.html (archived at https://perma.cc/67JK-PT5T)

22 Case—In re: Vioxx Products Liability Litigation, 501 F. Supp. 2d 789 (E.D. La. 2007)

23 United States District Court for the Southern District of Ohio (2020) In re: Davol, Inc./C.R. Bard, Inc., Polypropylene Hernia Mesh Products Liability Litigation, Opinion and Order No. 18, www.ohsd.uscourts.gov/sites/ohsd/files//MDL%202846%20MIL%20Opinion%20and%20Order%20No.%2018.pdf (archived at https://perma.cc/HR6Z-54RC)

24 Senanayake, N. (2024) Boeing under investigation after "several" employees failed to perform required wing attachment inspection, PEOPLE, https://people.com/boeing-under-investigation-after-employees-failed-to-perform-important-inspection-8644784 (archived at https://perma.cc/QXL4-FUJ7)

25 AlignMark (2024) The impact of poor hiring decisions on business performance, www.alignmark.com/2024/07/25/the-impact-of-poor-hiring-decisions-on-business-performance/ (archived at https://perma.cc/HC5P-B88A)

26 Fink, B. (2017) What's the cost of a bad hiring decision? LinkedIn, www.linkedin.com/pulse/whats-cost-bad-hiring-decision-brian-fink/ (archived at https://perma.cc/6TBK-Z4DN)

27 Chamorro-Premuzic, T. (2017) *The Talent Delusion: Why data, not intuition, is the key to unlocking human potential*, Piatkus

28 Fahey, S. (2022) The real cost of bad hiring decisions (and how to avoid making them), *Forbes* Human Resources Council, March 10, www.forbes.com/councils/forbeshumanresourcescouncil/2022/03/10/the-real-cost-of-bad-hiring-decisions-and-how-to-avoid-making-them/ (archived at https://perma.cc/8JXP-C6YP)

3

The Funnel

To ground this book in the broader context of recruitment and talent acquisition, let's take a look at the recruiting "funnel" illustrated in Figure 3.1.[1,2] This diagram outlines the key phases candidates move through before being hired. While this book focuses heavily on the screen and interview phase—where you directly engage with candidates to evaluate their strengths, weaknesses, and potential contributions—it's important to think strategically about how and where you assess candidates throughout the entire process.

At the "top of the funnel," the focus is on sourcing—identifying and persuading potential applicants to apply. The "bottom of the funnel" represents the final decision-making stage, where you select one candidate from a shortlist.

If you hire only a few people each year but receive a large volume of applications, it makes sense to incorporate screening tools early in the funnel to narrow down the list and save time. On the other hand, if you struggle to attract applicants, you might use less rigorous screening at the start to avoid deterring candidates. For high-demand roles, such as software engineers, the top of the funnel often resembles a sales pitch to attract talent, with the actual selection process happening closer to the bottom.

For positions with an abundance of applicants, the early stages of the funnel typically focus on efficiently sorting and eliminating unqualified candidates to avoid spending unnecessary time on them. By understanding the funnel, you can strategically determine where to apply different levels of assessment rigor to make the best use of your resources and maximize the candidate experience.

And remember, the time you spend assessing candidates isn't just an investment in finding the right hire—it's also equivalent to real dollars. Your time has value, so allocate it wisely!

FIGURE 3.1 The Recruiting Funnel

The funnel is a visual way to plan your time with candidates so that ideally you only screen and interview those who meet your required qualifications.

Notes

1 Symonds, C. (2023) Recruitment funnel explained: stages, metrics & practices, Factorial HR, https://factorialhr.com/blog/recruitment-funnel/ (archived at https://perma.cc/X8X2-EK3C)

2 Mbuvi, H. (2023) The Recruitment Funnel: A comprehensive guide, AIHR, www.aihr.com/blog/recruitment-funnel/ (archived at https://perma.cc/S6HB-RHLK)

4

Your Stakeholders

HR Stakeholders

Whether you're refining interview techniques for a small team or an entire function, the starting point is always the same: Identifying your key stakeholders and gathering information about your organization's approach to hiring.

- **Start with research**
  - o Begin by investigating if your company already has past or current interview processes in place. If so, find out who developed them, how they were created, and what data informed their design. This foundational knowledge will help you build on what already exists or identify gaps that need to be addressed.

- **Centralized HR teams: Guidance and guardrails**
  - o In companies with centralized HR teams, you'll likely receive more structured guidance on the hiring process. While this might feel restrictive, it's actually a safeguard against inconsistent or biased hiring practices. Centralized systems ensure hiring decisions are standardized and legally sound.
  - o Although these teams may be hesitant to embrace every new hiring innovation, don't be discouraged. Many HR tech solutions promise time-saving and accuracy improvements but often fall short due to poor underlying data, lack of customization, or overly simplistic functionality. Trust that your centralized HR team is protecting you from costly, ineffective tools and providing a stable framework for hiring.

- **Decentralized HR teams: Freedom and challenges**
  - o If your HR team operates more independently across functions, you may have greater flexibility but less direct support. Some leaders in

decentralized organizations invest in tools like applicant tracking systems or training programs. While these can be valuable, getting the most out of them is challenging without the right expertise or infrastructure.

o If you have limited HR support, consider prioritizing company-wide interviewer training. It's a high-impact investment that ensures consistency across hiring practices. This book is especially helpful for those navigating decentralized environments with minimal resources.

- **Build strong relationships with recruiters**

o Recruiters are essential allies in implementing your hiring processes. Involve them early and often as you develop your approach. Their cross-functional expertise and familiarity with the talent market will help ensure your process is both practical and effective.

- **Clarify role expectations**

o Do clear performance expectations already exist for the roles or levels you're hiring for? If so, trace them back to their source. Identify key contributors who helped establish these criteria and engage them for insights. If you're designing the process but aren't the hiring manager, the hiring manager is one of your most important stakeholders. You'll need their input at every stage and their help identifying other team members who can provide job-specific expertise (as discussed in Part 2).

- **Collaborate with HR experts**

o Collaboration with HR partners is critical, even if they're overwhelmed or slow to respond. Setting up structured feedback sessions before launching the process can ensure you get the necessary input and avoid missteps. While others may handle logistics and finer details, the upfront strategy and planning rest with you.

By engaging stakeholders thoughtfully and leveraging available resources, you'll set the stage for an effective and efficient hiring process.

What If You Don't Have an HR Team?
Advice for Small Business Owners and Entrepreneurs

For small business owners, operators, and entrepreneurs without an HR team, building a strong hiring process can seem daunting. However, you can still create effective practices to attract and select the right candidates—even without formal resources or large teams to rely on. The principles in this book are designed to be adaptable to any scale of operation. For example, when we mention gathering input from subject matter experts (SMEs) for a role, you might not have a team of experts to consult—perhaps there's only one, or maybe you're the SME yourself. That's perfectly fine. The key is identifying who, if anyone, can help you craft your hiring process. Even if you're building everything from scratch on your own, rest assured: You're fully capable of making it work. This book will guide you every step of the way.

- **Start simple: Define what you're looking for**
  - The first step is to clearly define what success looks like in the role. Follow the steps outlined in the subsequent chapters to write a straightforward job description that includes the specific knowledge, skills, experience, and abilities that align with the job and your company culture. Focus on what the role must have versus nice-to-have qualities, and be realistic about what the job entails.

- **Leverage your network**
  - In the absence of a formal recruiting process, your personal and professional networks can be invaluable. Spread the word about the role through friends, colleagues, and social media. Platforms like LinkedIn or industry-specific communities are excellent places to find referrals or attract candidates who are already familiar with your industry.

- **Borrow best practices from this book**
  - Use the guidance in this book to create your interview process. A structured interview framework ensures you're consistently assessing candidates against the same criteria, which minimizes bias and improves decision-making. Start with behavioral questions to explore past performance, and mix in hypothetical or problem-solving questions to assess potential in areas where candidates may lack direct experience.

- **Automate where you can**
  - Technology can help you manage some of the hiring workload. Free or low-cost applicant tracking tools like Google Forms or basic hiring features in platforms like Indeed or LinkedIn can help you organize applications and track candidate progress. While these tools aren't perfect, they can save time and create some structure.

- **Train yourself and your team**
  - o Without HR support, you and your team must become competent interviewers. Dedicate time to learning and practicing interview techniques, even for smaller teams. The more aligned you are as assessors, the stronger your hiring decisions will be.
- **Iterate and refine**
  - o After every hire, reflect on what worked and what didn't. Did the person match your expectations? Were there any surprises? Over time, this iterative approach will sharpen your instincts and help you fine-tune your process.

Even without an HR team, you can still approach hiring with rigor and thoughtfulness. By following these steps, you'll be equipped to attract the right talent, make confident decisions, and set your business up for sustainable growth.

Part 1 Summary: Key Learnings

From 2018 to 2022, the tech industry faced a hiring frenzy, leading to over-hiring without clear job descriptions and causing talent hoarding and inflated workloads. This resulted in artificial talent shortages, higher incomes, global inflation, and eventual layoffs, damaging trust and retention.

We highlighted the importance of clear job descriptions and proper hiring processes, and aligning roles with key skills, enhancing hiring efficiency and employee retention.

Small businesses and HR teams often lack resources to build effective hiring processes. *The Hiring Handbook* addresses these needs by providing a comprehensive guide to avoid common pitfalls, including inconsistent methods and systemic bias, which lead to poor hiring decisions and increased turnover. Our methodology emphasizes structured interviewing to reduce bias and ensure focus on job-related skills and behaviors. By replacing gut-level decisions with data-driven evaluations, you can improve hiring outcomes. Through real-world examples, like avoiding subjective "beer tests," we show how to implement fair, effective hiring practices that enhance organizational success.

Effective hiring, much like selecting athletes in football, relies on data and principles rather than charm or likability.

Our Three-Step Assessment Process draws from such data-driven approaches and aims to improve hiring processes. For example, we reduced hiring costs for a client by streamlining their process, cutting expenses from $10,000 to $3,000 per hire. Inefficient hiring not only wastes resources but can lead to costly lawsuits and negative impacts on morale and performance.

Poor hires can cause significant issues, from reduced team productivity to legal and reputational damage, underscoring the need for a structured, data-driven hiring approach to avoid these pitfalls and enhance overall organizational success.

In *The Hiring Handbook*, we outline a Three-Step Assessment Process for improving hiring processes: (1) defining what to assess, (2) developing how to assess, and (3) selecting who to hire. This guide will help you refine your interview practices and ensure fair, effective decisions, reducing legal risks. We focus on creating job profiles, crafting structured interview questions, and evaluating responses objectively. Additionally, we address legal considerations, candidate experience, and the role of AI in interviews. This book emphasizes structured interviews and practical assessment techniques, aiming to enhance hiring outcomes and reduce biases.

This book emphasizes the interview phase of the recruiting funnel, focusing on assessing candidates' strengths and potential contributions. The funnel illustrates the recruitment process from sourcing at the top to final hiring decisions at the bottom. For effective assessment, tailor the process based on applicant volume, balancing thoroughness with efficiency. For a robust interview process, identify existing processes, performance expectations, and engage key stakeholders, including hiring managers and recruiters. Collaboration with these stakeholders, despite potential challenges, is crucial for developing a successful hiring strategy and ensuring that interviews are both effective and efficient.

Quick Disclaimer

We have worked with a variety of large and small clients around the world. We hold the confidentiality of the work we have done with them to the highest possible standard. Any information naming a particular company comes from publicly available information sources, and NOT from work we did with them directly. Work we have done directly with clients is aggregated across job types or company types to protect confidential information.

Part 1 Key Terms

Applicant: An individual who has expressed interest in a job position within an organization by submitting an application for employment. This person typically submits their resume, cover letter, or application form to be considered for the role.

Assessment: Description of someone's existing skills, strengths, and development needs, as well as predicting what they would do based on these.

Candidate: An individual who has progressed beyond the initial application stage and is actively being considered for a specific job position within an organization.

Competencies: Competencies are measurable personal characteristics that differentiate levels of performance in a given job, role, organization, or culture. Any characteristic—mental, physical, or emotional—that leads to outstanding performance in a given job is considered a competency for that job.

- o This term can sometimes be confusing when compared to "Skills," so in this book, we will use the "Skills" term.

Job analysis: The process of systematically gathering, documenting, and analyzing information about a role to identify the tasks, responsibilities, skills, knowledge, and abilities required for successful performance. This foundational activity informs workforce planning, recruitment, performance evaluation, training, and compensation. Job analysis results are used to create both the job profile and job description.

Job description: A concise, candidate-facing summary derived from the job profile, emphasizing the essential duties, qualifications, and expectations of the role. It is designed to attract potential applicants by communicating the role's key aspects in a clear and engaging manner. The job description streamlines the information from the job profile for external use in recruitment materials.

Job profile: A comprehensive output of job analysis that details the key knowledge, skills, abilities, qualifications, responsibilities, and criteria needed for success in the role. This internally focused document serves as a guide for crafting interview questions, performance metrics, and recruitment strategies. It is dense and technical, providing the foundation for the candidate-facing job description and ultimately the interviewing and evaluation materials.

KSAs: Knowledge, skills, abilities. Note: experiences and other characteristics are sometimes also referenced.

o **Knowledge:**
  – Refers to the body of information an individual must possess to perform a job effectively.
  – Often involves theoretical or practical understanding of concepts.
  – Example: Knowledge of accounting principles for a financial analyst role.

o **Skills:**
  – Refers to the practical application of knowledge in performing specific tasks.
  – These are measurable and often task-specific proficiencies.
  – Example: Proficiency in using data analysis tools like Excel or Python.

o **Abilities:**
  – Refers to the innate or acquired capacity to perform an activity at a required level.
  – Abilities are broader and often combine cognitive, physical, or interpersonal capabilities.
  – Example: Problem-solving ability or the capacity to analyze complex systems.

Structured interviewing: A methodical approach to conducting interviews, where all candidates are asked the same predetermined set of questions in the same order, focused on specific knowledge, skills, and abilities (KSAs) required for success on the job. It involves:

o **Consistency:** Ensuring a uniform process across all interviews to allow for fair comparisons.

o **Job relevance:** Designing questions based on a thorough job analysis to focus only on what is most critical for success in the role.

o **Evaluation criteria:** Using standardized rating scales to objectively assess candidate responses, reducing subjectivity and bias.

Subject matter expert (SME): An individual who possesses deep expertise and knowledge in a specific field, subject, or area of expertise. SMEs are often consulted for their insights and guidance in decision-making, problem-solving, and project development within their domain of expertise.

The recruiting funnel: The recruiting process that sorts and selects candidates at different phases.

PART TWO

WHAT to Assess

In this part, we will discuss how to determine the specific qualities needed for successful performance in a particular job. In other words, we'll present a guideline for how to create your unique formula for job success.

5

Overview of Job Analysis
About Those Miraculous, Time-Saving Interviews

Can you actually predict job performance in any—and all—jobs through just one simple measure? Wouldn't that be fantastic? A regional managing director has gone viral for claiming that a candidate's likelihood of returning a coffee cup to the kitchen post-interview predicts "ownership" and thus future job performance (in all the jobs in his company).

In another example on social media, a company founder asks each candidate to estimate the height of their office building. We assumed that providing the actual, accurate height of the building would be the best answer, but this founder prefers to understand *how* they solve the problem without knowing the answer. According to the founder, a high-scoring candidate should do something like leverage the height of the building's shadow compared to their own height to estimate the size. The founder goes on to explain that this interview question accurately predicts a candidate's ability to solve ambiguous problems, and therefore is a silver bullet interview question for all jobs in his company. We like the second example slightly better than the first, but both of these outsized claims are suspiciously like writing high-dollar checks that can't be cashed. Our rationale is simple. Like with reading horoscopes, the suggestions are often general enough to be plausible. Is a Scorpio going to argue with a prophecy that something annoying will happen this week? No. Something annoying happens every single week to all of us, even if it's (hopefully) a small annoyance. But the problem is that Cancers, Geminis, and Libras (essentially all of the signs) *also* experience something annoying each week. Even if you spent your week on a remote island beach with perfect weather, something annoying is bound to occur, like getting bitten by a bug or finding it hard to fall asleep after too much sangria.

We want to be much more specific when it comes to predicting job performance. While you could convince us that something like *drives business results* is important for every single job, is it the *most* important thing for every job? For a financial trader, it's one of the most important things. For an airline pilot, it's not. Personally, we'd rather our pilots focus on process, safety, and mechanical comprehension than their airline's business results.

Both social media reels mentioned above containing the "be-all-end-all" assessment get a lot of clicks, because who doesn't appreciate the idea of a single-shot, quick measure that miraculously predicts a candidate's performance in a job? It should be so simple! Also, while these business influencers propose a vague idea of what they are trying to measure, neither make a clear case for *why* this sole quality is truly the silver bullet for the entire job performance prediction (whether it be *ownership* or *ambiguous problem solving*). We're a little skeptical to say the least, and you should be, too. Viewers are apt to quickly accept that ownership or ambiguous problem solving are logical qualities to seek in any job candidate, without considering that there may be differences depending on the actual job. Would you believe that having an excess of each of these qualities can actually derail performance in some jobs?

Absolutely, and here's why: While qualities like ownership and ambiguous problem solving are valuable in many contexts, their unchecked application or overemphasis can create blind spots. A candidate with an extreme sense of ownership may struggle to delegate effectively, leading to bottlenecks or burnout in roles where teamwork and collaboration are crucial. Similarly, someone who excels at ambiguous problem solving might overcomplicate straightforward tasks, wasting time and resources in roles that require precision and adherence to established processes.

The key is context: Different roles demand different competencies in varying degrees. For example, while pilots benefit from strong problem-solving skills for unexpected in-flight challenges, their primary success factors are grounded in safety protocols and mechanical precision. Conversely, a product manager's ability to navigate ambiguity and take ownership is often central to their effectiveness, but even here, too much ownership could alienate team members or stifle innovation.

A holistic approach to assessment considers the interplay of strengths and weaknesses in relation to the job's specific requirements. By failing to tailor assessments to the role, we risk hiring individuals whose dominant qualities might hinder rather than help performance.

We noticed that the influencers in both examples provide unclear definitions (if any) of the constructs. What does *ownership* really mean, anyhow? Does it equate to *action orientation*, or *collaboration*? We were certainly left with more questions than answers after watching these reels when considering how to implement this advice in real life. When preparing to conduct an interview, it may seem like a no-brainer to try out the *brand-new-simple-question-nobody-else-discovered* hack. The regret will kick in later, when you realize you've been making your hiring decisions based on random criteria that have little to do with the actual job. Or worse, you could find yourself in court needing to defend your hiring practices because you unfairly eliminated candidates for reasons unrelated to job performance.

David Pennington, our expert in job analysis methodology from Part 1, recalled an example in which he was asked complex math questions for an HR-related position early in his career:

> Clearly, a hiring manager was working to independently innovate new and interesting ways to select candidates for a financial services firm. The hiring manager enjoyed math puzzles, and so thought this would be a useful way to assess general problem-solving skills. In reality, however, the problem being solved was completely unrelated to the types of reasoning skills needed for the job.

When an interviewer asks questions to determine a more basic skill that looks less like the tasks performed on the job, it's difficult and sometimes impossible to determine which exact ability to target without a few years' experience as a psychologist or psychometrician. David advises that any questions asked should look very similar to the kinds of things someone would have to actually do on the job to avoid candidates launching complaints against the process.

Use Your Time Wisely...

The typical interview process allows between two and six hours with each candidate across all your interviewers. Of course the process (and lack thereof) across organizations varies significantly, but a typical funnel might include a phone screening, hiring manager interview, and technical or other interviews. Since you have such a limited time to gather data about a candidate, it's essential to use that time wisely. Being wise means asking candidates about the relevant knowledge, skills, and abilities that are most likely to result in success on the job. Maybe you're determined to measure *ownership* and *ambiguous problem solving*. But what if the job requires prior memorization of specialized knowledge and generating correct answers to problems on the spot (such as a surgeon in the middle of a surgery, a pilot experiencing an issue during their flight, or an elevator mechanic during an elevator emergency)? You will have spent your valuable interviewing time assessing all the wrong things. This, precisely, is the problem we are most concerned about in today's world of interviewing.

Many managers understand the importance of structuring interviews, using consistent question banks, and steering clear of illegal or problematic topics. However, we often see hiring managers fail to identify what's truly required for success in the role. This leads to a common pitfall we call "interviewing thoroughly but on all the wrong things."

We witnessed first-hand how the "war for talent" led companies to hire for really "nice to have" qualities such as graduation from a highly prestigious university, experience with similar companies, ability to solve obscure problems, or willingness to work any time of the day until the emotional needs of their bosses were satisfied. Nobody, including us, could convince these leaders that these traits or characteristics were irrelevant to job performance. Convincing someone that *working hard* is not the most important thing for job success is like trying to argue that the sky is not blue. Working hard is always important. But is that the most important thing for every job? And does graduating from an Ivy League school in the United States mean that person worked *harder*? Would you hire an airline pilot based on just that single metric of "working hard"? Are there other things that are more important?

Yes! We of course appreciate hard workers, but in the precious little time we have to interview a candidate, we want to focus that time on only the most important things for that unique job; and jobs are in fact uniquely distinct from one another. *Working hard* may be the most important thing for a project manager, but it's less important for an airline pilot. Instead, things like technical knowledge and sound decision-making will differentiate performance more effectively... and keep passengers safer.

When our clients asked us to challenge their hiring criteria, we found that someone's college selection is more predictive of their economic status in high school than anything else. We have noticed from our own experience reviewing resumes and interviewing leaders that those who went to public universities while working in paying jobs land in equally high-level roles 10 years post-university as those who were sponsored by their family wealth to attend prestigious universities. Truth be told, early work experience and dedication to self-improvement are excellent signals of ambition and long-term success.

We absolutely don't want to cast aspersions on prestigious university graduates. There are some outstanding people among them. However, we also spend much of our work time helping others see how matching the job criteria to the person is more important than a universal catch-all characteristic about someone's background. Will someone who graduated from Yale Law School be a more effective lawyer than someone who graduated from University of Kansas Law School? We have no idea, because we don't know enough about the schools or the candidates! Instead, we'd prefer to assess both lawyers based on their actual knowledge, skills, experience, and abilities; how they solve difficult problems, how well they negotiate, or how they present in court. The simplest way to predict their greatness is to ask them how they handle the things they will *actually* do on the job.

Start With the Job

When we work with a client to build a new assessment, they often jump directly to the development of their assessment or interviews. While that feels intuitively appropriate, you'll develop a better candidate prediction if you start by understanding the *job* before you decide how to interview the *candidate*. Let's figure out *what* to assess when building the interview process. This process of figuring out *what* to assess is called job analysis.

Uber was recognized early on by investors as a hot investment opportunity. Well documented in the book *Super Pumped: The battle for Uber* by Mike Isaac, Uber built its business during the early startup days by hiring like-minded "achieve at any cost" people who focused on ruthlessly beating competitors, and then rewarded them with obnoxious displays of hedonism, free-reign, and generous equity.[1] In describing the core values, Isaac painted the picture of wealth acquisition, power, land-grabbing, and aggression. The company leaders were directly and deeply involved in the hiring process and collaborated with recruiting experts to build a profile that enhanced focus on competitiveness and results.

To give credit where it's due, based on the descriptions we read, we found the science behind the profiles to be impressive. Uber targeted top college and business school grads and employees at top companies—not surprising, also not the impressive part. They tested candidates for skills related to "success at all costs." These statistics were entered into predictive algorithms meant to assess intelligence, future results, and absolute compliance with leadership. These core values were adhered to diligently and consistently, and their recruiters were excellent at finding people who fit the mold. Uber showed that when you use precise people-measurement tools to identify the candidates who fit a certain mold, you can find exactly those candidates you're seeking.

Here's the problem: The core values of the company were fundamentally flawed. While it seemed smart to focus on hiring the most intelligent and hardest-working individuals, this approach ultimately caused the company to collapse, along with its CEO. Though Mike Isaac did not directly link the recruiting strategy to the company's downfall, we believe that hiring employees based on a broader range of essential skills, relevant to their specific roles, could have prevented this outcome. For instance, a lawyer should be hired for their ability to stand up to executives and communicate critical information to protect the company—not just for being highly competitive or working long hours.

Uber has undergone significant transformation and recovery since 2016. One of the earliest steps they took was creating a comprehensive job profile for specific roles prior to actually recruiting or assessing any candidates. A visit to Uber's career site speaks to the diversity of positions and skills now available at the far more successful v2 of the enterprise. This core value of Uber summarizes nicely how far they have come: "Great minds don't think alike," evidence of the recognition that each role and person can be unique to thrive at Uber.[2]

Notes

1   Isaac, M. (2019) *Super Pumped: The battle for Uber*, New York: W.W. Norton & Company
2   Uber (2024) Careers, www.uber.com/us/en/careers/ (archived at https://perma.cc/GL79-3JNS)

6

Job Analysis

What Is a Job Analysis?

A job analysis refers to the study of a role, its activities, and the skills needed for success in that job. It's essentially everything that defines what this job is all *about*.[1]

Here is an overview of the specific information you can gain from job analysis in clear terms.

1 **Role:** A summary of the job.

2 **Activities:** A detailed breakdown of the specific responsibilities, duties, and tasks associated with the job role.

3 **KSAs:** Identification of the knowledge, skills, and abilities needed to perform the job effectively.
Note: Some industrial organizational psychologists were trained to refer to knowledge as knowledges in the plural sense. For our audience in this book, we'll refer to knowledge in the singular tense.

4 **Qualifications and requirements:** Understanding the minimum qualifications, certifications, education, and experience required.

5 **Challenges and improvement areas:** Any particular challenging aspects of the role or areas that would benefit from improvement.

6 **Work context:** Any aspects of the work environment that help or hinder their performance.

During our specialized training to become I-O psychologists, we wondered if job analysis was invented just to torture students, but we learned later that job analysis was created to ensure we fully understand a job before we go out and assess the candidates on all the wrong things.

To make it clear, we'll use a more unserious, perhaps obvious (but helpful) example. Imagine that we want to hire a dog walker for our respective dogs, Josie and Leia.

To hire our dog walker, we may be tempted to start by just coming up with good candidate questions. One of us might ask the dog walker: "Tell me what you like about dogs," and then ask: "How do you think dogs make the world a better place?" Since these dogs are our best friends, we might be tempted to focus on how this candidate will also be best friends with our dogs. We love our dogs so much that we likely hold some biases in how we select a dog walker. These types of questions might help us understand whether our dog walker has the same passion for dogs as us. After all, why would we trust someone to walk our dogs unless we knew that they loved dogs as much as we do?

Or perhaps we would do more of a work sample instead of wasting our time on interview questions. We could ask the dog walker to come over to our houses and introduce themselves to the dogs. If the dogs like the dog walker, then they pass the "sniff" test. If the dogs don't like the dog walker, then they fail. That seems like an ultimately efficient and realistic way to see how they could handle our dogs *in action*.

But alas… these are terrible questions. And it's a terrible test! Whether we agree with a dog walker about why dogs are great is not predictive of dog walker job performance. And furthermore, it's often the case that dogs don't respond well to new people, even when they meet the most wonderful dog walkers. In fact, the dog's initial response is likely more related to what the dog walker had to eat that day, how they react emotionally to the situation, or what other smells are covering the person!

Instead, we should start by understanding the *job*. We've both *been* dog walkers, because we both live with dogs and we walk them every day. We each have a pretty good idea of what the dog walker needs to do. They need to get the dog from our house, put a leash on the dog, take the dog on a walk, pick up any mess, and then place the dog safely back into the house after removing the leash.

If we were going to write a list of job activities, it would look like this:

JOB ACTIVITIES

1 Use a key to open the front door

2 Greet the dog (potentially with a treat)

3 Get a leash on the dog

4 Lock the front door

5 Walk the dog safely around the neighborhood, ensuring that the dog is safe and others are safe from the dog

6 Ensure that the dog has a chance to relieve themselves

7 Clean up any dog mess

8 Take the dog home, and ensure the dog is locked in the house, and the house is locked

---

Now we're making progress! Let's say we want to know more about what makes someone perform well on these tasks. It's fine that someone has done all this stuff before, but we're talking about caring for our *best friends in the world*. We need to know more about whether they are the kind of person to consistently do this well.

Let's write the knowledge, skills, and abilities that predict how well someone can do the things we listed above.

KSAs for the key activities:

1 Opening and locking the front door—they need to not lose our key, they need to be responsible about our home and dog safety. They need to be *conscientious and dependable.*

2 Greet the dog (potentially with a treat). They should bond and connect with Leia or Josie. They need to be *empathetic.*

3 Get a leash on the dog. Leia doesn't like it when new people put leashes on her. Therefore, this person needs to be *firm and in control* of the dog. They should be *consistent.* They should have *knowledge of how to get a dog to comply.*

4 Ensure that the dog has a chance to relieve themselves. They should have *knowledge of the signs* that a dog needs to go.

5 Clean up any dog mess. *Conscientious. Not easily disgusted.*

Gen AI Tip: Once you feel comfortable with developing skills, you may try to plug these sentences into your chatbot and prompt it to outline which skills are required to do each of these things as a second check.

Now that we know what the person needs to do, and what it takes to be good at these things, it's much easier to come up with relevant interview questions. We will cover this in the next section, but basically, we can simply ask our candidates for examples of times when they have done these things we listed above. We can also come up with questions to address the predictors of those activities, like:

"Tell me about a time when you had a hard time building a positive relationship with a dog. How did you handle it? What helped you and the dog to bond?"

"What are some of the ways you check that the dog is safe before leaving a house?"

"Do you have an example of when a dog you walked was aggressive towards another dog? What did you do? What happened?"

Those are some very predictive questions! And based on the analysis that we did, we can come up with examples of what good answers look like as well. We are looking for someone who has a strategy of some kind (and it may not be the same as what *we* do with our dogs) to bond with the dog. We are looking for someone who double checks that the doors are locked and ensures the dog is safe each time. And we need to hire someone who understands how to safely walk a dog in an area where other people and dogs may be and can express this clearly.

The last thing we'll do is determine if there are any basic qualifications for this job. Can our neighbor's nine-year-old child do the job? Probably not. Our dogs are big and strong, and they might be overwhelming and overpower a young, smaller person. Therefore, we could have a preferred qualification of being at least 14 years old and having had at least two years of hands-on dog experience. Having said that, we also avoided criteria that might eliminate people unfairly. Although the nine-year-old neighbor's sister is short for their age and doesn't look like a champion powerlifter, the kid has so much experience with dogs that she can command a dog to sit, lie down, and even be quiet when needed. She would likely pass the qualification to walk a strong dog. Done and done. Now, if the job required speaking in Spanish to the dog, that would need to be a minimum qualification, i.e. a requirement.

Activities

To recap, activities are simply a list of the things that the person in the job actually will do in the role. We find it easiest to use existing job-related data (like job descriptions) as a starting point for these, unless the job description does not exist, or isn't updated.

The following are examples of activities for some common roles.

FIGURE 6.1 Example Job Activities for Common Roles

CUSTOMER SERVICE REPRESENTATIVE

- Respond promptly and professionally to customer inquiries via phone, email, or chat.
- Resolve customer issues and complaints in a timely and effective manner.
- Maintain accurate records of customer interactions and transactions.
- Collaborate with other departments to address customer needs.
- Strive to meet or exceed customer satisfaction goals.

PROJECT MANAGER

- Develop and manage project plans, ensuring adherence to timelines and budget.
- Coordinate communication among team members and stakeholders.
- Conduct risk assessments and implement mitigation strategies.
- Monitor project progress and report on key performance indicators.
- Facilitate team meetings and provide leadership to ensure project success.

SALES ASSOCIATE

- Cultivate and maintain positive relationships with customers.
- Identify and pursue new sales opportunities.
- Provide product knowledge and assistance to customers.
- Meet or exceed monthly sales targets.
- Keep abreast of market trends and competitor activities.

FINANCIAL ANALYST

- Analyze financial data and trends to provide insights for decision-making.
- Prepare and present financial reports to management.
- Conduct budgeting and forecasting activities.
- Evaluate investment opportunities and assess risk.
- Collaborate with other departments to ensure financial goals are met.

Knowledge, Skills, and Abilities (KSAs)

We've referenced KSAs a few times now, but what are they? KSAs are what someone needs to excel at in order to do all the activities required for the job. It may be useful to create another column next to each activity, and note the type of KSAs they need in order to be good at that activity. In a moment, let's check out an example with one of the jobs listed in Figure 6.1. The KSAs should link back to the activities. There may be multiple KSAs for each activity. Sometimes, the same KSAs may measure multiple activities.

Knowledge

What stuff does someone need to know before they can do a job? Knowledge areas are the pieces of (sometimes theoretical) knowledge that someone must have to do their job. The more complex the job, the more knowledge areas required. How about a lawyer? There are lots of different kinds of lawyers, so this is a field that is differentiated by the type of knowledge that they gained. In their areas of expertise, lawyers use past case history to make arguments for new cases, which is loosely referred to as building a precedent. During law school and their job experience, they learn a lot about case history, so that they can reference specific instances to guide others in digging for more detail on specific case evidence that they can use. Some of the key knowledge required for a lawyer regardless of specialty is:

Legal systems and structures: Familiarity with the structure and operation of the legal system in their jurisdiction, including court hierarchies, legislative processes, and regulatory agencies.

Legal theory and philosophy: Understanding the foundational theories and philosophies that underpin the legal system.

Substantive law: In-depth knowledge of the specific laws and regulations applicable to their area of practice, including statutes, case law, and legal precedents.

The information above should help you to determine which knowledge concepts you want to focus on during your interviewing process. You'd likely remove knowledge areas that are guaranteed by the fact that they passed the US Bar exam, or that they completed an accredited law school.

When we hire someone to install a new roof on our house, we also expect them to have a lot of knowledge on roofing materials, roofing best practices, and pitfalls during installation. For example, we recently learned that if you use too much pressure in a nail gun when applying roofing materials, it causes the shingles to curl upwards, rendering the roof useless. Asking a candidate to explain proper use of a nail gun could be a legitimate knowledge question for a roofer interview. It's not practical to hire someone who could "figure it out" through problem solving, or "read up on it." We want our roofer to have the right information available at the moment so they can quickly make a recommendation and perform the installation.

The examples above point to situations where you would outline a list of knowledge areas for these jobs—those pieces of information that someone has to know intimately to do the job well. When you add knowledge to the job profile, you're indicating that *this is something they need to know and understand before you hire them*, and while they may get better at some of these on the job, you're generally not willing or able to train them on it.

If you're hiring someone for a tax law job and they're an expert in Brazil, but you also need them to handle tax law in Argentina, consider if they can get up to speed with what they know. Sometimes it's necessary to allow some knowledge leeway because perhaps there are few lawyers available who have any South American tax law expertise AND understand the complexity of a mining corporation. You'll be in a position to decide which of these you're more willing to forgo to get the right person. If it's something they could learn, make it a desirable, but not required, knowledge area.

Skills

Skills create a simple and common language around job performance.

Technical skills include things like "Excel" or "Python." Behavioral skills include things like influence, communication, strategic thinking, or action orientation, to name a few. We're bucketing all of these seemingly different things together in the broad category of "skills" because they are generally considered learnable, meaning someone can get better at them with practice and motivation. However, for the sake of hiring for your job, you're identifying the skills they need to possess at some minimum level on the very first day of their job. We often get asked: Is *MS Excel proficiency* a skill or a knowledge? Programming languages and computer skills are skills, because proficiency is gained through practice rather than theoretical knowledge. Understanding KSAs, something we would be interviewed on when we IOs

FIGURE 6.2 What Are Skills?

WHAT ARE SKILLS?

Skills refer to the specific learned abilities or proficiencies that enable an individual to perform tasks or duties effectively. Unlike inherent abilities, skills are typically acquired through practice, training, or experience and can be developed or improved over time.

Measurable personal characteristics that differentiate job, role, organization, or culture performance levels are considered skills.

Any **mental, physical**, or **emotional element** that **leads to outstanding performance** in a given position is considered a skill.

Because different jobs have widely differing demands, the skills contributing to excellent performance will **vary from job to job**.

apply for jobs, however, is a knowledge that we acquired during graduate school and used to hone our skills as interviewing trainers.

Your job may require a combination of technical and behavioral skills, and if you're lucky, your organization may already have a skills model. A *skills model* is the core language around the essential skills that matter across the organization. If you can find it, and it seems useful, then by all means, use it! If your organization lacks a model, or the model isn't what you need for your job, we'll guide you in identifying a shortlist of crucial skills for the desired role.

KEEP IT SIMPLE

Aim for simplicity by narrowing down the list of skills to 10 or fewer. That's hard to do! That means you need to identify only those that are absolutely necessary for minimum job performance, thus required for success on day one.

Using an existing, reputable, and validated model ensures that your skills model has research-backed skills that are distinct, observable in performance, and predictive of success. If we've done a good job of discouraging you from writing skills from scratch, go ahead and leverage a free set of validated skills. O*NET online, built by the Department of Labor, is probably the easiest starting point.[2]

Does generative AI create skills? Yes, your favorite chatbot will answer any questions you present. Where do they come from? We don't know. They could come from anywhere in the great World Wide Web. We would love to hope that they come from the Department of Labor, but they could also come from some random website a recruiter built for their startup somewhere in Tulsa, Oklahoma. It may not be bad, but it may not have all the best research behind it. In other words, confirm anything that generative AI builds for you against your own great knowledge, and against what the research says about the job. Just a few extra steps to ensure you have a really solid profile.

CAN I MAKE UP MY OWN SKILL NAMES?

Feel free to create a unique language to describe your skills—with some small caveats. Many clients love this approach because they feel a sense of ownership and affinity to the resulting job profile. Bob Eichinger, a founder of a firm now part of Korn Ferry, understood how important it was for each company to feel a sense of unique language to describe their high performers. Our personal experience has found some evidence to indicate that creating your own model increases the likelihood of widespread adoption in everyday communication amongst your leaders and staff. Plainly put, people like to name things and place their unique company brand on them. Many seek to infuse the unique culture of their company into the language describing effective job performance, especially for leadership roles.

However, having said this, Bob Eichinger also highlighted the drawbacks of this approach, noting that it's challenging to create entirely novel descriptions due to the finite nature of skills. He emphasized the time-consuming nature of the process, as individuals involved in the job often have numerous perspectives on how to articulate performance criteria.[3]

Even if you end up crafting your own skill names and descriptions, make sure they exist somehow in the universe of the official skills repository from O*NET. It's kind of like the laws of physics. The Law of Conservation of Mass by Antoine Lavoisier states that mass is neither created nor destroyed through chemical reactions.[4] Skills follow a similar set of rules. There is, in the large universe, a set number of things on which you can assess a person, and psychologists have done a pretty good job of defining them *in their entirety* at a basic level. So, although you may come up with some nifty new names to describe "collaboration," "influence," or "problem solving," it's actually a physical impossibility that you'll name something new that wasn't already named in a different way. However, some people still like going through this exercise because, honestly, giving things new names can be fun. If you prefer to call "Influence" "Impresario Impact," we won't stop you, and we applaud you for your unique name, as long as everyone clearly knows and can agree on what "Impresario Impact" actually means, and how to measure it during an interview. What matters is that the name chosen represents the construct and everyone understands and agrees on the meaning.

At Google, some people are still hired for the construct of "Googleyness," based on the preparation guide for a product manager, which was defined as of this writing in 2024 as:

> Google's Product Managers dream of the next moonshot idea, thrive in ambiguity, value feedback, effectively challenge the status quo, and do the right thing. They lead and influence effectively, manage projects, get things done, work as a team, and strive for self-development. They demonstrate curiosity to know more and are able to come up with novel product concepts and feature improvements.[5,6]

Thriving in ambiguity, valuing feedback, and doing the "right" thing (which is what, exactly?) sound to us like amazing qualities in a product manager, but we are skeptical of any construct that measures more than one unrelated thing. Since "Googleyness" measures three or more different and separate things, it's officially rendered impractical and prone to bias during any assessment process. One person could be interviewed by four different people, and half of them could see the "Googleyness" and the other half might see no evidence of it, because it's a loose definition which contains a variety of traits. How does that happen? Imagine a scenario where we are asked by our client to give a candidate a score on "Googleyness." We are often asked to replicate concepts such as these because many of our clients admire Google, understand that Google hires outstanding employees, and want to use a similar process to ensure that they also hire outstanding employees.

One of Mollie's former leaders once explained to her, "If someone can do one thing but not another, you're dealing with two separate constructs." In the example of Googleyness, if a candidate excels in handling ambiguity but doesn't value feedback, this indicates that the construct is not well defined and is actually measuring at least two distinct qualities.

Mollie interviews candidate A. Mollie notices that candidate A has excellent examples of managing projects. Therefore, Mollie gives Candidate A a high score on Googleyness. Kasey interviews Candidate B. Candidate B has excellent examples of dealing with ambiguity. Therefore, Kasey gives Candidate B a high score. Are Candidates A and B equally qualified? What if Mollie had interviewed Candidate B, would Candidate B have still gotten a high score, especially if Mollie places more value on examples related to project management? As you can imagine, the criteria end up lacking consistency and causing problems.

If we made the Googleyness interview more robust, we could ensure that candidates are all measured on separate subscales that relate to the areas listed above. Then, we could average all of these together and give them an overall score on Googleyness. While this improves the process significantly, we're still concerned about the fact that Googleyness is not meaningful. To meaningfully discuss a candidate, we need to discuss each of the components instead, ignoring the larger measure of Googleyness. At its best, therefore, the construct is simply distracting to the process. At its worst, it makes the interview process take a lot longer and many good candidates are likely left out in the shuffle. Before we leave the subject of Google, you may ask how they manage to hire such great people. Google's employees are indeed often high-performing, so something is going well in spite of all of our criticism. We believe that Google and firms such as Goldman Sachs hire high-quality staff by screening based on education, history of work results, and prestige associated with their past companies. We agree that these can be important qualifications, but in Part 3, we'll describe ways to ensure you don't limit your candidate pool to just the superstars who happened to have gotten the best opportunities in their lives, through their universities or in past jobs.

Instead of using successful companies as a model for building your skills, we recommend using skills and traits developed by the experts. As of the writing of this book, you'll find a section in O*NET called "work styles," which allows you to choose the areas most important to your job and flesh out the components you want to leverage for each. These are the most basic skills that you can select for any type of job.[7] They are distinct and separate from one another, which ensures you're only measuring one single thing at a time. If you're looking for more specific job-related skills, you can also look at the section on "soft skills," and investigate the various skills in each of the components, like *coordination* or *social perceptiveness*.

Abilities

About 100 years ago, researchers determined that cognitive ability (intelligence) was predictive of everything in life. Job success, education, income… you name it.[8,9,10] General intelligence is one of the most desirable and talked-about abilities amongst hiring managers. However, it's not a good measure to leverage for your own job profile, and we will explain more about the reasons for this.

Abilities are one of the few areas that are particularly challenging for individuals to improve or develop over time. In fact, they are often more difficult to enhance than knowledge, which can be acquired through education and training. Abilities refer to natural aptitudes or inherent capacities that significantly contribute to job performance and overall effectiveness in various roles. These abilities, such as analytical thinking, manual dexterity, or deeply ingrained personality traits, are typically stable over time and can influence how well a person can execute specific tasks. While skills can be cultivated through practice and experience, abilities represent the foundational traits that set the stage for an individual's capacity to excel in their job. As such, understanding and assessing these abilities is crucial in the context of KSAs, as they play a vital role in determining a person's potential for success in a given position.

Kasey scores below average on an ability called *spatial reasoning*. This didn't come as a surprise, given a lifetime of misreading maps, diagrams, and flat-pack assembly instructions. Rebuilding an entire Ikea dresser or Lego Galaxy Explorer ship due to a cognitive deficit in translating two dimensions to three dimensions is frustrating, to say the least. While disappointing, she also realizes this capability probably failed to develop from an early age. Based on our experience coaching leaders, we've found that if Kasey decided that she desperately wanted to become someone who excels at spatial reasoning, she may still not be able to up her score from the 15th percentile to the 75th in a short amount of time, compared to improving something like presentation skills. If she somehow did, it would take hard work. Even if she became better at it, she may need considerably more time to complete a task involving spatial reasoning than someone who already scored high on this.[11,12] Because of the less developable nature of abilities such as this and *reading comprehension*, *numerical reasoning*, and *logical problem solving*, we want to be particularly careful in assuming that any are needed for a job. In spite of excellent numerical and mathematical abilities, Kasey ruled out the field of mechanical engineering early in her career, to say the least.

Once again, O*NET will come in very handy here. In the section on O*NET called "Abilities," you'll find a list of abilities categories. For example, under "physical abilities," you'll see the requirements for jobs that involve lifting or other physical tasks.[13] Using other similar jobs as a guide, you can select applicable abilities that apply to your role. Per the example we provided above, however, it is especially important to only use abilities that you can prove are **absolutely necessary**. Although we discuss this in more detail in the final part of this book, some abilities have adverse or disparate impact against certain groups of people. If, for example, you post a job with a minimum lifting requirement of 100 pounds, that eliminates more women than men from the job. This means that your requirement has an adverse or disparate impact against women. In the United States, that impact is in violation of the Civil Rights Act, unless you can prove that someone cannot do the job without being able to lift 100 pounds (i.e. fire-fighters). Your proof of the requirement will be the documentation you retain after building your job profile.[14,15,16]

The studies correlating intelligence and *success-in-all-things* were done on massive samples of people—more than tens of thousands.[17] When researchers use a huge sample, it's often easier to see even smaller, incremental differences among the populations. For example, the sample included people who have top-level degrees, work in prestigious companies, and experienced a lifetime of practice in showing their intelligence in various ways. The sample also included the exact opposite, meaning individuals who did not have any advantage in their life or education and achieved far less financial or educational success on the whole. The stratification of those two groups is intense, and therefore it makes the factor of intelligence test scores also look more predictive. In the typical population of people applying for jobs of any kind, the stratification of applicants is far less. If we test 100 of your job applicants on intelligence, we'd see a large proportion of them fall around the middle with few differences, meaning that it wouldn't be a differentiator. Therefore, in spite of how broadly predictive intelligence is, it's less likely to help you differentiate among candidates for your specific roles.

Minimum and Preferred Qualifications (MQ and PQ)

Does your candidate absolutely need to have an *Underwater Welding Certification* to do this job? How about a certification from the *International Chocolate Awards* for individuals with a refined palate to evaluate and judge the quality of chocolate? Perhaps they must be a *Certified Forensic Handwriting Analyst*? A long-time favorite of this set of authors is the *Diploma Course in Professional Palmistry/Fortune Telling*. That must be important for a job out there, somewhere, and we imagine more than a few palm readers may have this proudly displayed on a front office wall.

If you can prove with absolute certainty that something is required for someone to be able to do their job, then we call this a minimum qualification

(MQ). Licensure requirements in healthcare jobs, an active driver's license for a role involving driving, or educational requirements for specific areas of work are most common. (You'll learn all about minimum qualifications, for example, should you accidentally sign up as an Uber driver when you meant to sign up as a rider.) Note, however, that if any of your existing employees have already succeeded in the job without these qualifications, then it's not easy to justify that it's an MQ. In that case, you can list it as a preferred qualification (PQ).

Here's how it works when you post your job. If you list an MQ of lifting more than 30 pounds for a warehouse job, that means anyone who can't lift more than 30 pounds may not even apply for the job. Thinking back to the funnel diagram in the introduction, think of your MQs as slicing off a number of applicants right at the top. If you do allow employees in the job who cannot lift 30 pounds, and list it as a PQ, and you end up with two equally qualified candidates, except that one can lift 30 pounds and one can only lift 25, you'd likely hire the one who can lift 30 pounds. However, if the candidate who can only lift 25 pounds has other qualifications that make them a better candidate, you could still hire them.

For an entry-level financial analyst role, we like to limit the MQs to ensure we don't eliminate candidates who may still have the skills needed for the job even if they didn't go to the most prestigious university or work in the most prestigious company. In this role, it's acceptable for candidates to receive their licenses and degrees within a certain number of months after hire.

Similar to the abilities, MQs should be your *absolute must-have qualifications* in terms of education, years of experience, or licenses.

FIGURE 6.3 Example of Minimum and Preferred Qualifications

FINANCIAL ANALYST MQs AND PQs	
MINIMUM QUALIFICATIONS	**PREFERRED QUALIFICATIONS**
None	Financial Modeling and Valuation Analyst (FMVA) A university degree in finance, accounting, economics, or a related field.

Methods for Conducting a Job Analysis

I-O psychologists leverage a combination of interviews, focus groups, and surveys with job experts in the job analysis process. In the earlier example, we are the job experts on dog walking. Since we are very knowledgeable about this job, we just listed out the job profile components and took them one step further to write our interview questions. Similarly, when you conduct a job analysis for a role on your own team, you may also be the job expert, or someone on your team will be. Whoever has sufficient knowledge of the job can help fill in the required information for the job analysis.

If you are the recruiter or HR representative, however, then you're conducting a job analysis for another team in your organization. In that case, you'll need a process to gather data from the experts. There are a few options. The easiest, and most likely solution is to sit down and have a conversation with your expert(s), in which you gather the data we'll describe.

Let's say you're the only recruiter for a 100-employee startup, and you need to hire for a variety of jobs that are constantly changing. You may develop a survey for your job expert to fill out each time you need to hire for a new team, since that's quicker and more efficient than using email or holding a meeting with each hiring manager or team. Even better, maybe you can integrate that survey into your applicant tracking process (ATS) so it's tracked together with all your other candidate data.

What if you can't get time with the leaders, any job incumbents, and they won't fill out a survey? Sometimes this happens because the analysis needs to be done yesterday, or because they are in jobs where it's difficult to get time with them (because actually doing their jobs is more important than analyzing their jobs). We have created job profiles for brand new jobs that have no incumbents or experts. Although it's not ideal and we would always recommend pulling out all the tricks to influence the appropriate people to help get you the information you need, you can conduct research to learn about the job. We do research by benchmarking—basically understanding how this job looks at other companies.

Benchmarking data about your job ensures you can safely say that you haven't spiraled out of control in your job creation and that it aligns sufficiently with other similar jobs in the industry. That is a legitimate basis for job analysis in the absence of expert data. We often start by looking up the job on O*NET, a site built by the US Department of Labor to describe each and every job in our economy. O*NET provides a list of the top skills, tasks, and background requirements, and can be a great resource for common roles.[18]

You can also search the web for job descriptions to understand how other companies post your job. As of the writing of this book, popular sites such as Indeed.com and LinkedIn.com have many job descriptions available for view.

If you're hiring for a role such as a driver, sales representative, or software engineer, the job profile may not vary a lot from one company to the next. You may be able to start with the content you found, then customize the content as needed for your specific team and organization. What about generative AI? It's worth seeing what is generated, but since we don't know the source of the data, the chatbot could just be pulling from some random person's resume online. We always check for consistency with known and researched sources such as O*NET.

To summarize, the commonly used data collection methods are shown in Figure 6.4.

When to Use Interviews and/or Focus Groups

In essence, the need to involve others in job analysis depends on how much you already know about the role. If you are the hiring manager and have a deep understanding of the job—especially for roles you've hired for or managed frequently—you may not need significant input from others. However, there are specific scenarios where looping in additional stakeholders becomes critical.

WHEN TO LOOP OTHERS IN

1 **Limited knowledge of the role:** If you're unfamiliar with the job's day-to-day responsibilities or its unique technical requirements, involving current role incumbents or team members can provide key insights.

2 **Broad or cross-functional roles:** For roles that span multiple departments or functions, gaining input from those who interact with the position is crucial to ensure an accurate understanding of its scope and impact.

3 **Newly created or evolving roles:** When the role is new, or its scope has changed significantly, stakeholders such as department heads, peers, or employees in adjacent roles can provide valuable perspectives.

FIGURE 6.4 Job Analysis Methods

JOB ANALYSIS METHODS

INTERVIEWS AND FOCUS GROUPS	• Conduct structured or semi-structured interviews with high-performing incumbents and supervisors to understand activities, skills, abilities, and knowledge required. These interviews can be one-on-one or in a group setting (i.e. a focus group.) • Ideal number of experts to meet with: 10% of job incumbents, no more than 30 people. • Participating incumbents should have been in the role for more than 6–12 months. • Any managers or supervisors included should have managed an incumbent in the position for more than one year. • All participants should have met or exceeded performance expectations in the previous performance cycle. • Participants should represent diversity in terms of race, ethnicity, gender, age, location, and tenure in the organization, as long as they have been with the organization for longer than 6 months.
QUESTIONNAIRES AND SURVEYS	• Helpful to use with larger-volume jobs with many incumbents we want to speak with and when we don't have a lot of information about the job without input from SMEs. • Send out questionnaires or surveys to job incumbents (and some supervisors) to understand activities, skills, abilities, and knowledge required for success on the job. • Surveys are sometimes used after the interviews and focus groups to rate how important and frequent the job activities, skills, etc. are to the job.
RESEARCH EXISTING JOB DATA	• Exploring any available information about the job in other companies or through the Department of Labor. This could include job postings on websites, performance reviews, job descriptions, or O*NET (https://www.onetonline.org/).
HIRING MANAGER-DRIVEN ANALYSIS	• A streamlined method where the hiring manager provides direct input about the role. The hiring manager completes a structured form or documents insights related to the key knowledge, skills, activities and abilities, required for the role.

4 **Collaborative decision-making cultures:** In organizations with a collaborative hiring process, gathering input ensures alignment and buy-in from all key stakeholders.

5 **Role misalignment concerns:** If there are past issues with role misalignment or unclear expectations, engaging a broader group can help clarify needs and avoid repeating mistakes.

WHEN IT MAY NOT BE NECESSARY

1 **Well-defined, repetitive roles:** For roles with stable, well-documented responsibilities (e.g. entry-level or operational jobs), a single stakeholder with strong knowledge of the role may suffice.

2 **Time constraints:** If timelines are tight and the job responsibilities are clear, focus groups may add unnecessary complexity. In such cases, prioritize direct, targeted interviews instead.

3 **Singular knowledge:** If you are the sole person who fully understands this job and the job requirements, then others are not likely to be helpful in defining the job.

USING FOCUS GROUPS

Focus groups are particularly useful when additional input is required but time and resources demand efficiency. They can bring together multiple perspectives in one session, fostering discussion and consensus.[19] Consider using a focus group if:

- you're seeking to validate job duties with a group of incumbents
- you need to identify overlapping responsibilities or gaps in role clarity
- multiple departments rely on the role's outputs, and alignment is critical.

By weighing these factors, you can decide whether looping in others is necessary and determine the most efficient way to gather the insights needed for a robust job analysis. See Table 6.1, which outlines some of the key considerations for using interviews and/or focus groups.

TABLE 6.1 Considerations for Using 1:1 Interviews and/or Focus Groups for a Job Analysis

1:1 Interviews		Focus Groups	
Pros	Cons	Pros	Cons
Depth of Insight: Individual interviews allow for deeper exploration of a participant's thoughts, experiences, and insights, leading to more detailed information.	Time-Consuming: Conducting individual interviews can be resource-intensive, requiring more time for both the interviewer and the participants.	Diverse Perspectives: Focus groups allow multiple participants to share their views simultaneously, leading to a richer, more varied discussion that can highlight common themes and differing opinions.	Dominance of Voices: Some participants may dominate the conversation, potentially overshadowing quieter individuals and leading to a biased understanding of the group's perspectives.

(continued)

TABLE 6.1 (Continued)

1:1 Interviews		Focus Groups	
Pros	Cons	Pros	Cons
Confidentiality: Participants may feel more comfortable sharing sensitive information or honest opinions in a one-on-one setting, leading to more candid responses.	Limited Perspectives: Each interview captures only one person's viewpoint, which may not represent the broader team or organization's perspective.	Group Dynamics: The interactive nature of focus groups can stimulate conversation and encourage participants to build on each other's ideas, often leading to insights that may not surface in 1:1 interviews.	Groupthink: The social dynamics of a group may lead to consensus-seeking behavior, where individuals conform to the dominant opinion rather than expressing their true feelings.
Customization: Interview questions can be tailored to the specific individual, allowing for follow-up questions that dig deeper into unique experiences or perspectives.		Efficiency: Gathering information from several individuals in a single session can be more time-efficient than conducting multiple individual interviews.	Logistical Challenges: Coordinating schedules for multiple participants can be difficult, and the group setting may introduce distractions that hinder effective discussion.
Flexibility: The interview format allows for adjustments based on the flow of conversation, enabling the interviewer to explore topics that may arise unexpectedly.			

Choosing between 1:1 interviews and focus groups for job analysis activities depends on the specific goals of the analysis, the nature of the information sought, and the resources and time available. When possible, a combination of both methods can be beneficial to gather comprehensive data. And you might consider supplementing them with surveys for quantifiable data or when seeking input from a broader audience. Combining methods ensures a comprehensive understanding of the job and its requirements.

When to Use Surveys or Questionnaires

While we don't expect surveys or questionnaires to be a primary tool for most readers, they can be a helpful method in certain scenarios. This approach is particularly beneficial for high-volume roles where there are many incumbents performing similar tasks and substantial hiring activity.

USING SURVEYS FOR JOB ANALYSIS
Best Use Cases, Purpose, and Efficiency

- **Best use cases:** Ideal for jobs with many incumbents or when you need input from multiple subject matter experts (SMEs) to fill knowledge gaps about the role.

- **Purpose:** Surveys or questionnaires allow job incumbents (and sometimes their supervisors) to provide input on the key activities, skills, abilities, and knowledge required for success in the role.

- **Supplementing other methods:** I-O psychologists often use surveys after interviews or focus groups to gather quantitative data. For example, they may ask respondents to rate the importance and frequency of specific job activities, skills, or competencies to validate earlier findings.

- **Efficiency:** This method streamlines data collection for large-scale hiring initiatives, enabling input from multiple individuals quickly and consistently.

While this method offers efficiency for high-volume scenarios, it's less relevant for niche or unique roles where detailed qualitative insights are more valuable.

When to Research Existing Job Data

Researching existing job-related data should be a foundational step for every role, every time. This method involves reviewing internal job documentation if you have any (like past job descriptions, performance evaluations, or competency frameworks) and external resources (such as comparable job descriptions, industry standards, professional certifications, and labor market data). It provides essential context for understanding the historical expectations, benchmarks, and evolving demands of a position.

This approach ensures accuracy, prevents redundancy in reinventing established standards, and sets a baseline for any further analysis. By anchoring the job analysis process in reliable, existing data, you save time and build a stronger foundation for identifying role-specific requirements and adapting to current organizational needs.

When to Use the Hiring Manager-Driven Analysis Approach?

The hiring manager-driven job analysis, or manager questionnaire, is a streamlined method where the hiring manager provides direct input about the role. This method is most effective in the following situations:

1   **When the manager is highly familiar with the role:** The hiring manager has a deep understanding of the position's tasks, responsibilities, and key success factors.

2   **For roles that are not highly complex:** When the role involves clear, well-defined, or standardized responsibilities, the manager's insights are typically sufficient without the need for broader input from other stakeholders.

3   **For complex roles with limited expertise:** When only a few experts are available, or when experts struggle to agree on the role's requirements, this method may not be ideal. In such cases, more comprehensive data gathering is needed.

4   **When time and resources are limited:** This method is efficient and requires minimal time and resources from other parts of the organization, making it ideal when quick decisions are needed.

This approach is most useful when simplicity or speed is a priority, but it may need to be supplemented with additional methods for highly complex or specialized roles.

HOW IT WORKS

The hiring manager completes a structured form or questionnaire detailing:

- key responsibilities and day-to-day tasks of the role
- the knowledge, skills, and abilities (KSAs) required for success
- relevant qualifications or certifications needed
- reporting relationships and position in the organizational structure
- expected outcomes or success metrics for the role.

The questionnaire may be designed by HR or I-O psychologists to ensure it captures critical job components. Or, if the hiring manager is driving this process, they can simply document the insights related to these key topics.

PROS AND CONS

- **Pros:**
    - o Fast and resource-efficient for straightforward roles.
    - o Provides insight from the person most familiar with the job's requirements.
- **Cons:**
    - o Risk of bias: The hiring manager might overemphasize specific attributes based on personal preferences.
    - o Limited perspective: Other important viewpoints, like those of current role incumbents or peers, are excluded.

While this method can be effective for simple roles, for more complex or collaborative positions, combining the hiring manager's input with data from incumbents, focus groups, or SMEs often results in a more comprehensive and accurate job analysis.

In summary, job analysis methods—such as interviews, focus groups, surveys, hiring manager-driven analysis, and researching existing job data—each provide valuable insights depending on the role's complexity and the resources available. Interviews and focus groups offer in-depth understanding from multiple perspectives, while surveys and questionnaires gather data from a wider group efficiently. The hiring manager-driven method is quicker but may be limited to roles with straightforward responsibilities, and researching existing job data ensures that decisions are based on relevant historical context and data for every role.

HOW DO WE DO IT?

If all the stars align, we have plenty of experts to choose from, there is abundant background information about the job, and we have willing participants to complete a survey… we could do it all!

We begin our process by benchmarking and researching the job. We create a test-case starting point of activities, skills, abilities, and knowledge as well as minimum qualifications. Then, we conduct one-on-one interviews with leaders or managers overseeing the role, especially those with a vision for the strategic nature and the mission of the job (meaning how the job may change in the future). We show them the materials we built so far and get alignment.

Next, we schedule focus groups with job incumbents and supervisors to discuss the details. How many job incumbents should we meet with? I-O psychologists recommend about 10 percent of the job holders, or about 30 individuals for large teams (whichever is fewer). These are not random numbers, but developed based on research about sampling strategies.[20] According to studies done by I-O psychologists, they found these figures to illustrate the maximum utility of time usage for yourself and for the incumbents. Among those 10 percent or 30 individuals discussing the job, ensure that you cover all the ways and places that the job is different. If you are analyzing a sales job with locations all around the world, include people from each of the offices. If the job is divided into different product types, include people who represent each of the different product types. That way, you've ensured that you have data across all the different ways the job could be performed.

Notes

1   SHRM (2023) How do I conduct a job analysis to ensure the job description matches the duties performed by the employee in the job?, SHRM, December 21, www.shrm.org/topics-tools/tools/hr-answers/how-conduct-job-analysis-to-ensure-job-description-matches-duties-performed-employee-job (archived at https://perma.cc/6CH4-M8ZR)

2   O*NET OnLine (n.d.) www.onetonline.org/ (archived at https://perma.cc/L5AG-XZWC)

3   Lombardo, M. M. and Eichinger, R. W. (2000) *FYI: For Your Improvement: A guide for development and coaching* (4th ed.) Lominger Inc.

4   Lavoisier, A. (1789) *Traité élémentaire de chimie*, Paris, Chez Cuchet

5   Project Management Institute (2020). Google interview prep guide product manager, google.com. https://d3no4ktch0fdq4.cloudfront.net/public/course/files/PM_Prep_Guide_2.pdf (archived at https://perma.cc/M5MA-Q8V3)

6   Meisenzahl, M. (2019) Google made a small but important change in 2017 to how it thinks about "Googleyness," a key value it looks for in new hires, *Business Insider*, www.businessinsider.com/google-googleyness-hiring-training-guide-change-2019-10 (archived at https://perma.cc/EKV7-FRF5)

7   O*NET OnLine (n.d.) Browse by ONET Data Descriptor, www.onetonline.org/find/descriptor/browse/1.C (archived at https://perma.cc/7P4M-BMGL)

8   Lang, J. W. B. and Kell, H. J. (2020) General mental ability and specific abilities: Their relative importance for extrinsic career success, *Journal of Applied Psychology*, 105(9), pp. 1047–61, https://doi.org/10.1037/apl0000472 (archived at https://perma.cc/6LUR-ME5P)

9 Tikhomirova, T., Malykh, A., and Malykh, S. (2020) Predicting academic achievement with cognitive abilities: Cross-sectional study across school education, *Behavioral Sciences (Basel)*, 10(10), p. 158, https://doi.org/10.3390/bs10100158 (archived at https://perma.cc/F2S7-25T8)

10 Tompsett J. and Knoester C. (2023) Family socioeconomic status and college attendance: A consideration of individual-level and school-level pathways, PLoS One, 11 April, 18 (4): e0284188, doi: 10.1371/journal.pone.0284188 (archived at https://perma.cc/P8RF-YB5K), PMID: 37040370, PMCID: PMC10089351

11 Uttal, D. H. et al (2013) The malleability of spatial skills: A meta-analysis of training studies, *Psychological Bulletin*, 139, pp. 352–402

12 Schultheis, H. and Carlson, L. A. (2013) Spatial reasoning. In *The Oxford Handbook of Cognitive Psychology*, Oxford University Press, https://academic.oup.com/edited-volume/34404/chapter/291768790 (archived at https://perma.cc/25XZ-PAB5)

13 O*NET OnLine (n.d.) www.onetonline.org/ (archived at https://perma.cc/C768-ENZK)

14 U.S. Equal Employment Opportunity Commission (1964) Title VII of the Civil Rights Act of 1964, www.eeoc.gov/statutes/title-vii-civil-rights-act-1964 (archived at https://perma.cc/5R2C-B96J)

15 Gutman, A. (2004) Ground rules for adverse impact, *Industrial-Organizational Psychologist*, 41, pp. 109–19

16 Fischer, R. J. (2018) The Uniform Guidelines on Employment Selection Procedures, on the occasion of the guidelines' 40th anniversary, *The Industrial-Organizational Psychologist*, October, www.siop.org/Research-Publications/TIP/TIP-Back-Issues/2018/October/ArtMID/20676/ArticleID/1344/The-Uniform-Guidelines-on-Employment-Selection-Procedures-on-the-Occasion-of-the-Guidelines%E2%80%99-40th-Anniversary (archived at https://perma.cc/8SQL-N6DL)

17 Strenze, T. (2007) Intelligence and socioeconomic success: A meta-analytic review of longitudinal research, *Intelligence*, 35(5), pp. 401–26

18 O*NET OnLine (n.d.) www.onetonline.org/ (archived at https://perma.cc/C768-ENZK)

19 Smithson, J. (2000) Using and analysing focus groups: limitations and possibilities, *International Journal of Social Research Methodology*, 3(2), pp. 103–19, www.sfu.ca/~palys/Smithson-2000-Using&AnalysingFocusGroups.pdf (archived at https://perma.cc/847J-PJD2)

20 Ibid

7

Job Analysis, Step by Step

Preparing to Conduct Your Job Analysis

Imagine that you need to build a job description to post on all the job boards, a job profile for internal/HR purposes, and ultimately interview guides. Is that why you're reading this book? We know that this can feel overwhelming, especially if you're a lean team of one tasked with this and with minimal HR support! Don't worry, you can do this.

We recommend you start by making a spreadsheet for each job you're conducting a job analysis for. This is where you'll track all the data you plan to collect and generate. If you prefer to use a document that's fine too. What matters is that you track and organize the key information regarding the job and what it takes to be successful.

Below are the job analysis components. If using a spreadsheet to organize this information, include the list of headings in Table 7.1.

Key Topics and Questions to Include in Your Job Analysis

Once you have your spreadsheet or document outlining the key headings and topics for your job analysis (such as activities, KSAs, minimum and preferred requirements, challenges, and work context), the next step is to create a document to capture and organize the questions you'll ask during job analysis interviews or focus groups. This will help structure your process and allow you to easily document insights from your job analysis discussions with subject matter experts (SMEs) and/or hiring managers.

We recommend creating a template for job analysis interviews or focus groups that you can reuse. Every time you conduct a job analysis interview or focus group for a new role, simply make a copy of this template. This keeps your approach consistent and efficient, while allowing flexibility for slight adjustments when necessary.

TABLE 7.1 Job Analysis Components

Job profile category	Description
Purpose	Why does this role exist? Why is this job essential? What's the mission for this job overall in terms of accomplishing goals for the company?
Levels	What levels exist for this job (like entry, junior, senior, or are they leveled by a number)? What level is in focus of the job analysis? Are there managers and different levels of managers as well? What differentiates each level? Ensure each level has reasonably distinct requirements.
Scope	How high up do they report in the organization? How much authority in decision-making do they have? What are their year-end goals or metrics?
Activities	What list of things do they actually do in this job? Consider what a person typically does in their work, both each day and throughout the weeks/ months. Describe the activities, such as "responds to queries that appear on the chat program."
Minimum and preferred experience	What experiences should candidates have before they start? Do they need customer service experience, and if so, how many years? Or is a positive attitude and a few retail jobs with good references enough? We find required experiences often inflated. Ensure all requirements are not trainable on the job, and ensure they are required for success on *day one*. Also, make sure you don't add requirements beyond what your current incumbents already have, unless they are expected to gain them in a certain amount of time.
Minimum and preferred education	Does the candidate need to have a degree? Can you prove that it's only possible to do the job effectively with this degree? Note that normally the job description shows "a degree in <certain field of study> or X years of experience to compensate." Also note that *very few* jobs actually require a Master's or PhD.
Knowledge	What knowledge does a candidate need to have on day one on the job? E.g. best practices in their subject, case law, or the history of xyz.
Skills	What technical or behavioral capabilities do they need? Understanding of arrays in software engineering is a *knowledge*, using python is a *skill*. Understanding best practices in accounting is a *knowledge*, using sequel queries is a *skill*.
	Hypnosis fundamentals is a *knowledge* area, but driving results and influence are *skills*. Selling strategies are *knowledge*, but negotiation is a *skill*.
	If you have too many skills, force a ranking to land on the top 7–10.

(continued)

TABLE 7.1 (Continued)

Job profile category	Description
Abilities	Abilities refer to the innate or developed capacities that enable someone to perform a task or activity. Unlike skills, which are learned and honed through practice, abilities are more long-term attributes that a person may possess and can apply across various tasks.

Here are some examples of abilities:
1. **Personal attributes:** The enduring traits or characteristics of an individual that influence their capacity to build relationships and perform a task or job effectively. Attributes are typically innate or deeply ingrained and serve as foundational components of abilities, influencing how a person approaches and performs work-related activities. A few examples:

   a. Interpersonal attributes:
      i. Traits that affect how individuals interact with others.
      ii. Examples: Empathy, adaptability, or emotional intelligence.
   b. Personal attributes:
      i. Broad, personality-driven traits that influence work behavior and performance.
      ii. Examples: Resilience, reliability, or initiative.

2. **Numerical reasoning ability:** The capacity to understand, interpret, and manipulate numerical data to solve problems. For example, a financial analyst may use numerical reasoning to analyze budget reports, forecast financial trends, and make data-driven recommendations.
3. **Analytical reasoning ability:** The capacity to break down complex problems, analyze information, and identify patterns or solutions. For example, being able to interpret data trends to make informed decisions.
4. **Verbal reasoning ability:** The capacity to communicate clearly and effectively using language. For instance, a teacher might rely on verbal ability to explain complex concepts to students.
5. **Physical strength and stamina:** The ability to exert force or maintain physical activity over extended periods. For instance, a firefighter may need the ability to carry heavy equipment and sustain high levels of activity during emergencies.
6. **Spatial awareness:** The ability to understand and remember the relationship between objects in space. For example, an architect may rely on spatial awareness to visualize how a building design will look in three dimensions.
7. **Manual dexterity:** The ability to use hands skillfully and precisely. For example, a surgeon needs manual dexterity to perform intricate operations.

Abilities are often harder to teach and can be crucial in determining overall job success when combined with relevant knowledge and skills.

Key Topics and Structure

While the main topics of a job analysis remain consistent, the way you phrase your questions and follow-up may vary depending on the job analysis method chosen and who you're speaking with. For example, when interviewing the job incumbent or SME, you may ask detailed questions about their specific experiences. For a hiring manager, however, you might reword those questions to align more with strategic or organizational needs. If conducting a survey, the questions and requested input will need to be formatted differently. The core topics you gather input on map directly to the components of the job profile you've documented in your preparation document or spreadsheet.

Capture and Document Insights

During each interview or focus group, ensure you document responses thoroughly. Use your template to organize notes under each topic, highlighting key insights and observations. This will make it easier to analyze the data later and develop comprehensive job descriptions or role specifications.

By maintaining consistency in your approach while adapting the language for each audience, you ensure that your job analysis interviews and focus groups provide relevant and actionable insights for the job role.

TABLE 7.2 Key Topics and Sample Questions for Your Job Analysis

	Interviews/focus groups	Surveys
Role questions (e.g. purpose, level, scope)	• "Why does the role exist? What critical need does it fulfill?" • "What are its key objectives and responsibilities?" • "How does this role interact with other teams, levels, or stakeholders?" • "What level of autonomy or decision-making authority does it involve?" • "How has the role evolved, and what future changes might affect it?"	• Primary purpose: "Select one or more options (e.g. Operations, Strategy, Client Interaction)." • Criticality to organizational goals: "Rate on a scale of 1–5." • Key interactions: "Check applicable levels or departments (e.g. Frontline, Executives)." • Autonomy: "Estimate percentage of independent decision-making (<25%, 25–50%, etc.)." • Open-ended questions: "Describe key responsibilities or future trends impacting this role."

(continued)

TABLE 7.2 (Continued)

	Interviews/focus groups	Surveys
Task-related questions (key activities)	• "Can you describe a typical day in your role? What activities and tasks do you focus on the most?" • "Are there any tasks you feel are particularly critical to the success of your job?" • "How do you prioritize your tasks or activities when under time pressure?" • "Indicate if these tasks are required to be successful on day one or learnable on the job."	• "List the primary tasks you perform in your job." • "Rate the importance of each task on a scale from 1 to 5." • "Indicate if these tasks are required to be successful on day one or learnable on the job."

Minimum and preferred qualifications	Minimum
	• "What qualifications (education, certifications, years of experience, etc.) are absolutely required for someone to perform this role effectively from day one? Can you provide examples of why these are essential?"
	• Follow-up: "Have there been any situations where someone lacking these qualifications succeeded? What made that possible?"
	Preferred
	• "Are there additional qualifications or experiences that are not strictly required but would make a candidate stand out? How do these qualifications enhance success in the role?"
	• Follow-up: "In what ways do these preferred qualifications impact performance or ease of onboarding?"
		Minimum
		• "What are the top three qualifications you believe are absolutely essential for this role? (select from the list or specify other)"
		  o Education level (e.g. Bachelor's, Master's)
		  o Years of experience
		  o Specific certifications or licenses
		  o Other (please specify)
		Preferred
		• "Which of the following qualifications would significantly enhance a candidate's potential for success in this role? (select all that apply)"
		  o Specialized technical skills
		  o Leadership experience
		  o Knowledge of specific tools or systems
		  o Other (please specify)

(continued)

TABLE 7.2 (Continued)

	Interviews/focus groups	Surveys
KSAs questions	• "What knowledge or expertise is essential to perform your role effectively?" • "Are there specific skills that set top performers apart in this job?" • "Can you think of an ability that makes a significant difference in your day-to-day performance?"	• "Rate the importance of the following skills for your role." • "Select the abilities you believe are critical for job success."
Challenges and improvements	• "What are the biggest challenges you face in your job? How do you address them?" • "If you could improve one aspect of your job, what would it be?"	• "Rank the following challenges in order of how frequently they impact your performance." • "Describe one area where additional support would improve your effectiveness."
Work context	• "What aspects of your work environment help or hinder your performance?" • "Are there any unique situational factors that influence how you perform your tasks?"	• "Indicate how often you encounter the following working conditions."

PRO TIP

If speaking with the hiring manager, ask, "What would success for the person in this role look like in one year? What would they have done?"

In the document or spreadsheet where you are capturing your job analysis data, list the most common activities of the job, like we did for the dog walker. Figure 7.1 shows a suggested template for capturing common activities required for a given role and determining if they are required for success on day one, or if they are learnable on the job.

FIGURE 7.1 Suggested Template for Capturing Common Activities

ACTIVITIES	REQUIRED DAY 1, OR LEARNABLE?

Make a note in the column next to each activity if the candidate needs to be able to perform the activity on their first day, or if it can be learned on the job. The activities necessary for day one on the job are the ones you'll assign KSAs to and ultimately evaluate candidates on. In the next section, we'll discuss how you can use the list you created to assess candidates.

Putting It All Together

Let's examine the full list for the example role of financial analyst. In Table 7.3 we've detailed the essential activities required for success in the role, followed by the corresponding KSAs necessary to perform those activities. Table 7.3 illustrates how these elements come together cohesively.

TABLE 7.3 Key Activities and KSAs for the Example Role of Financial Analyst

Activities	Knowledge	Skills	Abilities
Analyze financial data and trends to provide insights for decision-making.	Financial acumen: Understanding of financial principles, accounting standards, and financial modeling techniques to analyze data and trends.	1. Financial modeling: Proficiency in building and using financial models to analyze and interpret data.	Analytical reasoning: The capacity to critically analyze financial data and trends, and make recommendations based on insights.

(continued)

TABLE 7.3 (Continued)

Activities	Knowledge	Skills	Abilities
		2. Data analysis: Strong analytical skills to interpret financial data, identify trends, and draw meaningful insights.	Numerical reasoning: The capacity to understand, interpret, and manipulate numerical data to solve problems, e.g. to analyze budget reports, forecast financial trends, and make data-driven recommendations.
Prepare and present financial reports to management.		Presentation: Ability to create clear and compelling presentations to convey financial information to management and stakeholders.	
		Communication: Effective communication skills to articulate complex financial concepts to both financial and non-financial stakeholders.	
		Decision-making: Ability to make informed decisions based on financial analysis and risk assessments.	
Conduct budgeting and forecasting activities.		Budgeting and forecasting: Ability to develop, implement, and monitor budgets and forecasts.	Analytical reasoning: The capacity to critically analyze financial data and trends, and make recommendations based on insights.

(continued)

TABLE 7.3 (Continued)

Activities	Knowledge	Skills	Abilities
			Numerical reasoning: The capacity to understand, interpret, and manipulate numerical data to solve problems, e.g. to analyze budget reports, forecast financial trends, and make data-driven recommendations.
Evaluate investment opportunities and assess risk.	Investment acumen: Understanding of investment principles, financial markets, and methods for evaluating investment opportunities.	Risk management: Skill in assessing and quantifying financial risks associated with different business decisions.	
	Risk assessment: Knowledge of risk management principles and methods for assessing and mitigating financial risks.	Decision-making: Ability to make informed decisions based on financial analysis and risk assessments.	
Collaborate with other departments to ensure financial goals are met.		Collaboration: Ability to work collaboratively with other departments to align financial goals with overall organizational objectives.	

PRO TIP

When conducting this exercise, you may find that some skills are closely related to others or are even embedded within them. For example, you might discover that "presentation" skills can be mapped under the broader category of "communication." This is because effective communication encompasses a variety of methods and channels, such as verbal communication, writing, and delivering presentations.

Similarly, "risk management" might be mapped within "decision-making." This is because assessing risks and considering trade-offs is a key aspect of making informed decisions, particularly in situations where there are competing factors to balance. Recognizing these relationships between skills helps streamline the evaluation process and ensures a more holistic understanding of what's required for success in a role.

Final List of KSAs for This Role

After a final review, we've distilled this information into Figure 7.2, which will be included in the job profile. This figure serves as your blueprint for the KSAs you'll need to assess throughout the interview process.

Once you've gathered your job analysis information and consolidated the insights, don't forget to share the results with the SMEs you've spoken to, any hiring managers or supervisors, or HR professionals to verify accuracy and make any necessary adjustments.

FIGURE 7.2 Knowledge, Skills, Abilities (KSAs)

KNOWLEDGE (K)	SKILLS (S)	ABILITIES (A)
Financial Acumen	Communication	Analytical Reasoning
Investment Acumen	Collaboration	Numerical Reasoning
Risk Assessment	Financial Modeling	
	Data Analysis	
	Decision-Making	
	Budgeting and Forecasting	

Building Evaluation Criteria for Your Final KSAs

After finalizing the critical KSAs and other components of your job profile, the next step is to develop evaluation criteria to help interviewers assess candidates' proficiency in each area. It's worth noting that depending on your approach, you may need to involve SMEs in creating these evaluation criteria to ensure accuracy and alignment with the role's requirements.

In this book, we will explore several methods for developing evaluation criteria. Key considerations include deciding on the type of scale to use—such as a 3-point or 5-point scale (more about this in Part 4)—and determining the level of detail required (more about this later in this part). Regardless of the scale or format you choose, the most crucial step is getting alignment across SMEs and/or key decision-makers on what "good" looks like for each competency or KSA and ensuring that your interviewers are evaluating candidate interview data against those criteria.

Option 1 for Evaluation Criteria: Light and Universal Scale

One option is building light and somewhat generic evaluation criteria that can be used across any and all KSAs in a consistent way, if written a particular way. If using a 5-point scale, here is an example of this type of scale and the descriptors.

Communicates clearly: Communicates in a clear and concise manner across audiences and contexts. Actively listens to others and evolves dialogues based on new information shared. Skilled at picking up what matters to others and applies this to solutions and delivery.

Rating scale:

1 Poor
  o Displays minimal knowledge or experience with relevant principles, skills, and/or industry-specific standards and requirements.

2 Needs improvement
  o Displays limited knowledge or experience with relevant principles, skills, or industry-specific standards and requirements.

3 Solid
  o Demonstrates sufficient knowledge and experience with relevant principles, skills, and/or industry-specific standards and requirements.

4 Strong

- o Demonstrates strong understanding and extensive experience with relevant principles, skills, and/or industry-specific standards and requirements.

5 Exceptional

- o Demonstrates comprehensive mastery and significant experience with relevant principles, skills, and industry-specific standards and requirements.

Notice with this type of scale, the descriptions for the anchor points on the scale are not specific to the skill or other KSAs being measured—in this case, "Communicates clearly." So, this type of scale might be the easiest and most scalable (pun intended) method to implement, but lacks nuance across the KSAs you might use it for. This is a fine type of scale to implement if you need to build evaluation criteria quickly, as long as you and your interviewers align on "what good looks like" across any KSAs being measured, so all are evaluating consistently and fairly.

Option 2 for Evaluation Criteria: Basic Proficiency Scale

This option is still considered "lightweight" but provides more detail than Option 1. It includes definitions of basic proficiency for each KSA, clearly outlining what "good" performance looks like. Specifically, it defines the criteria for achieving a 3 rating on a 5-point scale. If you wish to build out a bit more detailed and KSAs-specific evaluation criteria, as overviewed with this option, we'd recommend doing so in partnership with your SMEs who you are working with during the job analysis work.

Start by listing out your KSAs. Then, we suggest listing out three bullets per KSA that describe what "solid" or "good" performance of that KSA looks like (this will become the 3 anchor point on the scale). When thinking about how to describe what "solid" or "good" looks like, think about "what behaviors would *meet* your expectation for a given KSA?" There has to be room for a candidate to exceed the 3 rating. The description for a 3 rating on a 5-point scale should not be exceptional performance. With this approach, interviewers can adjust their ratings up or down depending on candidate performance on each KSA assessed.

Communicates clearly: Communicates in a clear and concise manner across audiences and contexts. Actively listens to others and evolves dialogues based on new information shared. Skilled at picking up what matters to others and applies this to solutions and delivery:

- Communicates effectively in most situations, delivering clear and understandable written and verbal messages.
- Makes an effort to adapt communication style to different audiences and contexts.
- Demonstrates active listening by allowing others to speak and asking clarifying questions.

The bullets above reflect "solid" performance. However, there is room for potential improvement, such as consistently tailoring communication to resonate deeply and more actively evolving dialogues. See the notes below regarding what might be missing from each bullet. It's up to you if you want to include this type of detail in your descriptors. For less-experienced interviewers, it could be helpful to provide this extra level of detail:

- Communicates effectively in most situations, delivering clear and understandable written and verbal messages. (Use of "most" situations implies there is room for the candidate to do this more consistently across situations.)
- Makes an effort to adapt communication style to different audiences and contexts, though adjustments may not always fully resonate with all stakeholders.
- Demonstrates active listening by allowing others to speak and asking clarifying questions, though there may be occasional opportunities to enhance engagement or follow-up.

Option 3 for Evaluation Criteria: Behavioral Anchored Rating Scales (BARS) (most detailed)

This approach offers the most detailed and comprehensive evaluation criteria. While it requires more time to develop, input from SMEs, and may not be necessary for every role, it has significant advantages. By creating detailed descriptors, this method provides a robust framework for interviewers to make evidence-based ratings.

Here's how it works:

- Collaborate with SMEs to identify three to five key behaviors or qualities for each KSA being assessed.
- Develop behavioral examples for the low (1), mid (3), and high (5) points on a rating scale.
- Use a 5-point scale, with clear descriptors for the 1, 3, and 5 anchor points, ensuring interviewers have a detailed understanding of performance levels.

This method ensures consistency, supports objective evaluation, and allows for nuanced differentiation in candidate assessments. Additional guidance on selecting the number of anchor points for your scale is provided in Part 4. Table 7.4 is an example utilizing a 5-point scale with behavioral descriptors for key anchor points.

TABLE 7.4   Example Behavioral Anchored Rating Scales (BARS): Communicates Clearly

Communicates clearly: Communicates in a clear and concise manner across audiences and contexts. Actively listens to others and evolves dialogues based on new information shared. Skilled at picking up what matters to others and applies this to solutions and delivery.		
Does not meet expectations (1)	Meets expectations (3)	Exceeds expectations (5)
Listens actively: Engages fully in conversations, asks clarifying questions, and responds thoughtfully to ensure mutual understanding.		
Interrupts or disengages in conversations, rarely seeks clarification, and frequently misunderstands key points.	Listens attentively, occasionally asks clarifying questions, and demonstrates an understanding of key messages.	Fully engaged in conversations, asks insightful questions to deepen understanding, and accurately synthesizes and responds to key messages.
Structures information logically: Organizes messages clearly and coherently, making key points easy to follow and understand.		
Messages are disorganized, difficult to follow, and lack clear structure or key takeaways.	Organizes messages with a logical flow, presents key points clearly, and provides sufficient context.	Structures messages seamlessly, making complex information easy to understand, with clear takeaways and a compelling narrative.

(continued)

TABLE 7.4 (Continued)

Adapts to audience and format: Adjusts communication style, tone, and level of detail to suit different audiences and mediums effectively.		
Uses the same communication approach for all audiences and formats, leading to confusion or disengagement.	Adjusts tone, language, and level of detail based on audience and medium, ensuring effective communication.	Skillfully tailors communication style to different audiences and formats, ensuring clarity, engagement, and impact.

Summary of Evaluation Criteria Approaches: Key Differences, Considerations, and Implications

KEY CONSIDERATIONS FOR CHOOSING EVALUATION CRITERIA APPROACH

KEY TAKEAWAYS

Regardless of the approach, calibration among interviewers is critical to ensure shared understanding of "what good looks like" for each KSA and consistency in applying the evaluation criteria. The choice between these options depends on the organization's resources, time, and the complexity of the roles being evaluated:

- **Option 1** works well for speed and simplicity but risks lacking depth.
- **Option 2** strikes a balance between speed and specificity, offering a practical solution for many organizations.
- **Option 3** delivers the highest level of rigor and defensibility but requires significant investment in time and expertise.

For all options, clearly defined criteria and consistent use of pre-determined evaluation standards are essential for fair and evidence-based hiring decisions. Whichever option you decide on will go into an evaluation criteria document that will be shared with interviewers along with their interview guide.

FIGURE 7.3 Options for Evaluation Criteria

OPTION 1: LIGHT AND UNIVERSAL EVALUATION CRITERIA

DESCRIPTION	• Uses a single, generic scale that applies consistently across all KSAs. • Anchor point descriptors are not tailored to specific KSAs but instead represent general performance levels.
PROS	• Quick and easy to create, making it scalable and practical for organizations with limited time or resources. • Ensures consistency across all KSAs as long as interviewers are calibrated on "what good looks like." • Requires minimal involvement from SMEs during development.
CONS	• Lacks nuance, which may make it harder to capture KSA-specific strengths or development areas. • Could lead to less precise evaluations if interviewers don't clearly align on how generic criteria apply to specific KSAs.
IMPLICATIONS FOR USE	• Best for situations requiring a fast implementation or when evaluating KSAs that do not require deep differentiation. • Risk of less actionable feedback for candidates or hiring teams due to broad criteria.

OPTION 2: BASIC PROFICIENCY SCALE

DESCRIPTION	• Focuses on KSAs-specific criteria by defining 3 key descriptors for what "solid" or "good" performance looks like for each KSA. • Provides a foundation for a 5-point scale but emphasizes the mid-point (3) as a clear baseline for adequate performance.
PROS	• Balances ease of creation with increased specificity compared to Option 1. • Allows for a more tailored evaluation aligned with job analysis, improving accuracy and relevance. • Encourages SME involvement, leading to better alignment with organizational needs.
CONS	• Slightly more time-intensive to develop compared to generic scales. • Relies on interviewers to subjectively adjust ratings above or below the mid-point, which may introduce variability.
IMPLICATIONS FOR USE	• Suitable for teams looking for a moderately detailed approach without committing to fully behavioral anchors. • May require some calibration to ensure consistency when interpreting and applying descriptors across interviewers.

OPTION 3: BEHAVIORAL ANCHORED RATING SCALES (BARS)

DESCRIPTION	• Creates detailed, behaviorally anchored examples for each KSA at specific points (e.g. 1, 3, and 5) on a rating scale. • Behaviors are directly tied to the KSAs and provide clear expectations for performance levels.
PROS	• Provides the most detailed, consistent, and defensible evaluation criteria. • Ensures clarity for interviewers by describing specific behaviors for each rating level. • Encourages evidence-based decision-making by aligning ratings to observable behaviors.
CONS	• Time-consuming to develop, requiring significant input from SMEs. • May be overly detailed for organizations that don't need highly granular evaluations or are screening large applicant pools and unsure about asking interviewers to spend the time rating with BARS.
IMPLICATIONS FOR USE	• Ideal for high-stakes roles or hiring processes where precision and defensibility are critical. • Requires strong interviewer training to ensure consistent application of detailed criteria.

WHAT TO INCLUDE IN THE EVALUATION CRITERIA DOCUMENT

Once you determine the level of detail of your evaluation criteria (i.e. option 1, 2, or 3), then you will want to create a separate document that houses the evaluation criteria for your final list of KSAs. For an effective evaluation criteria document in a structured interview, include the following key elements:

- **KSAs definitions:** Define each KSA that was assessed in each interview to ensure interviewers understand what to assess.

- **Rating scale:** Provide the rating scale with descriptors for each anchor point on the scale for the KSAs being evaluated in the interview.

- **Evaluation guidelines:** Offer instructions on how to assess the candidate, including avoiding bias and ensuring objectivity.

- **Space for notes:** Allow room for interviewers to jot down specific observations and evidence that support their ratings for each KSA.

- **For a screen:** There should be a clear place for the interviewer to note if the candidate should move forward. This should NOT be included for onsite interviews, as based on our experience, we found that it is best practice to assess candidates on all KSAs being measured once they proceed from the screen before making a hiring decision.

- **Anything else relevant for hiring team:** Allow space for the interviewer to include critical notes that the hiring team should consider, e.g. "The candidate performed solid to strong on all KSAs measured in this interview, however, they spoke very poorly of their team throughout the interview and disrespected a few of their current team members, making personal jabs. I'm not sure how to capture this data since 'teamwork' or 'respect' was not assessed but wanted the hiring team to see this!"

How Much Effort Should I Put Into My Job Analysis?

We love our work and think it's essential, but don't let anyone, even rocket scientists, convince you that job analysis is rocket science—or brain surgery (we've analyzed both of these jobs, by the way).

Use Table 7.5 to identify how much sweat and tears you should put into your job analysis. Several factors should feed into your decision on how much effort to invest in your job analysis, e.g. the bigger the job population (how many incumbents the job has/will have once you hire), the criticality of the role, the seniority of the role, the scope and impact, etc.

If any of the conditions are in the *complex* or *highly complex* category, then you could conduct the job analysis process at that level of complexity.

Quick disclaimer for those of you in the United States! Table 7.5 has not been created by or approved by the Equal Employment Opportunity Commission (EEOC), one of the strictest entities when it comes to monitoring how employment decisions are made. We intend to help you figure out whether you should jump into this on your own or insist that your HR team step in with additional support for your job profile. We wrote this book to walk you through the easy option (not the complex option). We have consulted with countless startups and smaller businesses who didn't have an HR function and lacked the infrastructure, knowledge, and truthfully the bandwidth to figure this all out on their own. We conducted the easy version of the job analysis for them to help quickly put interviewing materials together and hire the right individuals for their needed roles.

You'll also notice that leadership roles fall into the *highly complex* option, and there's a proliferation of advice in the form of business books about how to hire leaders. Still, we have enough experience to say that hiring a leader without consulting, executive search, and HR support (including online surveys and assessment centers) can be pretty risky!

TABLE 7.5 Determining the Right Level of Effort for Job Analysis

	Minimal	Low	Moderate	Complex	Highly complex
# of incumbents (direct and indirect)	1–10	11–25	26–40	41–100	100+
Base salary	<$75k/ hourly	$76k–$125k	$126k–$180k	$181k–$300k	$300k+
Leadership	Individual contributor, early career talent	Individual contributor, frontline manager (still below middle management)	Mid-senior level individual contributor, frontline to mid-level manager	Senior management and executive	Senior executive and C-suite
Consequence of errors	Minimal, less than $1,000 loss	Insignificant, $1,000–$10k loss	Injury and accidents and/or $10k–$100k loss	Injury, accidents and death rarely and/or $100k to $1m loss	Injury, accidents, or death common, and/or more than $1m loss

When an I-O psychologist conducts a job analysis, it's because someone paid us for the analysis, and we go the entire length of the field to describe every single thing you could ever imagine about the job—the "exhaustive" option. The I-O psychology team at the US Department of Labor created O*NET as a fantastic resource for all who need to leverage job profiles and job descriptions. When we make a formal job analysis for a client, the resulting reports documenting the work can be close to 100 pages of obnoxiously dull text and charts, including excruciating detail about the tasks performed in the role, notes from interviews, focus groups, and surveys about the job or the job families. The whole process can take a month or two (or longer) for a single position, mainly because we spend so much time talking to experts about the job.

In this book, however, our aim is to offer an accessible, self-service solution for managing your hiring process independently or with your team, without relying on HR, recruiting, or consulting support. We'll focus on an approach acknowledging that while it may not cover every detail, it will effectively guide you in identifying job requirements and creating hiring materials and plans to support them.

Need more clarity? Check out Table 7.6 for insights into data rigor.

TABLE 7.6 Balancing Depth and Efficiency in Job Analysis

	Complexity scale for job analysis		
	Mini	Comprehensive	Exhaustive
Data review & collection	Uses existing data on similar jobs at a company or other companies (from O*NET, for example)	Uses existing data on similar positions at a company or other companies (from O*NET, for example)	Uses existing data on similar roles at a company or other companies (from O*NET, for example)
	Data from interviews with 1–2 experts in the job, plus HR/Recruiting	Data from interviews with 20–30 experts in the job, or 10% of the job population, plus HR/Recruiting	Data from interviews with 20–30 experts in the job, or 10% of the job population, plus HR/Recruiting
	No survey	Survey to collect information about the importance of skills and time spent on tasks	Survey to collect information about the importance of skills and time spent on tasks
Job profile output	2–3 pages or shorter	5–10 pages	11 pages or more (in the form of a Technical Report)
Legal value	When accurate, it's better in legal challenges than having nothing!	With good data, it can likely help in legal challenges	Done by a consulting firm with good data, it can probably hold up to or prevent legal challenges
When to use	It is useful when you only have 10 or fewer incumbents and/or only plan to hire < 10 employees	If possible, valid for any job	Useful in jobs with high risk of challenges, unions, and large volumes of employees
When NOT to use	Not for high-impact roles	Good for high-impact roles	Good for high-impact roles

8

Building Your Job Profile and Job Description

You've just conducted your job analysis (the heavy lifting)! Congrats! You can think of the **job profile** as a synthesis of all the information you gathered during the job analysis. This is an internally facing document that outlines the necessary skills, prerequisites, and any other characteristics necessary for success in the job. The **job description** is a summary of essential job duties and key skills pulled from the job profile. The job description is candidate-facing and is what you will post to external job boards and on LinkedIn. We recommend that you present your recruiting and HR team with the job profile so that they can then create the job description for candidates. If you're a small company and don't have HR/recruiting, then you will be creating the job profile and the job description!

A job profile....

1 Differentiates a successful performer from everyone else.

2 Explains what a new employee needs to know or do on day one of the job.

3 Ranges from 3 to 20 pages, depending on the job's complexity.

4 For complex jobs, it describes what skills, abilities, and knowledge areas are required to progress each step in the career ladder and when further training or knowledge shifts someone to a higher level.

5 Serves as evidence that your company took the time to study what your job needs, should someone in your HR or legal department need to justify reasons for hiring, promoting, or releasing someone. Your compensation team could also use it to justify pay for a particular role.

Job Profile

Let's get into the structure of a job profile. Your job profile should have the key sections as outlined in the box below. Since you created a spreadsheet, the job profile should mostly be a matter of copying and pasting the information.

INFORMATION TO INCLUDE IN THE JOB PROFILE

1 **Job title:** A job title that accurately reflects the position you are hiring for. Avoid using internal jargon or ambiguous terms.

2 **Date created:** The date you completed the job profile.

3 **List of experts:** List all the job experts, their job titles, and tenure.

4 **Job summary:** Provide a brief overview of the role's purpose and primary responsibilities. This summary should give the reader a clear understanding of the job.

5 **Reporting structure:** Clarify the position's hierarchical relationship within the organization. Indicate the immediate supervisor, any direct reports, and the position's place in the broader organizational structure.

6 **Working conditions:** Describe the working environment, including office location, remote work possibilities, travel requirements, or any physical demands associated with the role.

7 **Activities:** Outline the specific tasks and duties that we expect a successful candidate to perform. Focus on the most critical and impactful responsibilities, ensuring they align with the overall goals of the position.

8 **Qualifications and experience:** Specify the qualifications, skills, and experience necessary for the role, which may include educational background, certifications, technical skills, or industry-specific expertise.

9 **Knowledge:** Knowledge they need in order to do their job, which they gained from education or experience.

10 **Abilities:** Note the types of cognitive functioning requirements that drive success in the role, such as reading comprehension or numerical reasoning. This also may include any specific attributes required for success in a given role (e.g. empathy, resilience, etc.).

11 **Skills:** Write out the essential skills crucial for success in the role.

A quick note on terminology. We don't feel very strongly about what you call each "thing" that is measured, but the following represents the terms our clients find most intuitive and are most commonly used by other I-O psychologists. If you like the word "skills," that works for us. You can call them "superpowers," "capabilities," or "things that help you do a job better." If you like the term "stuff that's hard to learn but predicts job performance" instead of "abilities," feel free to use it.

Job Description

After you have created your job profile, we recommend creating a job description. This will be a candidate-facing document with the purpose of letting the world know you're hiring for your wonderful role, and letting candidates know about the role and company. A good job description has three components.

JOB DESCRIPTION COMPONENTS

1   Company details, including company mission, culture, and benefits.

2   Qualifications, including information about minimum requirements for education and experience.

3   Job summary, including a list of expected tasks, responsibilities, and behavioral characteristics in the form of skills and behaviors, with definitions.

Note: In some regions, you will need to provide a salary range.

Keeping a job description to less than two pages is ideal so that candidates can quickly identify the essential job needs.

Wait a minute! Why can't I just skip right to the job description? That's what many of us normally would do, right?

Our first response is always that any planful documentation about a job is a step up from nothing. If you've been in the habit of writing out a job description for each of your roles, you're very close to a job analysis already.

However, we recommend you go the extra mile and still conduct the more "formal" job analysis study as we outlined it.

First, the analysis of work activities goes beyond a simple list of job duties. When you identify each of the specific actions, procedures, and processes involved in completing each activity, the details promote a deeper understanding of your job's intricacies. These will then lead to a more accurate set of questions and evaluation guidelines. As a bonus, you can leverage these for aids in training, performance evaluation, and process improvement.

The analysis of knowledge, skills, and abilities provides a more comprehensive overview of predicted success in the role, including technical and soft skills. Similarly, your interview questions and evaluation are likely to better differentiate candidates with the extra detail.

In summary, job analysis is the process of gathering and organizing detailed information about a role. The job profile, developed from this analysis, is an internally focused document that outlines the role's key requirements and qualifications for success. The job description, derived directly from the job profile, is an externally facing document used to attract candidates. It presents a clear and accurate overview of the role's tasks and responsibilities, enabling potential candidates to assess their fit for the position.

9

Food for Thought

Any specific job usually has no more than seven or eight *most* relevant skills and about three or four that are also *somewhat* relevant. How do we know this? Psychologists recognize a balance point between trying to gather too much data about a person versus getting the correct data. It's difficult to absorb more about a candidate than we can handle; even if some of these are "nice to have" qualities, we can't expect to ask questions about all of them and process all the data from these to efficiently make a decision.

Focus only on the essentials and let the rest go. Truly, the hardest part of building a job profile is narrowing it down to the most critical KSAs.

If someone can't do the job on day one without this, that means it's critically essential. As an example, education is often overrated (yes, sometimes we get laughed at for saying this since many of us have PhDs). Make sure you don't overvalue education when people may have achieved equivalent experience to do the job just as well.

If you have seen someone do a job without this thing, it's automatically a "nice to have" and *not* critical. Save your interviewing time for the most essential things only.

After creating your job profile, if you're the hiring manager and job expert, review it with your HR business partner, recruiter, and other members of the HR team and maybe your employment lawyer. They may add some content or clarify further to improve your job profile.

To Weight or Not to Weight

We're often asked whether it's a good idea to assign different weights to the skills and other qualities you assess. While weighting can be valuable, it's a complex process that requires extensive research, far beyond what this book covers. It's also difficult to score accurately. For that reason, we recommend focusing on identifying the most critical aspects of the job and treating them equally. Trust us, we've seen job experts get excited about creating the perfect job prediction algorithm, only to use it for three hires a year. In our experience, we've only used weighting when working with an online assessment tool and after gathering data from at least 200 job holders to ensure that the weights are meaningful.

Where Else Can Job Analysis Be Useful?

Pre-employment hiring is not the only place where job analysis adds value. It will also help you build your onboarding, employee development, performance management, succession planning, compensation and benefits, and even give a sense of broader job architecture. Your future self will absolutely thank you for all that up-front work.

Point of Diminishing Returns in Data Collection

While it may seem appealing to understand everything in the world about the job, we have also found a point of diminishing returns when collecting data.

If you need more people to understand the position, it's a sign that you are dealing with different roles, not a single job. Or it's a sign that they disagree about how to do the job, which is likely causing problems that your job analysis can help unpack.

POINT OF DIMINISHING RETURNS

If you find that you're including more than 15 percent of the job incumbents, or more than 50 job incumbents for a large job, that's likely too many people.

For small teams with fewer than 10 people, try to get one-third to a half of the incumbents to participate.

Job Profiles Have Expiration Dates

Regularly review and update the job profile to ensure its accuracy and relevance. In today's world of constantly changing technology, jobs also change. When Kasey first learned about job analysis, plumbers did not have such a thing as digital cameras. This simple innovation turns a plumber into a diagnostician and type of "radiologist," discovering the mysteries of clogs and leaks in an entirely different way. Along with this change, plumbers had to display new skills. In another example, surgeons underwent significant adaptation to robotics equipment in the early 2000s, drastically altering the skills required for successful surgery, from hand-eye coordination to understanding machine operation and even some programming. Today, many of you are finding ways to incorporate various forms of artificial intelligence into your own work, changing the way you think through solving your own problems. Regularly consider if your job profile is still up to date.

Will My Job Change Due to AI?

One of the things we've noticed since the dawn of time—as was nicely put by the CEO of JP Morgan Chase, Jamie Dimon—whether it's about the printing press or the advent of AI, is that jobs invariably change with technology.[1] He points out that in 2024–2025, we're in a rapid change period. As a result, the job profile you create may not be relevant in a year or even less. Or perhaps the job profile will be relevant, but still significantly change, even if the core tenets of the job remain the same. What kinds of changes can you expect? How do you prepare for these and still hire the right people? Job activities or the KSAs might change due to technology. New skills and knowledge are likely required, while old skills and knowledge might be replaced. There is so much complexity involved in predicting whether or how much a job will change. Yet, we want to impart to you some sort of method and guide to determine whether you need to monitor your jobs and how frequently to update your profile.[2,3]

To help you prepare for this, we're providing a short checklist that will help you determine the likelihood that your job might change. If a large part of the role is encompassed by any item in Table 9.1, then we recommend creating a new job profile at least every year.[4,5,6]

The simple answer is that the more activities in the job that can be done by artificial intelligence, the sooner you'll need to update the job profile. What sorts of activities are most likely to be handed to AI?

TABLE 9.1 Adapting to AI and Technology: When to Refresh Job Profiles

O*NET Activity ID	More than 25% of activities related to the following indicates likelihood of automation	☑
4.A.1.a.1	Getting information	
4.A.1.a.2	Monitoring processes, materials, or surroundings	
4.A.2.a.2	Processing information	
4.A.2.a.3	Evaluating information to determine compliance with standards	
4.A.2.a.4	Analyzing data or information	
4.A.2.a.3	Making decisions and solving problems	
4.A.2.b.3	Thinking creatively	
4.A.2.b.5	Scheduling work and activities	
4.A.3.a.3	Controlling machines and processes	
4.A.3.a.4	Operating vehicles, mechanized devices, or equipment	
4.A.3.b.1	Working with computers	
4.A.3.b.2	Drafting, laying out, and specifying technical devices, parts, and equipment	
4.A.3.b.6	Documenting/recording information	
4.A.4.b.8	Performing for or working directly with the public	
4.A.4.c.1	Performing administrative activities	
4.A.4.c.3	Monitoring and controlling resources	

What happens if you have a job with a high chance of change? In that case, try to do a job analysis that is future-proofed, meaning that it takes into account the new skills needed. Let's walk through a couple of examples.

Quality assurance engineer: Before the rise of modern AI technologies, these engineers would define test requirements and check code for adherence to certain quality guidelines and make fixes. After AI, they clearly define test requirements and automate test procedures using generative AI tools, which may also be programmed to fix the code.

Customer service representative: Before the rise of modern AI technologies, a customer service rep would read a chat from a customer and respond to the chat. After AI, the customer service rep would see fewer messages, since initial requests were handled through the AI process. They would focus their effort on handling second- or even third-tier requests.

Radiologist: Before the rise of modern AI technologies, a radiologist examined every image and returned an analysis for the patient. After the rise of modern AI technologies, the radiologist audits inputs from the AI mechanism, which searches through patterns for suspicious findings that humans cannot detect.[7]

If you're noticing a trend in how AI transforms these very different jobs, you're absolutely correct. One of the reasons we discuss job *change*, versus job *elimination*, is that we see humans placing themselves more strategically in the best spot to leverage the AI tools. Data analysis was severely restricted by human brains in the past, needing a lot of time and cognitive energy to accomplish lines and lines of data. Now, assuming that our chatbots continue to be improved to avoid inaccuracies and data truncation, we can use the tool to quickly process much more information, much like the advent of the machine computer in the 1960s to make calculations.[8] The transformed jobs will call upon us to be increasingly strategic and process-oriented, versus carrying out tasks assigned to us.

Because the job has changed, your job profile should include the new knowledge, skills, and abilities needed to manage the AI, versus managing whatever task was done before. Here are just some examples of KSAs needed to work in the AI world.[9]

Knowledge:

- AI and machine learning: Understanding AI models, algorithms, and machine learning frameworks.

- Data science: Knowledge of data preprocessing, statistical analysis, and data mining techniques.

- Programming: Proficiency in relevant programming languages.

- Mathematics and statistics: Strong foundation in linear algebra, probability, calculus, and optimization methods.

Skills:

- Problem solving: Ability to apply AI tools and techniques to solve business problems or optimize operations.

- Data manipulation: Skilled in cleaning, processing, and analyzing large datasets.

- Modeling and simulation: Creating, training, testing, and fine-tuning AI models for predictive analysis or automation tasks.

- Critical thinking: Analyzing the implications of AI models and identifying potential limitations or biases.

- Communication: Ability to translate complex AI concepts into layman's terms for non-technical stakeholders.

- Collaboration: Working with cross-functional teams (e.g. data engineers, developers, domain experts) to implement AI solutions effectively.

- Creativity: Innovating new applications or improving existing AI processes to meet business needs.

- Project management: Managing timelines and resources to develop and deploy AI initiatives.

Abilities:

- Analytical thinking: Quickly interpreting data and model outputs to draw insights and make data-driven decisions.

- Adaptability: Ability to stay updated with rapidly evolving AI technologies and methods.

- Attention to detail: Ensuring precision in data analysis, model development, and system implementation to avoid errors or bias.

- Learning agility: Comfort with learning new tools and algorithms as AI evolves.

- System design and integration: Ability to design AI systems and integrate them into existing business processes.

- Pattern recognition: Recognizing trends and patterns within datasets to derive meaningful insights.

This is just a starting point, but some general areas to consider as you build your updated profile.

Documentation

In the event that a candidate doesn't like the interview process and feels it was unfair, you may be asked to prove that the process was based on solid research. That research is your "job analysis"! Make sure that you and your HR team have access to the job analysis spreadsheet or other documentation made, the job profile, and a log of who created or gave input to these job criteria. Having that documented goes a long way toward showing the legitimacy of the hiring process. Whenever you meet with an expert, document the names and information noted above for each expert in your job profile in a file that you and your HR team retain.

Part 2 Summary: Key Learnings

In this part, you learned how to conduct a systematic job analysis—a process for identifying what it takes to excel in a given role. By completing a mini-study of the tasks and skills required, you can define the critical knowledge, skills, and abilities (KSAs) necessary for success on day one. For example, instead of simply asking if a dog walker loves dogs, a proper job analysis identifies specific responsibilities, such as safely walking the dog and cleaning up afterward. You also learned how to build evaluation criteria for those KSAs.

Effective job analysis involves gathering input through interviews, surveys, and research to create accurate job profiles. These profiles allow you to craft relevant, role-specific interview questions and avoid relying on ineffective single-measure tools like ambiguous problem-solving tests. By focusing on candidates' demonstrated skills and experiences relevant to the job, you can make better hiring decisions.

Job Profiles Are Your Guide

A key outcome of job analysis is the creation of a job profile—an internal document summarizing the role's required skills, qualifications, and key details. This profile serves as:

- a record of your analysis
- a resource for creating hiring materials
- evidence to support HR decisions around hiring, training, and compensation

The job profile includes essential sections like job title, summary, reporting structure, working conditions, primary activities, and qualifications. This contrasts with a job description, which is candidate-facing and highlights key qualifications, responsibilities, and company details. Together, these tools ensure alignment between your hiring process and the role's specific needs.

Striking the Right Balance

Job analysis can range from concise to detailed, but the goal is to strike the right balance:

- rushing risks missing important KSAs, which may lead to poorly aligned interviews
- overcomplicating wastes time and can reduce engagement from subject matter experts (SMEs)

The most successful approach is thorough but practical, ensuring critical KSAs are captured without losing momentum or buy-in. Skipping job analysis entirely is the most significant pitfall, as it undermines the foundation of an evidence-based hiring process.

With your job analysis complete, you're ready to move on to the next part, where you'll use the job profile to build a structured interview guide. This will ensure your interviews are focused, consistent, and effective in identifying the best candidates for your role.

Part 2 Key Terms

Applicant tracking system (ATS): Software to collect, organize, and track job applications and candidate information.

EEOC guidelines: The Equal Employment Opportunity Commission's published guidelines on how to legally assess candidates for a job.

Job analysis: The process of systematically gathering, documenting, and analyzing information about a role to identify the tasks, responsibilities, skills, knowledge, and abilities required for successful performance. This foundational activity informs workforce planning, recruitment, performance evaluation, training, and compensation. Job analysis results are used to create both the job profile and job description.

Job description: A concise, candidate-facing summary derived from the job profile, emphasizing the essential duties, qualifications, and expectations of the role. It is designed to attract potential applicants by communicating the role's key aspects in a clear and engaging manner. The job description streamlines the information from the job profile for external use in recruitment materials.

Job expert: Someone who knows details about the job, the job requirements, and leads to success on the job.

Job profile: A comprehensive output of job analysis that details the key knowledge, skills, abilities, qualifications, responsibilities, and criteria needed for success in the role. This internally focused document serves as a guide for crafting interview questions, performance metrics, and recruitment strategies. It is dense and technical, providing the foundation for the candidate-facing job description and ultimately the interviewing and evaluation materials.

Minimum qualification: A specific experience, license, or other qualification that someone must have to do the job.

Preferred qualification: A "nice to have" qualification that helps someone do the job better.

Weighting: Determining which skills may be more connected to successful job performance and giving them more credence in the selection process.

Notes

1   Volenik, A. (2024) J.P.Morgan CEO Jamie Dimon says we shouldn't put our heads in the sand, "We have to find a better way to help the people who get hurt by AI," Bezinga, October 15, www.benzinga.com/startups/24/10/41338251/jpmorgan-ceo-jamie-dimon-says-we-shouldnt-put-our-heads-in-the-sand-we-have-to-find-a-better-way-to?utm_campaign=partner_feed&utm_source=aol&utm_medium=partner_feed&utm_content=site (archived at https://perma.cc/4XZD-6VRF)

2   Rus, D. and Mone, G. (2024) How to know if AI will steal your job, according to an MIT professor, Fast Company, www.fastcompany.com/91167830/how-to-know-if-ai-will-steal-your-job-according-to-an-mit-professor (archived at https://perma.cc/U8S6-LCSV)

3   Benítez-Rueda, M. and Parrado, E. (2024) Mirror, mirror on the wall: Which jobs will AI replace after all?: A new index of occupational exposure, Department of Research and Chief Economist, Working Paper No. IDB-WP-1624, http://dx.doi.org/10.18235/0013125 (archived at https://perma.cc/BB42-4RJP)

4 Kochhar, R. (2023) Methodology for ONET analysis, Pew Research Center, www.pewresearch.org/?p=38539 (archived at https://perma.cc/7G7A-R5DA)

5 Pew Research Center (2023) Work activities with high exposure to AI, www.pewresearch.org /?p=46745 (archived at https://perma.cc/7QXK-JU4J)

6 Schendstok, M. and Schreiner Wertz, S. (2024) Occupational exposure to artificial intelligence by geography and education, https://home.treasury.gov/system/files/136/AI-Combined-PDF.pdf (archived at https://perma.cc/42CR-WGDW)

7 Derevianko, A. et al (2023) The use of artificial intelligence (AI) in the radiology field: What is the state of doctor-patient communication in cancer diagnosis? *Cancers*, 15(2), p. 470

8 Gavett, G. (2016) Today's automation anxiety was alive and well in 1960, *Harvard Business Review*, https://hbr.org/2016/02/todays-automation-anxiety-was-alive-and-well-in-1960 (archived at https://perma.cc/YP6F-2QJW)

9 National Center for O*NET Development (2024) O*NET online, www.onetonline.org/ (archived at https://perma.cc/V2RW-DQZE)

PART THREE

HOW to Assess

In this section, we will discuss different interviewing methods with their respective question types, pros, cons, and considerations for use. You will also learn how to establish measurement and evaluation criteria, as well as what to do during and after an interview.

10

Out-of-the-Box Questions

*Why the Beer Test and Guessing Games
Don't Belong in Interviews*

While interviewing for an HR job with a financial firm, David Pennington described that he was asked a hypothetical mathematics problem-solving question: "How many ping pong balls can you fit into a Boeing 747?" He explained:

> While the question does assess general problem solving and contributes to eliminating candidates from the selection pool, it's important to keep in mind the alignment of the question with the work expected to be performed on the job. Knowledge of volume equations does not relate to human resources responsibilities or the knowledge, skills, and abilities required to effectively perform them. A more valid approach to generating interview questions is knowing which difficult situations the job incumbent might face on the job or the competencies required to effectively perform the job, then building questions based on either.

What Is the "Beer Test?"

In one of Kasey's prior roles, she happened to be doing an audit of the comments left in the company's applicant tracking system (ATS), a database where information about candidates and the recruiting process is stored. One of the comments read: "I would definitely not have a beer with this candidate. I recommend we do *not* extend an offer."

Kasey had many questions for the interviewer. How does a candidate get invited to have a beer? Should they be fun? Interesting? Kind? Or just "smart," whatever that means? *It could literally be anything*, she thought to herself!

Let's imagine that a job profile outcome was "worthiness of an invite to have a beer." What makes someone a worthy socializing friend? If we found 20 I-O psychologists and asked them to reach an agreement on this topic, we would likely fail to reach a consensus. Would we "need to like the person"? Or do we "need to enjoy spending time with them"? Are those valid criteria for hiring? No. Ultimately, the simple beer test endorsed by one of our favorite and most recognizable tech founders, Steve Jobs, is difficult to carry out in a structured and consistent way and could lead you to hire only your friends.

Plus, they may all end up drinking too much beer to be productive.

The same applies to asking all sorts of interesting questions that happen to be irrelevant to the job. Whether you're asking yourself about socializing with a candidate or how much you like those red shoes that they found on sale at the discount department store, you are failing to start your interview process with a description and measure of need for job-related skills and behaviors. Thus, you're still doing the "Could I have a beer with this candidate?" test.[1]

What's Happening in Our Brains When We Do the Beer Test?

In any assessment process, personal characteristics and behavior will, and should, be evaluated. However, if you don't set up a structured process to assess these systematically, they will *still* be assessed, albeit subconsciously and inconsistently—such is human nature. Your brain will automatically try to figure out how much you like the candidate, hopefully in addition to comparing them to job-related skills.[2] For example, studies have shown that managers give higher ratings to their subordinates who are most similar to themselves.[3,4] The beer test is an excellent example of favoring people who are like themselves. During interviews, "higher interview ratings are given towards interviewees who possess similar attitudes and demographics as the interviewer."[5] That's only helpful for people whose friends are all coincidentally experts at the exact job they need to hire for. Even in situations when that is the case, those can be risky hires. If you've ever been part of a startup hiring process or hired for a department in a university setting, you have potentially seen this in action. If nothing else, a team hired based on the beer test may not be as productive as they should be.

Instead, let's say you are asked to evaluate someone on innovation. You ask them to describe some of their recent innovations and give them scores on their volume of ideas, the usefulness of their ideas, and the successful implementation of their ideas. When your brain is busy putting a score on the example of the innovation they gave you, it's less likely for your brain to also consider how much you like them (or whether you want to drink beer with them). Our brains are terrible at systematically evaluating data at the same time as deciding who we like and how we feel around them. Effectively using structured evaluation reduces the friendship-and-beer part of your brain until you need it later (like when your sister wants to introduce you to her third new boyfriend in a month). The structure makes it less likely for your gut to take over a data-driven decision because you have a plan to evaluate data in advance.

The brain won't ever stop trying to make gut-level decisions; even trained assessors like us find it easier to make quick judgments about our sisters' boyfriends than to use scoring and evaluation guides. The beer test is likely to select candidates similar to the interviewers and therefore narrows the job relatedness. That's why we consistently use clear rating evaluation criteria *every single time*, even after our many years of assessing candidates.

In case you're curious about the beer test, Kasey reached out to the interviewer who wrote the comments in the ATS and asked them what the qualifications were for passing the beer test. Once the interviewer figured out that she wasn't trying to just get a free beer out of the conversation, the interviewer explained that they wanted the candidate to have interesting and unique ideas. Kasey's version of the beer test looked different. She likes having beers with people who share common interests, such as trading stocks or hiking with dogs. The interviewer then understood the subjectivity of the beer test.

Over the next few months, that same interviewer joined a panel of engineers to refine the interview process further. The panel worked together to define how the quality of "interesting and unique ideas" was related to future job performance. The team was pleased with the new interview process and the objective evaluation measures. The "beer test" was never mentioned in the ATS again. We hope to enable you to have an equally productive outcome in your own conversations.

Notes

1   Evison, J. (2023) Steve Jobs had a "beer test" for Apple interviews, The Drinks Business, www.thedrinksbusiness.com/2023/08/steve-jobs-had-a-beer-test-for-apple-interviews/ (archived at https://perma.cc/7AJ4-DQWA)

2 Kahneman, D. (2011) *Thinking, Fast and Slow*, New York: Farrar, Straus and Giroux

3 Greenberg, J. (2010) Perception and learning: Understanding and adapting to the work environment. In *Behavior in Organizations*, Student Value Edition, Prentice Hall

4 The Pennsylvania State University (2015) Similar-to-me effect in the workplace, Applied Social Psychology (ASP), https://sites.psu.edu/aspsy/2015/04/17/similar-to-me-effect-in-the-workplace/ (archived at https://perma.cc/25BZ-F2DT)

5 Sears, G. J. and Rowe, P. M. (2003) A personality-based similar-to-me effect in the employment interview: Conscientiousness, affect-versus competence-mediated interpretations, and the role of job relevance, *Canadian Journal of Behavioural Science/Revue Canadienne des Sciences du Comportement*, 35(1), pp. 13–24, doi: 10.1037/h0087182 (archived at https://perma.cc/CMT3-DUUR)

11

Screen to Focus on
the Most Qualified

Before we start writing questions, we will review each of the phases of the interview process.

Remember when we introduced the recruiting funnel in Part 1?

Screening is a foundational step in the hiring process, significantly influencing the quality and diversity of your candidate pool.[1,2,3] While cognitive error is often discussed in the context of selecting the final top candidates, its potential to impact decisions exists at every stage of hiring. In fact, the risk of cognitive error is especially pronounced early in the process when you're screening large numbers of applicants. At this stage, decisions are often made quickly, using limited information, which can inadvertently lead to overreliance on unconscious biases or heuristics. These early screening decisions shape the overall pool of candidates moving forward, making it essential to implement strategies to mitigate bias from the outset.

Imagine you have 100 applicants, and 10 are strong matches for the role. A flawed screening process could eliminate half of them, leaving only five qualified candidates. As the process continues, some may disengage or be eliminated, leaving just three strong finalists.

Now, consider the impact: If qualified candidates are screened out too early, you not only reduce the overall talent pool but also miss out on diverse perspectives. Starting with six strong candidates instead of three significantly improves your chances of finding the best hire, setting the process up for success from the start.

Hiring managers and small businesses often struggle with evaluating the effectiveness of their screening process and figuring out how to improve it. Here's a breakdown of common screening methods that can help, whether used

FIGURE 11.1 The Recruiting Funnel

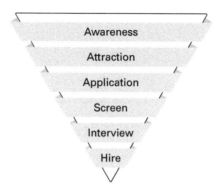

individually or together. If you're operating without a dedicated HR or recruiting team, don't worry—there are still ways to efficiently assess candidates:

1 **Resume screen:** The hiring manager reviews resumes and selects candidates to move forward to onsite interviews.

2 **Resume screen + recruiter phone screening:** The hiring manager shortlists resumes, and a recruiter conducts a phone screening to verify that candidates meet the minimum qualifications before inviting them for onsite interviews.

3 **Recruiter screen:** A recruiter reviews resumes based on feedback from the hiring manager, conducts a screening call to assess eligibility, and decides which candidates are suitable for onsite interviews.

4 **Applicant tracking system (ATS) screen:** Candidates answer qualification questions in an ATS. Those who meet the criteria are automatically scheduled for an interview with the recruiter or hiring manager.

5 **ATS and skills assessment screen:** Candidates respond to qualification questions and complete a skills assessment. Those who match the profile are invited for onsite interviews.

6 **Automated resume screen:** An automated system scans resumes and determines candidate eligibility. Qualified candidates are then passed to the recruiter and hiring manager for further evaluation.

For businesses without a dedicated HR team or recruiter, the simplest option is to review resumes and applications against your defined job requirements. This can help identify candidates who meet the basic expectations for the role, allowing you to start the process without advanced screening tools.

Screening practices can vary significantly depending on your business size and available resources. Even larger businesses with centralized HR teams often experience inconsistencies in their processes. The key is to find a method that works for your team's needs and resources while still ensuring you select the right candidates.

Screening in Action

Let's walk through an example with a Manila-based call center. A large call center may receive a few hundred applicants per day.[4] The ATS allows any applicant to enter their information into a database through a web form. The system checks for "yes" answers to the minimum qualifications (MQs). Sometimes, the system asks the candidates to confirm that they have an interest in the particular aspects of the role. For example, if the job involves credit collections, they might be asked to check off what we'll call *realistic job preview screening questions* like the following.[5]

Handling conflict: "This role requires communication with customers who may be upset or unwilling to comply with the payment process. Are you comfortable managing potentially difficult or hostile interactions?" (y/n)

Persistence in collections: "Part of this role could include repeatedly and persuasively following up on delinquent accounts. Are you comfortable with a job that requires persistence and determination?" (y/n)

Negotiation and disputes: "This role requires negotiation with customers over payments and disputes. Sometimes the customers face personally challenging situations. Are you comfortable with a job that requires negotiating with customers who are personally in challenging situations?" (y/n)

To create realistic job preview screening questions, you would use your list of activities from Part 2. In the collections call center scenario, since you want to emphasize that this job is tough, we choose the most challenging parts of this job in an effort for candidates to self-select out of the process. This approach saves our hiring team significant screening time. Truth be told, in a high-volume situation, our goal is to gently and kindly kick as many unqualified candidates *out* of the process as early as possible, while retaining those who are most motivated, qualified, and represent a diversity of applicants.

Our clients often find that pilot studies are a useful way to understand their applicant pool before fully committing to a screening process. For example, you could spend two months testing how realistic job preview screening questions impact screening results. To do this without excluding qualified candidates, simply add the questions but continue interviewing candidates who answer "no." After interviewing over 100 candidates, you can analyze whether "no" responses were linked to lower interview performance. If they are, the questions are likely effective and can be kept. If not, you can adjust or remove them before making them a permanent screening step. While this approach takes time and resources, it helps you refine the process with minimal risk.

Now we'll go through a different job example. Imagine hiring actuaries for an insurance company. Actuaries are certified in accounting and statistics specialty areas and often hold advanced degrees. Applicants are often solicited by recruiters and rarely fill out applications. In fact, in a job like this where applicants are in high demand, they'd *refuse* to spend time on an application until they know they are going through a full interview process. Actuaries are not easy to find due to their very specific skill set.[6,7] That means we're stuck reviewing resumes and can't easily rely on an automated screen, like with our collections call center.

Screening Methodology Without Applicant Tracking Systems

For this, you'll need to set up some way to sort through the potential candidates using plain old human brains and faulty human judgment.

The first step is to gather applicants. Generally, these are passive applicants, meaning that they didn't reach out to a job advertisement. Instead, they are often already employed, and you hope to convince them to leave their current job and work for you instead. We've heard many recruiters state that employees who left an existing job are higher-quality employees. There isn't research to prove whether this is true or false, so we would avoid using that as a criterion, even if it's a firm belief amongst people we work with.

Using some automated searching and sorting, recruiters comb through LinkedIn or similar websites for qualified candidates with the right expertise. LinkedIn, as an example of the most used resume repository for college educated job seekers, uses well-researched fields to collect profile and job data. As a result, sorting on LinkedIn can help narrow down candidates with the right years of experience.

Important note: "Years of experience" might seem like a solid way to gauge whether someone's ready for a job, but it's not always the best predictor of performance. Just because someone's been in a role for a long time doesn't mean they've been doing it well—or even doing the parts of the job that matter most to your business. Someone with fewer years might bring fresh ideas, advanced skills, or a more relevant background. Plus, when you put a hard number on experience, you risk shutting out great candidates who've taken a different career path or had fewer traditional opportunities. Instead of focusing on time, look at what a candidate has actually accomplished and whether they have the skills to tackle the challenges of the job. It's a much better way to find the right person for your team.

Besides years of experience, however, the sorting some recruiters use can miss many qualified candidates. Here are some specific fields that are more difficult to use in sorting.

SORTING FIELDS THAT NARROW THE TALENT POOL UNNECESSARILY

- **Past company:** Some hiring teams at tech companies claim they will only hire people who used to work for "Class A" or "Top Tech" (or whatever fancy term they use for this...) companies. They list out the highest-earning companies such as Facebook (Meta, as of this writing in 2024), Amazon, Apple, Netflix, or Google. It was such an ingrained bias that the list of companies had an acronym that software engineering managers loved to quote: "Get me someone from a FAANG!" Oddly, Microsoft is not on the list, nor are Cisco, Oracle, or WalMart, which hires more engineers than any of the FAANG companies. How was the determination made that FAANG companies are the best? In speaking to recruiters and hiring managers in tech, we discovered that it was because they have more stringent hiring criteria and perhaps more stringent performance goals. However, if you hire from a FAANG company and not from WalMart, based on our experience, your applicant pool is more likely to live in major metropolitan areas (such as London, Bangalore, San Francisco, Seattle, Shenzhen, New York), and are more likely to be men.

  o Perhaps that argument doesn't sway your hiring team—they still insist on getting only the "best." Fine. What if we told you that candidates show the same technical capabilities at all of these companies? What if their employees outside of the traditional "tech" industries experience lower burnout rates and produce steady, consistent quality work over longer periods of time?[8] Because of this, many of our clients have taken steps to remove the FAANG bias.

○ Ultimately, it's just not good practice to rely on other companies to do your screening for you.[9] We know many hiring managers who swear all their greatest employees came from Apple, but when we actually look at the data, we found no difference in performance from the Apple employee versus the employee who worked at four small startups between Chicago and Indianapolis. In fact, the applicants who came from unknown startups were shown to have more perseverance, creativity, and ambiguity tolerance.[10]

- **Job titles:** Job titles for even very standard jobs like "Software Engineer" vary considerably. It's feasible to try to figure out all the different ways someone might have been named in their job with an engineering role. But in our closely related field of Talent Management it's all over the place. Finding all the I-O psychologists or those with related experience on LinkedIn is almost impossible. We have job titles ranging from Workforce Insights Analyst to People Analytics Manager. Rarely would we ever have a title including the word "Psychologist," since we are not licensed like clinical psychologists. Recruiters find it very aggravating to identify a pool of people with our experience.

- **Degree:** You may not be considering identifying candidates based on what they majored in during college. But what about advanced degrees? Can we assume that a search for Actuarial Science will find us all the qualified actuaries? It may get at most, just like a degree in Industrial-Organizational Psychology will get a fair amount of us too. It's better than the job title search. However, some talented assessors we've met do not have an I-O degree. Some have an MBA, others have weird degrees we hadn't heard of like "Org Design Practitioner," and then one very brilliant consultant we worked with had a Master's in Comparative Literature. There are likely good actuaries out there with alternative degrees. They would have had to work their way through certifications and job training without the advantage of the degree. Often, those people are highly qualified due to their ability to learn quickly and pivot where they are needed.

Ultimately, our recommendation is to use the search for a job title, make note of the names, then do a new search for a degree, and see where you can find intersections. As a hiring manager, you may also reach out to people you know in the actuarial field and ask for referrals. We hope that this has given you some food for thought about what you're missing when we do initial searches for candidates.

Is There a Shortcut?

Here is where you may be inundated with offers for automated, easy-fast-reliable screening using the latest in AI technology. We'll explain why we don't endorse those solutions given the technology currently in place (as of the writing of this book in 2024).

Technology Isn't a One-Stop Fix

We are fans of technology to aid the selection process, but technology in the screening process has been riddled with problems as we discussed above. Even back in the 2000s, recruiting companies and applicant tracking providers toyed with automated resume reviews. The purpose of these efforts was to both save time during the screening process and ensure an approach without cognitive error. As an example, credit reporting agencies in the United States used automation to generate credit scores. After studying the impact of the automated scoring process, it was found that the process generated significant bias against low-income individuals and minorities, resulting in fewer opportunities for those individuals to be approved for mortgages.[11]

In this study, Blattner and Nelson investigated the differing treatment of minority and majority groups by mortgage lenders by analyzing credit reports for 50 million anonymized US consumers. They linked these reports to socioeconomic information from a marketing dataset, property deeds, mortgage transactions, and details about the lenders who issued the loans.

Jora Stixrud, PhD, is a labor economist, specializing in the statistical analysis of data, and a vice president in the Labor & Employment Practice of Charles River Associates (CRA). She regularly consults on matters analyzing race, gender, and age differences in employment outcomes within the context of litigation, proactive pay audits, and other initiatives. We have consulted Dr. Stixrud to better understand the impacts of utilizing automation in screening initiatives.

Dr. Stixrud accounts excess noise in the algorithm as a significant factor in a resume screening. Noise is any kind of error that impacts the score, but which is not directly related to someone's true capability.[12] Examples of noise that can impact someone's overall qualification score include things such as typos, formatting issues (which may be the fault of the AI), unconventional job titles, or gaps in employment. A person's actual experiences or skills may be lost amongst this other data. Noise is a problem in automated screening, but when correlated with gender or other personal characteristics, it becomes a potential legal issue.

This type of noise may be correlated with a difference in how candidates present themselves on a resume. Assessing a resume screen for example, women are less likely to promote a knowledge, skill, or ability until they feel completely certain of their ability. Men, however, are more likely to add such data when they feel confident enough to discuss the idea in an interview.[13,14] Therefore, in a situation such as this, a resume screen may incorrectly determine that women are less qualified.

We'd love to see equivalent confidence across all our job applicants, but it's a tall order for us to rectify without targeted training for multiple generations. We're better off ensuring that our measurements don't risk picking up on characteristics that are not helpful in making job decisions. In case someone is tempted to say that confidence is a required job qualification, and why don't we see this as a good signal of job success, we'll add that we cannot find research linking willingness to inflate or be conservative in how people present their skills to be predictive of job performance... even when that job requires a degree of confidence. We promise that there are excellent ways to measure confidence later in the process.

Companies who stand to make significant revenue from you by promising a bias-free, automation- or AI-driven resume screen may offer that their technology isn't the real problem. We named this dream-world the *Artificial Intelligence (AI) Utopia*. Like science fiction TV shows and movies that promise idealistic technology such as travel through wormholes or light speed (or even travel outside of our solar system), reality is riddled with unforeseen complications. We'll explain why.

Resume screeners use technology in two different ways to screen candidates. A reliable means is to screen for keywords using natural language processing (NLP).[15] The more complex way is to build a machine learning system that leverages artificial intelligence to increasingly learn and improve how it "reads" and interprets resumes, providing recommendations to reviewers based on the criteria that it has developed.

NLP in Action

Let's look at an example of resume screening with NLP. Imagine you're hiring a customer service representative and receive hundreds of applications per week. The job requires high school graduation (or equivalent), two or more years of customer service experience, basic computer proficiency, and familiarity with standard office software. An NLP program "reads" a resume and searches for keywords matching the experience you need for the role. To build an NLP program, we start by listing out all the different types of words and phrases that could capture the requirements.

We'll stop there for a moment, because now NLP has presented our first potential challenge. Ideally, we want to give our algorithm really specific guidance, so the phrases should look as much as possible like what we want to see in our candidates. If we say to our program, "Find all the candidates with '2 years' customer service experience'," the program will find only candidates who wrote the phrase in the exact way we requested it (we'll find very few candidates). We solve this by adding all the different iterations of how this phrase might exist, which is hard to do because we have to comb through resumes to find them, or we have to think of them proactively. That's the issue—ultimately it's likely we'll miss someone who has this experience but noted it in a different way on their resume (i.e. "worked at *xyz* customer solutions in a sales engineer role from 2021–2023"). There are a number of other ways our NLP program can miss people or include the wrong people, but this is a relatively straightforward example. It's worth noting that with more sophisticated NLP tools, many of these challenges can be mitigated.

Various companies offering automated resume screens have therefore become creative in fixing this issue with NLP by introducing a form of machine learning which then projects new phrases and adjusts the approach based on the data. In an AI Utopia, this miraculous algorithm will realize that the original phrases from the NLP formula are not perfect, so it will diligently try to fix them. How do they get fixed? They get fixed by reading many, many resumes, and making decisions on which new phrases to include from having learned from this vast amount of data. It sounds completely amazing.

There's the Rub...

Unfortunately, the machine learning/AI system is never given enough good information to evaluate the efficacy of these solutions. First, most of these systems do not tell us where they found the data they're using or what criteria are being used. When you hear people talk about the "black box" of AI, that's what they mean.[16] If, after looking at 20,000 resumes, the system decides that a phrase like "enjoys helping people" qualifies as two years of customer service experience, we won't know that this phrase is being used until we are presented with resumes that have this phrase, and we won't know how or why the algorithm even chose to use this phrase. Obviously, this phrase is not what we want to justify someone's experience, so it's providing useless information, hence additional "noise." The risk of inaccurate data is significant, but actually we're most worried about bias, in which certain candidates is systematically screened out for irrelevant reasons. We've seen examples of AI algorithms reviewing resumes and then deciding that men are better candidates than women. Obviously, this is not the kind of learning and automation that will help meet our goals, since gender is not a job qualification.

> One example can be seen in the example of Amazon's experimental AI recruiting tool from 2014. It had a tendency to penalize resumes that included the word "women." For instance, candidates who mentioned involvement in "women's chess club" were downgraded because the AI was trained on 10 years of predominantly male-dominated hiring data. This historical bias led the system to favor resumes reflecting traditionally male-dominated language and experiences, reinforcing existing inequalities.[17]
>
> Amazon ultimately scrapped the AI recruiting tool after discovering its bias against women and recognizing it couldn't guarantee fairness in hiring decisions. Despite attempts to adjust the algorithm and remove bias, the team couldn't ensure the tool wouldn't pick up on other discriminatory patterns. Amazon shifted focus to using human oversight and refining its hiring processes to avoid relying solely on automated tools. The experience highlighted the risks of deploying AI in sensitive areas like recruitment without rigorous safeguards.

A company hoping to sell you on their AI Resume Screens claims that the issue is the integrity of the information provided by candidates. Therefore, if all candidates could just be nice enough to provide straightforward and truthful information on a resume or their online job profile, then there is no reason the automated screening wouldn't appropriately distinguish them from each other. While they are not entirely wrong, the feasibility of this is mostly impossible in today's economy. Social networking sites for jobs such as LinkedIn or Indeed have tried incredibly hard with all the best of intentions to make it happen. If everyone interpreted and entered their LinkedIn CV experiences in the same way then we could get a lot closer to the *AI Utopia*. But even with the structured data entry formats of these social networking sites, we keep finding obnoxious levels of variety in how candidates enter information. This could solve the issue of "how many years of experience do you have," but only if the job title is very standard. Because companies and employees like to get super creative with job titles, it's nothing more than a pipedream to realize total standardization.

If you choose to review resumes with AI, it is recommended to ensure that you have the capability to trace and audit the algorithm decisions. Ask your vendor to document and show the criteria in a transparent way, so that you may be able to foresee any potential problems in the system. Above all, Dr. Stixrud reminds us that:

> … even the most thought-out and best-planned systems often come with unintended consequences. Therefore, it is imperative to pilot and test your systems more than once to uncover any unintentional disparities in outcomes, to verify that hiring decisions are accurate, fair, and bring in the best talent for your company.

Final Thoughts

Once you've determined your applicant pool, convinced them to apply, and are about to talk to them, it's time for the next step in screening. This screening step determines who goes to an onsite interview. Whether we're working with a call center or our actuaries, the screening interview is quite similar (but on different topics).

A screening interview can be done by a recruiter, a hiring manager, or both (either separately or together). The more complex and difficult your job, meaning the job needs specialized skills and experience and it is not easy to train, the more time you'll likely spend interviewing to find the right candidate.

That should make complete sense, since a difficult and complex job also carries more risk of terrible mistakes. If you hire a poor customer service representative, you've lost about three weeks of training and maybe a few customers. If you hire a poor nurse, however, then the risk of patient injury increases. It also likely took longer to establish that the nurse was bad at their role, so it may have wasted an entire year of work, not to mention the risk to patients!

If you hire for a job with stiff recruiting competition, a screening interview with a hiring manager is a must. Candidates are interested in knowing if the full interview process is worth their precious time, and they will make a decision about whether or not to proceed based on the screening call with the manager. It's also critical that the hiring manager is able to assess what matters most for success on day one in this role early on in the process. Therefore, this is another great reason to be as nice as possible to your candidates while you're screening them.

Regardless of who is conducting the screen, the same methodology applies. You can still choose to use any of the types of questions we outline in the next section. The interviews are generally shorter, however, and include information about the candidate's interest in the role as well as what skills are mission critical for success in the role. If there are experiences and/or skills that are required for day one success in the role, they should be assessed initially during this screen. Let's break down a potential screening interview into five-minute chunks:

---

5 minutes: Introductions to one another and explanation of the role."Hi, it's great to meet you. Thanks for meeting with me today. My name is (name), and I'm the manager for the (team) team. Let me start by telling you a bit more about this role (explain more about the role).

5 minutes: Candidate provides a brief career history."I have a copy of your profile here, and I'd appreciate learning more about the role you're in now, and what brought you there."

5 minutes: Candidate explains why they are interested in this particular role, which is an opportunity to assess if they understood what the role involves."Can you give me a couple of specific reasons why you find this role interesting?"

5 minutes: Question 1: (Use a behavior-based question to gauge specific experience demonstrating required behaviors and skill for success on day one on the job).

5 minutes: Question 2: (Use another behavior-based question to gauge specific experience demonstrating required behaviors and skill for success on day one on the job).

5 minutes: Conclude the interview, and give the candidate a chance to ask any questions.

Take thorough notes, and after the interview concludes, you will evaluate the candidate's performance on the criteria assessed and ultimately make a determination on whether they will progress to the next step or not. We will go into more detail on capturing notes, evaluating criteria, and determining a candidate's overall interview performance in screens and onsite interviews in Part 4.

Notes

1 Mbuvi, H. (2023) The Recruitment Funnel: A comprehensive guide, AIHR, www.aihr.com/blog/recruitment-funnel/ (archived at https://perma.cc/7UYG-VXJ5)

2 Symonds, C. (2023) The Recruitment Funnel: A step-by-step guide, Factorial HR, https://factorialhr.com/blog/recruitment-funnel/ (archived at https://perma.cc/ZT5F-298C)

3 Heaslip, E. (2024) 7 candidate screening methods for better hiring, Vervoe, https://vervoe.com/screening-candidates/ (archived at https://perma.cc/44R5-XSBS)

4 Harver (2024) Contact Center Volume Hiring Strategy, https://harver.com/blog/contact-center-volume-hiring-strategy/ (archived at https://perma.cc/XM47-LPUK)

5 Landis, R. S., Earnest, D. R., and Allen, D. G. (2014) Realistic job previews: Past, present, and future. In K. Y. T. Yu and D. M. Cable (Eds.) *The Oxford Handbook of Recruitment* (pp. 423–36), Oxford University Press

6 DW Simpson (2024) 2024 market trends in actuarial recruiting, www.dwsimpson.com/2024/03/06/2024-market-trends-in-actuarial-recruiting/ (archived at https://perma.cc/Q633-84D6)

7 BambooHR (n.d.) Passive candidate, www.bamboohr.com/resources/hr-glossary/passive-candidate (archived at https://perma.cc/Q45E-WSG3)

8 Talkspace (n.d.) Tech burnout: An ongoing mental health crisis in the industry, https://business.talkspace.com/articles/tech-burnout-an-ongoing-mental-health-crisis-in-the-industry (archived at https://perma.cc/MAH4-KFBV)

9 Sackett, P. R., Zhang, C., Berry, C. M., and Lievens, F. (2021) Revisiting meta-analytic estimates of validity in personnel selection: Addressing systematic overcorrection for restriction of range, *Journal of Applied Psychology*, 107(11), https://doi.org/10.1037/apl0000994 (archived at https://perma.cc/E4DF-RPK8)

10 Gulati, R. (2019) The soul of a start-up, *Harvard Business Review*, July 1 https://hbr.org/2019/07/the-soul-of-a-start-up (archived at https://perma.cc/2WL9-V92A)

11 Heaven, W. (2021) Bias isn't the only problem with credit scores—and no, AI can't help, *MIT Technology Review*, June 17, www.technologyreview.com/2021/06/17/1026519/racial-bias-noisy-data-credit-scores-mortgage-loans-fairness-machine-learning/ (archived at https://perma.cc/78SH-L36S)

12 Kahneman, D. and Sibony, O. (2023) Sounding the alarm on system noise, McKinsey, www.mckinsey.com/capabilities/strategy-and-corporate-finance/our-insights/sounding-the-alarm-on-system-noise (archived at https://perma.cc/7FSA-8CZ3)

13 Smith, C. (2019) Why don't women self-promote as much as men? *Harvard Business Review*, https://hbr.org/2019/12/why-dont-women-self-promote-as-much-as-men (archived at https://perma.cc/M8R2-NP78)

14 Reynolds, P. (2022) Women don't self-promote, but maybe they should, https://professional.dce.harvard.edu/blog/women-dont-self-promote-but-maybe-they-should/ (archived at https://perma.cc/9LH7-7TAB)

15 Pandey, V. (2024) The power of natural language processing (NLP) and its business applications, LinkedIn, www.linkedin.com/pulse/power-natural-language-processing-nlp-its-business-dr-vivek- (archived at https://perma.cc/SU7F-YFYF)

16 University of Michigan-Dearborn (2023) AI's mysterious "black box" problem, explained, https://umdearborn.edu/news/ais-mysterious-black-box-problem-explained (archived at https://perma.cc/T2KC-KWU5)

17 Dastin, J. (2018) Insight – Amazon scraps secret AI recruiting tool that showed bias against women, Reuters, www.reuters.com/article/world/insight-amazon-scraps-secret-ai-recruiting-tool-that-showed-bias-against-women-idUSKCN1MK0AG/ (archived at https://perma.cc/BC6Q-UDS5)

12

Structure Focuses on
What Matters Most

Whether you've been on both sides of the interview table or you're preparing to hire your first team member, the process likely feels familiar. It's a task we've all navigated at some point—either as candidates or interviewers. Yet, despite its familiarity, why is it often so difficult to get right? Interviewing can seem simple, but there are many potential missteps that can derail the process. From biased judgments to overlooking key skills, it's easy to make errors. However, there are only a few proven strategies to truly master the art of interviewing. In this chapter, we'll dive into what makes interviewing so challenging and how you can increase your chances of success.

It may come as no surprise that interview questions are highly valuable in the HR consulting world. Some say a comprehensive question bank can be the key to uncovering a candidate's potential performance. In fact, a license for a generic question library can cost your company hundreds of thousands of dollars (or more, depending on the provider). We know this from our experience managing similar sales for customers in the past. Customized interview questions can be even pricier, with consultants charging between $200 and $800 (or more) per hour for their expertise. But rest assured—you have everything you need to craft strong interview questions tailored to your roles, without spending a dollar on consultants. We even suggest calculating how much you've saved by building your own!

Worried about asking ineffective questions? Maybe you're concerned that your questions might reflect poorly on your company, drive away candidates, or even risk legal issues. What makes a bad interview question? Bad questions typically stem from untrained interviewers who lack a clear understanding of the role and fail to connect their questions to job-related skills. The simplest safeguard: If your question directly addresses a task the candidate will need to perform on the job, it's likely a good one.

Interview questions that are *not* related to the job can lead to biased decisions being made and the potential for adverse impact, that is, adversely impacting candidates from a protected group (e.g. based on race, gender, age, or disability). This is oftentimes done unconsciously. To state the methodology again, the simplest way to avoid bad interviews is to ask questions that are related to the job. Also, please don't ask about things that happen outside of work.

Similar to when we said that the actual questions are less important than having a great job profile (although the questions still matter a little bit), what *also* matters even more than the quality of your questions is how responses are evaluated. This will be covered in Part 4.

Structured Interviews Are Popular for a Reason...

Structured interviews are the gold standard of hiring when it comes to fairness and consistency. To reduce risk and simplify hiring, we recommend using structured interviews. In structured interviews, interviewers follow a set list of questions focused on the essential skills and characteristics needed to succeed from day one. This approach also provides clear evaluation criteria, making it easier to assess candidates fairly. Structured interviewing ensures that every interview is planned, consistent, and directly relevant to the job for each candidate and role. In short, structured interviews bring order to the chaos of hiring and help you make more informed, fair decisions.

Unstructured interviews are the opposite. They can feel more spontaneous and conversational, but they also come with potential downsides. While unstructured interviews can feel more natural and flexible, they introduce more bias and less consistency, making them less reliable for evaluating candidates fairly. Unstructured interviews are informal, open-ended conversations that don't require interviewers to use a predefined list of questions. While this approach allows for flexibility and spontaneity, it can introduce risks. Without a structured framework, interviewers might inadvertently ask questions that are not directly related to the job, which can lead to inconsistent evaluations and even potential legal issues if the questions are perceived as biased or discriminatory. Ensuring job-related focus and fairness is critical to mitigating these risks.

Did you know that structured interviews can be up to twice as predictive of job performance when compared to unstructured interviews?[1] Lucky for you, if you follow the guidance in this book, all of your interviews will be structured!

FIGURE 12.1 Structured vs. Unstructured Interviews

STRUCTURED INTERVIEWS	UNSTRUCTURED INTERVIEWS
• **Planning Ahead:** You decide what to ask candidates before the interview begins, using the job profile to guide your questions. • **Consistency Across Candidates:** Every candidate for the same role answers the same set of questions, creating a level playing field. • **Job-Relevant Questions:** The questions focus on what someone actually needs to do well in the role and fit into the organization's environment. • **Objective Decision-Making:** You score candidates using a predefined system, relying on notes and evidence rather than just memory or gut feelings.	• **No Set Plan:** You don't prepare a consistent question list in advance, and what you ask might depend on how you feel in the moment. • **Different Questions for Different People:** Each candidate might get a different set of questions, which makes comparing them later tricky. • **Candidate-Led Flow:** The conversation often follows the candidate's lead, and you base your next question on what they've just said. • **Gut-Based Decisions:** Instead of relying on structured notes and scoring, decisions are often based on what stands out most in your memory.

It's easy to think that unstructured interviews are better because they feel more conversational. But here's the thing: Structure doesn't mean you can't have a friendly chat. It just means you're being intentional. By having a plan and sticking to it, you're giving every candidate an equal shot, which makes for a better process and, ultimately, better hiring decisions.

Note: There are other interviewing methodologies that, while less structured, can be highly effective when conducted by trained assessors, such as I-O psychologists. These advanced techniques often require specialized expertise to ensure validity and can provide valuable insights in certain hiring contexts. However, as these methods are complex and require a high level of training, we will not be covering them in this book. This guide will focus instead on structured interviewing, which is more accessible and effective for a broad range of hiring situations.

When we conducted client training sessions, our clients sometimes worried about two *Structured Interview Myths*. We are now going to dispel these.

Common Points of Resistance With Structured Interviewing

AVOID BEING ROBOTIC

Each time we get invited to parties and talk about what we do for a living, someone will tell us about the horrendous, most terrible, worst-ever interview experience they were subjected to. Beyond the times when the questions were not job related, we also hear about times when the interviewer was robotic, overly scripted, and detached from the candidate. In those cases, the interview did appear to be structured, but failed on an important need, which is to connect to the candidate. Trained interviewers are instructed to follow the structure as a guide to cover necessary topics while communicating in an accessible, friendly, and accommodating way to each different candidate—*as long as they measure the same things with each candidate.*

Our optimistic view is that interviewers mostly have good intentions. They seek to make the candidate feel comfortable, open up about themselves, and learn more about the candidate in a conversational style. A conversational style helps the candidates build trust, and trust helps them to perform better during the interview. Candidate trust is tremendously important, and we can only achieve this through connecting with them. While doing so, however, remember to always cover the same topics for each candidate and cover all the topics you intended to cover. That's where a structured interview guide becomes handy.

We sometimes get pushback from our hiring managers when we introduce structured interviewing. Our hiring managers sometimes explain that the real "magic" in the interview process comes from an unstructured approach, one that allows them to adapt to the candidate and probe on the most critical areas for the job. When the managers go through a corporate structured interviewer training program,[2] they feel like the focus on consistency and standard questions restricts their ability to build rapport or dig deeply on important areas, which is not the intention or effect, when following the methodology as designed.

CONSISTENCY

The first argument has to do with consistency. Does a structured interview process mean that you must ask the exact same questions of each candidate in the exact same way? Not always. Often, an interview library will offer a choice of three or more questions to get at each skill. The three questions are seen as equal in their ability to gather useful information, but also allow you as the interviewer to choose the best question and phrasing for your particular need. We agree with interviewing experts that variation can enhance opportunities for diverse candidates by helping us to choose the context for them.[3] For example, let's say you're asking candidates to describe a time they solved a difficult problem. The questions to select from are:

1 Tell me about a time you had to solve a difficult problem.

2 Describe a situation when you were unable to complete your work due to an obstacle or roadblock.

3 Give an example of a situation where you tried multiple approaches to solving a problem, but none worked.

Answers to these questions would all lead you to gather the same information, but some candidates may find it easier to think of a generic problem, versus others who can think of their work in terms of roadblocks or obstacles (which are more often related to people than technical issues). A third candidate may find it easier to describe a trial-and-error situation like in question 3. You are welcome to use any of these three questions for your candidates, even if they apply for the same job, as long as you measure their answers against the same criteria. Therefore, consistency in interviewing is more about using a predetermined set of questions and applying uniform scoring rather than using identical phrasing for each question.

Now you know that it's acceptable to vary how you ask questions. Next, how can we put your mind at ease about your ability to dive deep with a candidate on important topics?

In the last section, you determined what was most important for the job. What happens if you get to the interview and realize that you forgot to add an important component to your job profile? In the example where we interviewed our dog walker, imagine that the candidate triggered a thought about the importance of checking for parasites? By this time, you've potentially already interviewed two candidates, but failed to ask them about checking for ticks after each walk. Although we don't like to add ad-hoc questions or topics to a structured interview process, if you realize that you need this information to make a decision, you can add it to the interview. Just make a note about the skill you're measuring and write down your question. That may require you to pause the interview for just a moment to document the process. Then, later, it is important to ask the other candidates for the same job the same question (or similar question) to ensure that you didn't make the process harder or easier for one candidate over another. It probably goes without saying that this situation would come up very rarely if you build a thorough job profile.

PROBING, AKA FOLLOW-UP QUESTIONS

When it comes to digging deep on topics, probes or follow-up questions are generally pretty unstructured compared to your skills lists and the prompting questions, and that's okay. Similar to making a painting, you might use a pencil to outline the main shapes and figures of the painting. By the end of that process, someone else should be able to see that it's a group of buildings, sky, and a river. But when you pull out your watercolors or oils, you have the freedom to adjust the color, details, and textures beyond what you sketched in the outline. The probes are more like the colors and the textures, while the outline is your job analysis and initial prompts. Giving depth to your river may require a number of layers of blue, white, and green paint. To fully understand how one of your candidates addressed a roadblock at work might need a few extra questions as well. A different candidate may easily answer one question with sufficient detail, but struggle when you ask them about collaborating with a team member. Use your details and the questions where you need them most—as long as you're doing what you can to effectively understand everything about how the candidate handled that particular situation and demonstrated a given skill.

THIS TAKES FOREVER!

We often hear interviewers say that a structured interview takes too much time. Why not just ask a few favorite questions and make a quick decision based on the responses? Each time an interviewer relies on a gut decision right after the interview, it may seem like a time-saver, but it often leads to far more time spent later on addressing performance issues, managing improvement plans, or even dealing with layoffs and backfilling the position.

Have you ever been on a hiring panel where it's difficult to get everyone to align on how to assess a candidate? Or, if you're a small business owner or entrepreneur, have you struggled to bring your team together when discussing a potential hire? We've seen situations where one panel member focuses entirely on the candidate's technical experience, while another is fixated on their communication style. This lack of alignment can significantly delay decision-making. The time spent reaching a consensus increases when there's no clear structure in place, such as when additional interviews are needed because one or more interviewers missed key data points or didn't assess the candidate as expected. Without a consistent process, these inefficiencies can hinder your hiring decisions. Additionally, structured interviews take far less time when you consider the time spent in negotiating a hiring decision among a team, or the time spent reversing a poor hiring decision. Figuring out what's important for a job is easier with fewer cooks in the kitchen. We recommend that you build your job profile and hold everyone in the interview process accountable to specific knowledge, skills, and abilities listed in that job profile.

When it comes to time savings, you can also leverage generative AI to produce initial ideas for your questions, as long as you vet these with common sense and your own knowledge of the job, and ensure you aren't missing anything! Just keep in mind, whatever you think of your favorite generative AI tool, it is likely less of a subject matter expert in the job than you are.

We define structured interviewing as the process of assessing candidates on the skills that matter most for success on day one of the job. A structured interview measures the candidate's skills in a fair, equitable, accurate, and consistent way. Lack of consistency can increase the likelihood of biased decisions, so by increasing consistency, we are also reducing the likelihood of biased practices and decisions that can increase the likelihood of adverse impact.

> If you truly follow a structured interview process that includes a valid job profile, then you have significantly reduced bias in your hiring system.[4]

We wish that this eliminated all bias from the human brain, but that's not possible (or advisable—bias can be useful for other things in life not covered in our book). What this means, instead, is that the structured process enables you to make decisions driven by the relevant data, instead of the decisions driven by your emotions.

Most people in corporate jobs have gone through some sort of training intended to help them understand and remove the bias that impacts their decision-making about other people. There is a range of quality and impact offered by these courses, but the ones that have the most impact are those that replace illogical/biased thoughts ("A person from XYZ can't possibly have the mental capacity to deal with flying this plane in an emergency") with a more logical thought ("The ability to fly during an emergency is predicted by processing speed, prior training and experience, and knowledge of the plane").[5,6]

Bias in Action

When Lion Air's Boeing 737 Max crashed in Indonesia in 2018, Boeing leadership blamed the pilot. Aviation specialists, who were mostly older white men, claimed that the pilot was ineffective, presumably on account of being younger and not having been trained in a Western country. In fact, Boeing had a history of shared private jokes about incompetent crews overseas. Later, as we now know, it was determined that faulty mechanics, systematically hidden and denied by Boeing, caused the Lion Air crash.[7] To add to the tragedy, just six months later, another plane crashed for the same reason.

Boeing prides itself on providing training and resources to encourage and promote accurate assessment of others and reduce cognitive errors.[8] Yet employees at Boeing acted in a way that contradicted this (although we do not disclose details beyond what is posted on their website regarding employee training). Why, then, were they so quick to make an assessment of incompetence of pilots who came from non-Western cultures? The beliefs they held were not grounded in facts. Pilots are required to receive equivalent training in all parts of the world. Federal Aviation Administration (FAA) training is equivalent for all commercial pilots.[9] There are equally low rates of plane crashes due to pilot error (most plane crashes are due to pilot error) on commercial airlines in Western or Eastern regions.[10] Ultimately, the assessment of poor pilot performance in the Lion Air crash was based on prejudice.

If we were asked to fix and rectify perspectives of men like those aviation specialists at Boeing in 2018, we would add to their onboarding with a more detailed training on how to replace their faulty assumptions about people with analysis of facts. When our brains are preoccupied with analyzing data, we find it harder to allow assumptions to lead the decisions. Eventually, when a separate team of aviation specialists were asked to list out the qualifications for handling a plane during an emergency, they confirmed that the pilots at Lion Air took all effective actions per the training provided. The origin of their training or the airline they worked for did not turn out to be an important consideration. Although cognitive errors may have a sneaky way of emerging into our brains at any time, it has less opportunity to hijack our decisions when we start with the data.[11]

Table 12.1 shows some of the most common types of cognitive errors that can influence interviews and hiring processes, along with a brief description and example for each.[12]

Awareness of these cognitive errors is crucial to ensuring a fair and effective hiring process. Structured interviews, standardized evaluation criteria, and training on unconscious bias can help mitigate their impact.

TABLE 12.1 Common Types of Cognitive Errors

Common interviewer biases	Description	Example
Confirmation Bias	The tendency to seek out or interpret information in a way that confirms preexisting beliefs or assumptions.	An interviewer who assumes a candidate from a prestigious university is highly competent might focus on positive aspects of their answers while overlooking weaker responses.
Similarity Bias (Affinity Bias)	Favoring candidates who share similarities with the interviewer, such as background, interests, or demographics.	An interviewer might prefer a candidate who shares their alma mater or hobbies, regardless of whether those factors relate to job performance.
Halo Effect	Allowing one positive attribute or impression to influence overall judgment of the candidate.	If a candidate has a confident demeanor, the interviewer might assume they are also highly skilled and competent in other areas.
Horns Effect	The opposite of the Halo Effect, where one negative attribute unduly influences overall judgment.	A candidate who fumbles one question early in the interview might be perceived as less competent throughout, even if they perform well on other questions.
First Impressions Bias	Making snap judgments about a candidate based on initial impressions rather than substantive evidence.	A candidate dressed in an unconventional way might be dismissed as unprofessional before the interview even begins.
Anchoring Bias	Overreliance on the first piece of information encountered about a candidate, such as their resume or an initial answer.	If a candidate's resume lists an impressive achievement, an interviewer might anchor on that and overlook weaker qualifications.
Contrast Effect	Comparing candidates to each other rather than evaluating them against the job criteria.	A mediocre candidate might seem exceptional if interviewed after a particularly poor one.
Recency Bias	Placing more weight on information or impressions from the latter part of the interview.	A candidate who answers the final question strongly might leave a disproportionately positive impression.
Leniency or Severity Bias	Consistently rating candidates too leniently or harshly.	An interviewer with a lenient tendency might rate all candidates higher than warranted, diluting meaningful distinctions.

The Interview Sequence

During your interview, you'll present a series of questions based on the job profile. You'll allow the candidate to answer, you'll take comprehensive notes, and then you'll follow up with further probes to the candidate. For each question you build, you will want to have probes ready on the following topics:

- What was the **Situation**?
- What **Action** did you take?
- What was the **Result**?

However, some of the probes will be hard to plan in advance, and only come from what the candidate has just told you. For example, if a candidate explains that they had to figure out how an accounting error occurred, but simply says, "I was able to successfully resolve it," you will want to ask the candidate to detail the specific *action* they took. If they don't give you enough detail to assess your KSAs, then you might probe further by saying, "You mentioned that you checked some of the accounting records from May of 2023. What other information was available for you to check?" or "What led you to check those records, what were you looking for?" Obviously, you didn't know that the candidate had accounting records from May of 2023 until you talked to them, so being prepared to come up with the questions in advance is not always possible.

At the end of an interview, you'll likely allow the candidates five or so minutes to ask questions, and then you'll conclude by thanking them for their time and interest in the position and inform them of any next steps.

Notes

1 Schmidt, F. L. and Hunter, J. E. (1998) The validity and utility of selection methods in personnel psychology: Practical and theoretical implications of 85 years of research findings, *Psychological Bulletin*, 124(2), pp. 262–74

2 Development Dimensions International (DDI) (n.d.) Targeted Selection®, www.ddiworld.com/solutions/targeted-selection (archived at https://perma.cc/N2H4-MQPR)

3 Carnahan, B. (2023) 6 best practices for creating an inclusive and equitable interview process, Harvard Business School, May 25, www.hbs.edu/recruiting/insights-and-advice/blog/post/6-best-practices-to-creating-inclusive-and-equitable-interview-processes (archived at https://perma.cc/A4GT-98K3)

4   Huffcutt, A. I. and Culbertson, S. S. (2011) Interviews. In S. Zedeck (ed.) *APA Handbook of Industrial and Organizational Psychology, Vol. 2: Selecting and developing members for the organization* (pp. 185–203), American Psychological Association, https://doi.org/10.1037/12170-006 (archived at https://perma.cc/L63Z-CRE5)

5   Bergelson, I., Tracy, C., and Takacs, E. (2022) Best practices for reducing bias in the interview process, *Current Urology Reports*, 23(11), pp. 319–25, https://doi.org/10.1007/s11934-022-01116-7 (archived at https://perma.cc/EM38-PMD4)

6   Dobbin, F. and Kalev, A. (2018) Does diversity training work the way it's supposed to? *Harvard Business Review*, https://hbr.org/2019/07/does-diversity-training-work-the-way-its-supposed-to (archived at https://perma.cc/5MQU-BYT7)

7   Robison, P. (2021) Boeing built an unsafe plane, and blamed the pilots when it crashed, Bloomberg, www.bloomberg.com/news/features/2021-11-16/are-boeing-planes-unsafe-pilots-blamed-for-corporate-errors-in-max-737-crash (archived at https://perma.cc/N4NL-CAYT)

8   The Boeing Company (2024) People and culture, www.boeing.com/sustainability/diversity-and-inclusion (archived at https://perma.cc/NKD2-746F)

9   Stock, S., Putnam, J., and Escamilla, F. (2013) Foreign airline pilots: US flight schools—do they get enough training time in the cockpit? NBC Bay Area, www.nbcbayarea.com/news/local/foreign-airline-pilots-us-flight-schools-do-they-get-enough-training-time-in-cockpit/1958500/ (archived at https://perma.cc/Y4RE-GSLN)

10 Wikipedia (2024) Category: Airliner accidents and incidents caused by pilot error, https://en.wikipedia.org/wiki/Category:Airliner_accidents_and_incidents_caused_by_pilot_error (archived at https://perma.cc/7YYW-CWF8)

11 Kahneman, D. (2011) *Thinking, Fast and Slow*, New York: Farrar, Straus and Giroux

12 Tversky, A. and Kahneman, D. (1974) Judgment under uncertainty: Heuristics and biases, *Science*, 185 (4157), pp. 1124–31, Bibcode:1974Sci...185.1124T, doi: 10.1126/science.185.4157.1124, PMID 17835457, S2CID 143452957 (archived at https://perma.cc/Z9VM-5FW3)

13

Building Structured Interviews

Interviewing Methods

Past Behavior or Behavioral Interviews

Past behavior interviews, also referred to as behavioral interviews, are based on the idea that a candidate's past behaviors and experiences are the strong indicators of their future performance. Have you heard the expression: "Past behavior is the best predictor of future behavior?" Psychologists internalize this quote on their first day in graduate school and repeat it like a mantra or verse. Where did the expression come from? One of the core tenets of psychology, psychologists accomplish three important goals in their work. First, we attempt to understand, define, and describe human behavior. Second, we attempt to predict human behavior. Third, we attempt to change or improve human behavior.[1]

The intention of this statement (predicting human behavior) stems from studies that show that in general, across large population groups, the way someone handled things in the past is a good estimate of how they will handle things in the future.[2] And in truth, if you forced us to nail the one single best predictor of future job performance, we would agree that the past behavior is indeed the most solid evidence for interview validity.[3] For that reason, we think you'll do your best hiring with questions that target how a candidate behaved in past situations.

Behavioral questions are simple. You will ask the candidate to describe a situation like the ones you want them to take on in the new job. As they describe what they did, how they handled things, and their results, you'll learn a lot about how they might handle similar situations on the job. That's it! The questions look like this.

"Tell me about a time when you…"

"Describe a situation where you had to…"

"Help us understand how you have done…"

If you've been through DDI's "Targeted Selection®" interviewer training,[4] questions like these should be really familiar to you.

Remember when we built the job profile for the dog walker? We developed questions for the following:

1 Empathy: "Tell me about a time when you had a hard time building a positive relationship with a dog. How did you handle it? What helped you and the dog to bond?"

2 Conscientiousness: "What are some ways you check that the dog is safe before leaving a house?"

3 Dog control: "Do you have an example of when a dog you walked was aggressive toward another dog? What did you do? What happened?"

Notice that each time you ask a candidate a question about past behavior, you're prompting them to share specific examples of how they demonstrated a job skill or other key indicator of success in a previous situation.

GenAI TIP

You could plug in *empathy*, *conscientiousness*, and *dog control* to gain a starting point for questions to ask related to these. We recommend closely reviewing and then revising the questions after the GenAI provides ideas.[5]

When you use these, keep in mind that GenAI can probably get you about 85–95 percent of what you need in terms of questions, but you may need to get more natural-sounding texts or revise them before you ask them out loud. Why not just use whatever was generated? It's such a time-saver! The content in sites like ChatGPT or Gemini pulls from a massive list of sources. Each site and each search you conduct could yield new and different results. At times, based on our personal experimentation and also in the recent blogs and literature on GenAI, the results are erroneous and nonsensical. Auditing the questions carefully will ensure you don't end up with something unrelated to your job.

Let's move on from our dog walker example and return to the financial analyst. Figure 13.1 demonstrates how we converted job activities for the financial analyst role into behavioral interview questions. Interestingly, in this case, it's questionable whether using the GenAI app saved much time, as creating these questions primarily involved adding simple phrases like "Tell me about a time…" or "Describe a situation where…" in front of the identified activities.

FIGURE 13.1 Example of How to Translate Key Activities Required for a Role Into a Structured Interview Question

ACTIVITIES	QUESTION
Analyze financial data and trends to provide insights for decision-making.	Tell me about a time when you needed to analyze financial data and trends to provide insights for decision-making.
Prepare and present financial reports to management.	Describe a situation when you prepared and presented financial reports to management.
Conduct budgeting and forecasting activities.	How have you conducted budgeting and forecasting activities in your last role?
Evaluate investment opportunities and assess risk.	Tell me about a time when you evaluated investment opportunities and assessed risk.
Collaborate with other departments to ensure financial goals are met.	Describe a time when it was difficult to collaborate with other departments to ensure financial goals are met.

If you decide to use a GenAI app for assistance, always review its output critically. Tailoring interview questions to the specific skills and nuances of the job is crucial to ensure the questions effectively assess what matters most. While these tools can be helpful, they often require thoughtful revisions to align with your job's unique requirements.

In other words, we sort of "skipped to the front of the line" by copying the activity directly into the question format. Is it cheating? No! This is a logical progression that clearly shows that the job requirements are exactly being asked in your interview! We're trying to keep it simple by just asking the candidate about specific times that they needed to do these exact things.

We truly value that these interviews are both easy to develop and guide candidates to provide precisely the information needed for the job. They're also more legally defensible, as there's a clear connection between the job profile and the interview questions.[6] Now, let's explore an alternative approach for gathering information about past experience—a method that's commonly used, intuitive, and well-liked by many.

Biographical Interviews

A **biographical interview** focuses on a person's career experiences, achievements, and significant events, in the order that they occurred. In this interview, you'll ask questions that prompt your candidate to share their full career story.[7,8]

The trick is, however, that you still need answers to the questions that we created for the past behavior interview above. In this interview, since you're asking them to describe their career chronologically, your candidates won't answer the questions in the order you created your job profile topics. That makes it a bit harder work for an interviewer who is not trained in this specific methodology.

So why do we do it? Candidates often find these interviews easier and more enjoyable, because most of us are generally prepared to talk through our career in chronological order. It also feels like a "get to know you"-type conversation, in which your prompts ensure that the candidate provides details on each milestone or step.

When do we use it? We prefer this type of interview with more senior-level roles, or roles where you're concerned with creating the best possible candidate experience, maybe because you have to "court" your candidates more directly for example.

A standard prompt for these questions might be:

> "Tell me about yourself, focusing on your work background, educational journey, professional experiences, and any significant milestones or accomplishments that have shaped your life and career."

Such questions are useful in understanding a leader's 20-year career, or that of someone who has encountered a variety of complex situations in their career and learned from them.

However, there's a drawback to biographical questions, and it impacts you, the interviewer. You probably won't be able to build out a list of question prompts or probes for the entire interview in advance. Instead, you have your list of skills and activities, and you'll need to check those off as you hear evidence for them and ask probing questions on the fly based on what you're missing. Even the most effective communicators will find it difficult to speak to *everything* you want to know in the course of telling you their career history, so you'll need to listen and adjust what you ask based on what you already learned and what you still need to learn.

You're interviewing an attorney for an advocacy role in your 20-person clean energy lobbying company. You want to know about their successes, their failures, their learnings, and their passions, particularly as they relate to clean energy lobbying. You prompt them with the initial question, and the candidate wishes to pontificate for 20 minutes about their philosophy studies at Penn State University. Since you only booked 45 minutes with the candidate, you will need to move them forward quite a bit faster. But you want to know how philosophy brought them to environmental law, and why they didn't actually study environmental law at university. So, you ask them: "Philosophy sounds like a great grounding for your subsequent studies. Tell me how you made this transition during law school, and what brought you to environmental law?" It then turns out that the candidate wanted to study international relations but ended up being admitted to law school and not the London School of Economics, as they had hoped. Therefore, they quickly adapted and realized that they had more of a knack for understanding the technical aspects of energy than they had previously thought (adding that perhaps it was as a result of a single terrible physics professor in their first year of university that they had falsely believed science was not right for them). After this point, the candidate became wildly passionate about policy related to energy production and educated themself while in law school. In addition, they thus secured a prestigious internship at a top three environmental law firm before graduating.

Now you're getting somewhere, although this has not even taken you to their 15-year work experience! Subsequently, you'll probably pivot your questions to how they leveraged their unique knowledge in philosophy as they argued policies with senators and congress members, coming to understand that the logical reasoning process actually underlies a key influence strategy that they carefully honed over the next years of their career. Perhaps you could glean some of the points of interest and jot down some questions from their resume.

Overall, the candidate will get a sense that the interview was customized for their unique and specific experience, and this often helps to gather deeper details about a person, especially for unique and highly complex roles.

Situational Interviews

Sometimes, you'll need to understand how well your candidate is likely to work in a job that they've never done before. A **situation-based interview** is when candidates are presented with hypothetical situations relevant to the job they are interviewing for and then are asked how they would respond or behave in a hypothetical situation.[9,10] The goal is generally to assess the candidate's problem-solving abilities, decision-making skills, and their capacity to apply knowledge to practical scenarios. Situational interviews provide insight into a candidate's thought process and problem-solving approach, even if they haven't previously done that exact thing you need them to do.

For example, let's say you need to hire individuals who have government and security training, but in a private sector role. They will need to use their knowledge in the context of protecting people from fraud or danger. Their past experience does not translate well enough to the new private sector job, so you'll need to leverage situational questions to understand how they would *likely* handle something new, given their past experience and training.

Another good example of such employees exists in finance and law, and other jobs that require a lot of knowledge and certifications/exams. In those situations, a stockbroker cannot actually trade stocks until they pass the exams, but they are often hired in a financial institution while they study for the exam. During the job application process, the employer needs to understand how they will apply their theoretical knowledge in real-world situations.

Finally, hiring students for early career ("graduate") jobs and internships is a great place to leverage these questions.

Situational questions look a lot like behavioral questions and are developed the same way, except they start with:

"Explain how you would handle the following situation."

"What if this happened… what would you do? Walk through each step and your rationale."

Just as you created behavioral questions based on the skills and activities from Part 1, you can easily structure situational questions by starting with prompts like "Tell me how you would handle…" or "Describe how you would…" followed by the specific topic you want to assess. Unlike behavioral questions, situational questions often require you to provide more context, as the scenario is new to the candidate and they may have follow-up questions. To keep things consistent, the person designing the interview should prepare each scenario in advance, deciding which details will or won't be provided initially or if a candidate asks for more information. This ensures that all candidates have the same context for responding.

FIGURE 13.2 Strengths and Limitations of Common Interview Approaches

BEHAVIORAL (PAST BEHAVIOR) QUESTIONS

STRENGTHS	LIMITATIONS
• Shows how candidates have demonstrated relevant skills or behaviors in real-world situations. • Hard to fake since examples are based on actual experiences. • Creates a positive candidate experience by focusing on authentic storytelling. • Offers a realistic preview of the job and its demands. • Reveals how candidates approach challenges, providing insights into problem solving and teamwork.	• Requires candidates to have relevant experience, which may disadvantage early-career professionals or career changers. • Relies on candidates' memory, which can result in incomplete or unclear examples. • Without training, interviewers may struggle to detect exaggerations or fabrications. • Candidates may find it hard to think of examples on the spot without preparation. • Demands interviewer skill to focus discussions on relevant data tied to the role's competencies. • May favor articulate or confident candidates over quieter but equally capable ones. • Focusing on detailed examples can reduce topic coverage, requiring skilled interviewers to extract evidence across multiple competencies from a single response—or risk leaving key skills unassessed.

BIOGRAPHICAL INTERVIEW

STRENGTHS	LIMITATIONS
• More enjoyable for the candidate. • Easier experience for the candidate. • Easier for the interviewer to build the questions. • Uncovers situations you may not have thought to ask about. • Candidate responses may be more truthful since it feels less like a "test" with right or wrong answers.	• Interviewer needs to do a lot of digging to get to the details, thus can be more time consuming. • Interviewer cannot easily plan the probing and gathering of more details. • Tying the examples back to the activities and KSAs from the job profile is time consuming after the interview and requires some training.

SITUATIONAL QUESTIONS

STRENGTHS	LIMITATIONS
• Allows candidates with less direct experience to showcase how they'd handle a situation, leveling the playing field for newer professionals. • Tests theoretical knowledge, free from constraints of past experiences. • Offers a realistic preview of job demands by presenting real-world scenarios. • Reveals how candidates think on their feet and approach novel, unexpected situations. • Can surface creative problem-solving abilities and adaptability.	• Easier for candidates to "fake" answers or describe ideal behaviors without actual experience to back them up. • High verbal intelligence may allow candidates to craft convincing answers, even if they wouldn't act that way in practice. • Assessing sincerity or true behavioral alignment requires strong interviewer skill and probing follow-up questions.

When to Choose Which Interviewing Method and Question Type

Figure 13.2 summarize the key strengths and limitations of the three common interview approaches overviewed—behavioral (past behavior), situational, and biographical interviews. These methods each offer unique insights into a candidate's abilities and fit for a role, while also presenting specific challenges. Use these comparisons to determine the best approach for your hiring needs

Importance of Interviewer Training

Regardless of the interview method chosen, interviewers need to understand how to use any given methodology.

When conducting a biographical interview or a behavioral interview for instance, either could yield valuable results when conducted by a trained, calibrated interviewer. On the other hand, if not conducted properly, both could yield data that may be used or interpreted less ideally. When you're trained in a given methodology, the relative risks with each become lessened, because you're trained to use the methodology to extract, assess, and evaluate key criteria.

Our recommendation

The easiest interview type to train newer interviewers on, especially when launching structured interviewing, is typically behavioral interviewing.

WHY BEHAVIORAL INTERVIEWS TEND TO BE "EASIER"

1 **Clear framework:** Behavioral interviews rely on asking candidates to share specific past experiences (e.g. "Tell me about a time you…"), making it straightforward for interviewers to follow.

2 **Consistency:** The STAR framework (Situation, Task, Action, Result) provides a simple and repeatable structure for interviewers to use during both training and live interviews.

3 **Predictability:** Questions are less hypothetical and more grounded in concrete examples, which is easier for interviewers to evaluate compared to scenario-based answers.

4 **Immediate relevance:** Evaluating past behavior often feels intuitive for newer interviewers because it connects directly to observable results or actions.

SCENARIO-BASED OR BIOGRAPHICAL ALTERNATIVES

- Scenario-based interviews require more experience and judgment to evaluate hypothetical responses accurately.
- Biographical interviews may lead to overly surface-level conversations if interviewers aren't skilled at asking probing follow-ups.

Notes

1 Cherry, K. (2019) How the goals of psychology are used to study behavior, Verywellmind

2 Janz, T. (1989) The patterned behavior description interview: The best prophet of the future is the past. In R. W. Eder and G. R. Ferris (Eds.) *The Employment Interview: Theory, research, and practice* (pp. 158–68) Sage Publications, Inc.

3 Sackett, P. R., Zhang, C., Berry, C. M., and Lievens, F. (2022) Revisiting meta-analytic estimates of validity in personnel selection: Addressing systematic overcorrection for restriction of range, *Journal of Applied Psychology*, 107(11), pp. 2040–68

4 Development Dimensions International (DDI) (n.d.) Targeted Selection®, www.ddiworld.com/solutions/targeted-selection (archived at https://perma.cc/9BSX-NMHM)

5 OpenAI (2024) ChatGPT (3.5) [Large language model] https://chat.openai.com (archived at https://perma.cc/X87V-V9BU)

6 Borden, L. W. and Sharf, J. C. (2007) Developing legally defensible content valid selection procedures. In D. L. Whetzel and G. R. Wheaton (Eds.) *Applied Measurement: Industrial psychology in human resources management* (pp. 385–401) Taylor & Francis Group/Lawrence Erlbaum Associates

7 Borden, L. W. and Sharf, J. C. (2007) Developing Legally defensible content valid selection procedures. In D. L. Whetzel and G. R. Wheaton (Eds.) *Applied Measurement: Industrial psychology in human resources management* (pp. 385–401) Taylor & Francis Group/Lawrence Erlbaum Associates

8 Mael, F. A. (1991) A conceptual rationale for the domain and attributes of biodata items, *Personnel Psychology*, 44, pp. 763–92

9 Latham, G. P., Saari, L. M., Pursell, E. D., and Campion, M. A. (1980) The situational interview, *Journal of Applied Psychology*, 65(4), pp. 422–27, https://doi.org/10.1037/0021-9010.65.4.422 (archived at https://perma.cc/AQ3P-PCVH)

10 Becker, T. E. and Colquitt, A. L. (1992) Potential versus actual faking of a biodata form: An analysis along several dimensions of item type, *Personnel Psychology*, 45(2), pp. 389–406

14

Other Interviewing Methods and Assessment Types

When hiring for roles that demand specialized expertise, technical interview questions play a critical role in the selection process. These questions go beyond the behavioral, situational, and biographical approaches commonly used in broader interviews. Instead, they aim to assess a candidate's proficiency in a specific domain—be it software engineering, data analysis, mechanical design, or another technical field.

Technical interview questions are designed to evaluate how well a candidate can apply their knowledge to solve real-world problems they're likely to encounter in the role. Unlike hypothetical or past-focused questions, these often require practical demonstrations of skill, such as coding exercises, case studies, or problem-solving scenarios. For instance, in a software development interview, a candidate might be asked to write and debug a piece of code in real time. For a data analyst, it could involve cleaning and interpreting a messy dataset to identify trends.

The goal isn't just to see if the candidate knows the right answers; it's also about understanding their thought process, approach to problem solving, and ability to adapt under pressure. This chapter focuses on how to design technical interview questions that are not only effective at identifying the right candidate but also align closely with the real demands of the job. By the end, you'll have a clear framework for crafting questions that help separate genuine expertise from surface-level familiarity.

Technical Questions

Do you need to understand how well a candidate can operate a radiology device? How about detailed planning for a construction project? Or solving a data science research problem? For this, we'd recommend using technical questions, which evaluate domain-specific knowledge and expertise in the particular field or specialty required for the job. You may create questions or even practical exercises and assessments (e.g. coding assessments are common for data scientists and engineers). In other jobs, candidates might be asked to analyze a dataset created for an interview or conduct a financial statement/forecast for the past quarter based on specific data provided. For a technical job, one or two detailed technical scenarios for each candidate should give you a sense of their capabilities.

To create effective technical or knowledge-based interview questions or exercises, focus on three approaches:

- **Hands-on tasks:** Have the candidate perform a job-relevant activity, such as writing code in a coding interview.

- **Experience-based descriptions:** Ask the candidate to explain how they previously executed a critical task, like managing the delivery of a technical program.

- **Hypothetical problem solving:** Present a relevant scenario and have the candidate walk through how they would approach and organize the work to solve it.

Ensure your job profile clearly outlines all required knowledge areas at an appropriate level of detail. This helps craft questions.

Make it job related: The technical questions should mirror the specific work, skills, and behaviors required for success in the role. Our goal is to assess candidates on aspects directly relevant to their job responsibilities. For example, we invest significant time in reviewing coding exercises for software engineers to ensure they simulate realistic, job-related tasks. While basic problem-solving skills could be assessed by asking someone to write a function to find two numbers that sum up to a target value in an array of integers, this type of algorithmic problem isn't commonly encountered in day-to-day engineering work. Instead, we focus on practical tasks that better reflect real-world challenges engineers face on the job.

Know the right answer: Whatever technical problem or question you create, make sure you have most of the possible right answers listed out, so that you can score the candidate responses. You will likely also want to create answers that are easy, moderate, and advanced. You can also create problem extensions for advanced candidates who too quickly solve the initial problem. For example, here is a question for a software engineer:

> You are tasked with developing a program to manage inventory for an online marketplace. You should design and implement the core functionality of the inventory management system, including classes, methods, and data structures as necessary. Consider factors such as scalability, concurrency, and data integrity in your implementation.

If a candidate can build this code quickly, then you could have a few alternative options ready, such as "How do you ensure that each product is deducted from the seller's inventory only once, regardless of the number of concurrent checkout attempts?"

With GenAI readily available, coding interviews are transformed significantly. There have long been services to aid candidates in preparing for technical interviews, especially coding. Now, many of these companies offer assistance using GenAI to create responses to the interview questions. Does this mean that the candidate is cheating? Our view is that we have an opportunity to revise the way we assess our candidates. Since GenAI is also available on the job, pivot the interview task in a way that helps you to understand how they would prompt engineer an effective solution. Ensure you know what the commonly generated responses are for the question, and then ask the candidate to explain the results verbally. Use probing questions to test the boundaries of their understanding and vary components of the problem to ensure they can adapt and adjust. These techniques will help you to test out how they handle real-world scenarios with the newly available tools.

Guidelines

Whatever you ask your candidates, make sure that you also know all possible correct answers. Document them for all interviewers who are using this content as well as for interviewer training.

Make sure you really need it: As a side note, people love to share their "nightmare interview" stories with us. Being asked to solve problems and then not being hired often creates a negative experience for candidates. If you must put candidates through a "day in the life" technical assessment, be sure that there is no other way to assess for this skill and make it clear to candidates that their answers will be stored safely by HR and not used for purposes other than assessment and selection.

A hiring manager once presented us with an exercise in which the candidate had to come up with new ideas and categories for an aspect of the user experience. They wanted to assess the candidate on the quality of their ideas and designs. We were unable to approve the question, however, because it could have been interpreted as asking for consulting or "free work" from a candidate. Your employment lawyers will be unhappy if you ask candidates for free advice, especially since all but a few of the candidates will be ultimately rejected for the job.

Keep it confidential: When building a technical problem, however, avoid sharing proprietary information about specific code being worked on. Software engineering is a fast-changing field, so any general question that shows candidates' ability to solve a problem can likely translate to the specific problems on the job (sorting data, debugging, etc.). Also, avoid asking the candidate to share proprietary information about their current or past employers. Make it possible for them to showcase technical skills without revealing too much and encourage them openly to maintain confidentiality. You'd want them to do the same for you.

Role Plays

Imagine that you're hiring a regional sales manager for a pharmaceutical company. A significant part of this regional manager's job involves monitoring and improving performance among their sales team members to drive overall performance goals, while also managing their own stakeholders and key performance indicators (KPIs). While past behavior/behavioral and situational questions will give you a sense of candidates' experience in past roles and ability to forge a hypothetical plan forward, there's another excellent method that would help assess candidates' ability to succeed in the role: Role plays.

Role play means precisely what it says: The candidate is asked to play a role in which they pretend they are doing something job-relevant, and then you can decide how well they performed against predetermined criteria. During a role play, candidates typically receive some contextual information about a situation as well as the role they are designated to play, and then are put into scenarios where they demonstrate observable behaviors in line with the job requirements in real time and under similar work conditions and pressures.

Most of the guidelines we noted for the technical assessments apply here, except that role plays are more commonly used for managers instead of individual contributors, so we measure things like *presentation skills*, *negotiation*, and *managing others* rather than solving a specific problem.

Similarly, you'll want to avoid giving anyone real company data or assignments that the team or company could potentially use to improve, since that would be like asking them for free consulting. For that reason, the role plays are often based on a fictitious company, or on your company data with key information and names scrubbed and edited. Some complained to us that this feels counterintuitive, since we really want to predict how they will act here, in our very own real-life company.

We get it, and we understand!

But you will save headaches later on if you create a fake company with fake problems, because this will make it harder for a candidate to later accuse you of trying to get free advice or work out of them. We know you're not trying to get anything for free, but candidates don't know that. It comes back to doing everything you can to establish candidate trust.

Hiring in Action

Let's say you're hiring a business-to-business (b2b) sales representative. The sales rep needs to negotiate the lowest possible price from a supplier. The supplier needs to negotiate the highest possible price from your sales rep. In addition, they both need to work well together for many years. Your company depends on the supplier for good service and consultation. Your supplier depends on the sales rep to maintain this relationship rather than going to other suppliers. Your job profile has the following skills.

SKILLS REQUIRED FOR SALES REPRESENTATIVE OF PRECISIONTECH

Negotiation: Secure the best possible prices and terms from suppliers, including market knowledge, pricing trends, and competitive insights.

Relationship building: Cultivate and maintain positive relationships over the long term; establish rapport, trust, and mutual respect, understanding suppliers' needs and motivations.

Strategic thinking: Develop and implement strategic sourcing strategies to optimize costs while ensuring quality and reliability; analyze market dynamics, supplier performance, and industry trends to identify opportunities for cost savings and process improvements.

Communication: Articulate requirements, expectations, and value propositions, listen actively, clarify expectations and ensure mutual understanding, convey complex pricing structures, contract terms, and negotiation outcomes.

Just like building your interview questions, the activities, knowledge, skills, and abilities are your guide to creating the scenario for a role play. Think about how to design a scenario that allows the candidate to demonstrate each skill listed above in a realistic context—perhaps by having them engage with a "supplier," where you play the supplier role. Prepare a briefing guide for the candidate that includes information about the company, relevant background, current pricing, high and low price points, and a target goal. This setup will provide the candidate with the context they need to respond effectively.

SCENARIO OVERVIEW

You are playing the role of a B2B sales representative for a manufacturing company called PrecisionTech Industries, which specializes in producing industrial equipment. Your task is to negotiate a contract renewal with one of your key suppliers, a raw materials provider. The supplier has been a reliable partner in the past, but you need to secure lower prices to meet cost-saving targets while maintaining a positive relationship.

PrecisionTech Industries is a leading manufacturer specializing in the production of high-tech precision machinery and equipment for industrial applications.

PrecisionTech is committed to delivering innovative and reliable solutions that meet the evolving needs of its customers across a wide range of industries, including automotive, aerospace, electronics, and more.

Your goal is to negotiate a resin price for Industrial 3D Printing Solutions (Photopolymer Resins for Stereolithography).

Prices range from $50 to $200 per liter, depending on the material properties and curing process. Last year, you purchased 20,000 liters, and paid $34 per liter. You know that pricing will need to go up, due to a materials shortage, but you need to keep it as close as possible to last year's price. Your demand has also increased, so you can commit to over 30,000 liters for the following year.

The role player/interviewer also receives their own guide. This should overview relevant context for the supplier (role player) to know as it should outline what the supplier should say and provide in relation to key topics, along with ideal candidate responses and contributions to the scenario based on the data. Train assessors to use the role play, unless you are the only assessor. Everyone role playing with candidates should be calibrated, meaning that they know the boundaries of the role they are playing (i.e. they do not go "off script") and they use the same guide to score all candidates on all skills measured. Assessors should not introduce new information into the role play beyond what is written in the guide to ensure the same experience for each candidate.

We suggest timing your role play time at about 30 minutes. Depending on the amount of information provided in the candidate briefing, preparation time for candidates could range from 15 to 60 minutes. For the amount of information provided above, 15 to 20 minutes is sufficient. The goal is to give candidates appropriate time to read any information you've shared about the company and prepare a strategy.

KEY INFORMATION FOR CANDIDATE BRIEFING MATERIALS

- Overview of candidates' role, description of any other participants in the role play and their relevant background information, any relevant contextual information about the scenario, and clear task instructions.
  - Your goal is to provide candidates with sufficient information to prepare for and engage successfully in the exercise.
- Duration of the role play (e.g. "This will be a 30-minute role play.").
- Preparation time (e.g. "It is advised that you spend between XX and XX minutes preparing for this role play. Do not spend more than X hours preparing.").
- Use of outside materials. Let the candidate know if they are allowed to use external research, e.g. are they encouraged to browse the web in preparation for the role play?

In Part 4, we'll discuss how to score the candidate's responses.

Presentation Assessment

For roles that require strong presentation skills—like sales, leadership, or client-facing positions—presentation exercises can be a powerful assessment tool. These exercises ask candidates to prepare and deliver a presentation on a specific topic, offering a direct glimpse into their ability to organize information, convey ideas clearly, and engage an audience. While the entire interview could be seen as a "presentation," this exercise focuses specifically on formal presentation skills critical to the role.

FIGURE 14.1 Examples of Presentation Types Across Functions

BUSINESS DEVELOPMENT OR SALES	PRODUCT MANAGEMENT, DESIGN, ENGINEERING	HR AND PEOPLE TEAMS	LEADERSHIP AND FINANCIAL
Stakeholder Updates	Design Review	Training	Quarterly Business Reviews (QBRs)
Quarterly Business Reviews (QBRs)	Project Proposals	Onboarding	Financial Reports
	Go/No-Go	Seminars And Workshops	
Marketing Campaign	Product Requirements Document Review		Investor Relations
Customer Success Reports		Conferences	Board Meetings

To design an effective presentation assessment, start by listing the types of presentations employees in the role are likely to give. Are they presenting strategic plans to leadership, pitching products to clients, or delivering training to internal teams? Each type requires different skills, so clarity about expectations is crucial. Figure 14.1 shows some examples of presentations across a few functions.

Once you've identified the key presentation types, craft a realistic scenario that includes:

- **Background information:** Provide context, such as the audience and purpose of the presentation.
- **Objective:** Define what the candidate should achieve, like persuading a client, sharing data insights, or proposing a solution.
- **Instructions:** Give clear guidance on the content they need to prepare, the format to use, and any materials they can leverage.

For example, you might ask a sales candidate to pitch a fictional product to a prospective client, or a leadership candidate to present a strategy to solve a business challenge. Provide enough detail to allow them to demonstrate creativity and insight while staying grounded in the scenario.

Finally, use structured evaluation criteria to assess their performance. Criteria could include clarity, persuasiveness, organization, and ability to handle questions—ensuring consistency and fairness across candidates. Presentation assessments can highlight a candidate's readiness for the communication demands of the job, offering a valuable complement to other interview methods.

Considerations

Some clients prefer to assign take-home exercises, such as problem-solving tasks, presentations, or technical assignments. However, we see two main issues with this approach. First, it's difficult to confirm whether the candidate completed the work themselves unless they return to discuss it. Second, these exercises can require significant time, which can unintentionally harm the candidate experience. For example, if a candidate invests many hours in a task and is ultimately not hired, it can erode their trust in the process.

There's also a fairness concern: If you set a one-hour preparation limit but one candidate spends six hours on it, while another—a single parent working two jobs—can only commit the designated hour, this can create an unfair advantage. By instead conducting the exercise in real time via video conference or in person, you can control the time commitment, maintain consistency across candidates, and gather insights comparable to a standard interview.

15

Let's Write Some Questions!

If you've conducted your job analysis and have your job profile with the shortlist of critical skills necessary for success on the job on day one, the questions will flow naturally. Here's an example. Let's dive into the "negotiation" skill for your lead attorney role and turn the associated behaviors into questions. Good news, it's an exercise of rewording, not recreating. Even without your favorite chatbot.

Let's explore negotiation.

Negotiation: Influencing stakeholders to gain agreement on specific courses of action or plans.

> **Key behaviors:**

1 Using influence strategies to gain agreement.

2 Leveraging knowledge of larger goals and needs, ensuring solutions accomplish these.

3 Ensuring consistently strong relationships and building consensus.

Here's a simple way to turn three behaviors into questions:

Question 1: "Tell me about a time when you needed to influence someone else."

Question 2: "Describe a situation where you needed to navigate a negotiation to a specific goal or objective."

Question 3: "Help us understand how you researched information to guide your negotiation toward your objectives."

Do you see a trend? There is no reason to beat around the bush with your candidate. Just go right in there and ask away about the *exact thing you need to know*. Simplicity is always a key to successful questions for any job, regardless of the complexity of the job.

We can also write interview questions for the collections call center we discussed in Chapter 11. The key competencies for the call center are in the box below, along with suggested questions for the onsite.

BEHAVIORAL QUESTIONS FOR A CONTACT CENTER REPRESENTATIVE

Key skills:

- Handling conflict
- Persistence in collections
- Negotiations and disputes

Behavioral questions:

- **Handling conflict:** "Tell me about a time when you had to navigate a conflict with a customer. What was the conflict about, and how did you handle it? What happened at the end of the call?"
- **Persistence in collections:** "Describe a time when you struggled to convince a customer to comply with a policy. What did you do/say? How did it turn out?"
- **Negotiation and disputes:** "Tell me about a situation when you needed to strike a win-win solution with a difficult customer. How did you go about engaging them and influencing them? What was the result?"

These questions will allow us to imagine our candidate in action as they navigate the same kinds of situations they will face when working with us. In Part 4, using the job analysis information, we will discuss how to score the candidate responses to such questions.

The questions we created all get at behaviors. Do our candidates need to have certain types of knowledge as well? See examples of questions to target technical or specific job knowledge referenced in Chapter 14.

Building the Interview Guide

Now you have your interview questions built out, including the knowledge, skills, and abilities (KSAs) being assessed, it's time to put together your interview guides. We recommend building an interview guide template and then just pasting in the KSAs you decide should be assessed per interview and the relevant questions and evaluation criteria. In a 45-minute interview, we recommend including three to four KSAs to be assessed. Including more may make it difficult for novice interviewers to capture enough data and detail necessary to provide detailed and substantial ratings.

There are a few things that an interview guide should have:

- **Overview of the interview:** This should be a two/three-sentence summary outlining the key information about the interview, e.g. interview length, purpose, guidance on who should conduct it, and any other relevant information or resources the interviewer should review or reference ahead of this interview.

- **List of KSAs being assessed:** Include the names and definitions of anything the interviewer will be assessing. This will be helpful for them to study ahead of the interview so they are clear on what they are "on the hook" for assessing.

- **Agenda:** The interviewer should share with the candidate the plan for the interview, i.e. how the time will be spent, any housekeeping items that should be covered before jumping into the interview questions, as well as next steps following the interview. This is helpful for the interviewer to reference to make sure they set the stage properly for the interview, as well as help them manage the time effectively.

- **Interview questions:** Whomever is building the interview guide (e.g. the hiring manager or HR team member) should paste in questions relevant for each KSA being assessed.

  o Note for whomever is building the interview guide: Include a few questions per KSA and give the interviewer a choice in which one they leverage per KSA.

- **Evaluation criteria:** Whomever is building the interview guide, e.g. the hiring manager or HR team member, should paste in the evaluation criteria relevant for each KSA being assessed.

Here is an example of information that should be provided to interviewers in advance of their interviews, either in a document, through training, or both.

INTERVIEWER GUIDANCE: REVIEW PRIOR TO CONDUCTING YOUR INTERVIEW

Step 1: Understand the KSAs definitions

- **Review the KSAs definitions before the interview:** Before evaluating a candidate, familiarize yourself with the KSAs being assessed. Each KSA should have a clear definition to ensure you know what behaviors, actions, or outcomes to look for in the candidate's responses.

- **Review the interview guide and evaluation criteria ahead of your interview:** Get familiar with the questions and evaluation criteria for each KSA you are assessing. Understand what "solid" performance (a rating of 3) looks like for each KSA based on its three key descriptors. These descriptors set a standard for adequate performance, ensuring consistency in your evaluations.

Step 2: Apply the rating scale

- **Anchor points for objectivity:** If using a 5-point scale, use the three key descriptors to guide your evaluation. This helps ground your evaluation in objective criteria rather than personal impressions.

- **Mid-point emphasis (3):** Remember that on a 5-point scale, a rating of 3 for a given KSA represents meeting expectations for the role. A rating of 3 with this type of scale should be considered a baseline for adequate capability with room for continued refinement and improvement.

- **Compare evidence to descriptors:** Compare the candidate's demonstrated behaviors and outcomes with the descriptors. If the candidate's performance on a given KSA seems to exceed the descriptors provided, that would suggest a higher score than 3. If the candidate's performance on a given KSA does not meet the expectation for a 3, that suggests a lower score.

Step 3: Follow evaluation guidelines

- **Take detailed notes during the interview:** Record the candidate's responses verbatim or in detailed summaries. This minimizes reliance on memory, which can introduce error.

- **Avoid bias:** Be aware of common cognitive errors, such as halo/horns effects, similarity bias, or confirmation bias. Focus strictly on the evidence presented during the interview.

- **Ensure consistency across KSAs:** Apply the same rigor and standards when rating each KSA. Avoid allowing performance in one area to disproportionately influence ratings in another.
- **Provide rationale for ratings:** For each score, document specific evidence from the candidate's responses that supports your evaluation. This not only ensures transparency but also aids in final decision-making.

What an Interview Guide Template Could Look Like

The following is an example interview guide template that highlights the key details to include in both the interview guide itself and the accompanying evaluation criteria document. To provide additional clarity, we've included a sample question and evaluation criteria for the *Problem Solving* skill. This demonstrates how the guide's structure integrates with the evaluation framework to create a cohesive and actionable tool for interviewers.

Name of Interview

DURATION (E.G. "45-MINUTE TECHNICAL INTERVIEW")

This interview is for *<insert role>* and should be conducted by *<insert person or role who is qualified to conduct this interview>*. Please review the competencies you are responsible for assessing below, as well as their associated evaluation criteria at the end of this document. Capture notes throughout the interview so you are prepared to evaluate the competencies or KSAs immediately after the interview. Please submit your evaluation criteria document with ratings and supporting evidence to *<insert person/email address>* no more than 24 hours after your interview.

KSAs BEING ASSESSED

- KSA name and definition: Definition of KSA
- KSA name and definition: Definition of KSA
- KSA name and definition: Definition of KSA

INTERVIEWER INSTRUCTIONS

- **Opening, introductions, and setting expectations: 2–3 min**
  - o Facilitate brief introductions, let the candidate know a bit about your role and time with the organization, rapport-building.

o Inform the candidate about the level of detail you will be looking for in the interview; e.g. if I'm asking you a "tell me about a time when" question, imagine I am following you around with a video camera making a documentary about the situation you're sharing with me. I'll want to be able to capture the level of detail necessary to explain what you did, said, and felt in a given situation.

– If conducting a behavioral interview ("tell me about a time when" questions), you might consider overviewing the STAR framework for candidates so they can aim to organize their responses within that approach. The STAR framework stands for Situation, Task, Action, and Results. Providing this framework to candidates can help them outline situations, their actions, and results for us in a way that allows us to capture the most relevant data.

o Inform the candidate that you will be taking notes throughout.

o Apologize in advance if you need to interrupt them to extract more detail or redirect them throughout their responses. This is to help ensure they provide the most relevant information in the limited time you have with them.

- **Interview questions: XX min** *(dependent on length of interview. In a 45-min interview, this would be ~35–40 min)*

o Ask the candidate competency-based questions or questions aligned with the KSAs you are measuring.

- **Closing: ~3–5 min**

o Inform candidate of any next steps and allow them to ask any questions.

RATING GUIDANCE

KSAs will be evaluated on a 5-point rating scale. Please review the evaluation criteria at the end of this document ahead of your interview to get familiar with the rating scale and descriptors.

INTERVIEW QUESTIONS

Choose one question for each KSA below. Optional follow-up probes are beneath each main question to help you probe for sufficient data.

> Problem Solving: Ability to make sense of new and complex information, and design tailored solutions. Leverages analytical and critical thinking to solve problems and drive solutions.

- Describe a situation where you had to solve a new problem (build a solution for a client, achieve some goal working through obstacles, etc.).
  - o What was the situation?
  - o Who were the key stakeholders?
  - o What obstacles did you run into?
  - o How did you handle this?
  - o What was the outcome?
  - o What would you do differently knowing what you know now? How have you applied that learning since? (gets at Learning Agility)
- \<insert "main" interview question>
- Include optional probing questions, e.g.
  - o What was the situation?
  - o Who were the key stakeholders?
  - o What was your objective?
  - o What obstacles did you run into?
  - o What was the outcome?
  - o What would you do differently knowing what you know now?

KSA name: Definition

- \<insert "main" interview question>
- Include optional probing questions, e.g.
  - o What was the situation?
  - o Who were the key stakeholders?
  - o What was your objective?
  - o What obstacles did you run into?
  - o What was the outcome?
  - o What would you do differently knowing what you know now?
- \<insert "main" interview question>
- Include optional probing questions, e.g.
  - o What was the situation?

- o Who were the key stakeholders?
- o What was your objective?
- o What obstacles did you run into?
- o What was the outcome?
- o What would you do differently knowing what you know now?

KSA name: Definition

- <insert "main" interview question>
- Include optional probing questions, e.g.
  - o What was the situation?
  - o Who were the key stakeholders?
  - o What was your objective?
  - o What obstacles did you run into?
  - o What was the outcome?
  - o What would you do differently knowing what you know now?
- <insert "main" interview question>
- Include optional probing questions, e.g.
  - o What was the situation?
  - o Who were the key stakeholders?
  - o What was your objective?
  - o What obstacles did you run into?
  - o What was the outcome?
  - o What would you do differently knowing what you know now?

Evaluation Criteria

Interviewers: Please review the evidence collected during your interview and compare against the evaluation criteria provided below. Using the full range on a 5-point scale where 1 = does not meet expectations and 5 = exceeds expectations.

In this sample document, we will provide you with two examples of evaluation criteria, based on the options we overviewed in Part 2.

If using Option 2 from Part 2, which defines what meeting expectations looks like for a specific KSA (i.e. a 3 rating on a 5-point scale) while allowing interviewers flexibility to adjust ratings based on candidate performance, refer to the example provided below.

Guidance for Using "Basic Proficiency Scale"

- **Compare evidence to descriptors:** With this type of 5-point scale, descriptions are only provided for the 3 rating, where 3 = meets expectations. You will need to compare the evidence gathered from the interview against the descriptors provided and determine if the candidate's performance should be rated below or above that descriptor.

- **Mid-point emphasis (3):** Remember that a score of 3 represents meeting expectations for the role. It is not a sign of underperformance, but rather a baseline for adequate capability.

- **Use the full range of the scale:** Behavioral descriptions are only provided for the 3 anchor point on the rating scale, but the full range of the scale should be used (1, 2, 3, 4, and 5 ratings).

Problem solving Ability to make sense of new and complex information, and design tailored solutions. Leverages analytical and critical thinking to solve problems and drive solutions.

- **Breaks down complex problems:** Analyzes new and complex situations by breaking them into manageable components. Identifies key issues but may occasionally overlook less obvious factors.

- **Applies logical thinking:** Uses critical thinking and analysis to develop practical solutions that address immediate needs. Solutions are effective but may not always anticipate secondary impacts or longer-term implications.

- **Adapts existing knowledge:** Draws from past experiences and known strategies to tackle unfamiliar problems. Adapts existing frameworks with some degree of innovation but could more consistently create truly novel solutions.

If using Behavioral Anchored Rating Scales (BARS), please reference the example in Table 15.1.

TABLE 15.1 Example Behavioral Anchored Rating Scales (BARS): Problem Solving

Problem solving: Ability to make sense of new and complex information, and design tailored solutions. Leverages analytical and critical thinking to solve problems and drive solutions.

Does not meet expectations (1)	Meets expectations (3)	Exceeds expectations (5)
Analyzes information logically		
Struggles to analyze new information; ideas lack logic.	Analyzes information sufficiently and does so logically.	Skillful in analyzing new information; shows creativity and interdependencies while maintaining logic.
Generates ideas to resolve issues and drive solutions		
Does not generate ideas or propose solutions.	Generates a few solid ideas.	Generates long list of ideas, may bring outside-in perspective, shaping solutions more comprehensively.
Applies relevant concepts and principles to address problems		
Overlooks chances to incorporate new concepts into own problem-solving approach.	Makes use of new concepts and principles when addressing problems.	Swiftly incorporates new concepts and principles into own expertise; skillfully uses these fresh insights to solve problems.

Guidance for Using "Behavioral Anchored Rating Scales (BARS)"

- **Anchor points for objectivity:** Use the 5-point scale provided, with specific descriptors for each anchor point (e.g. 1 = does not meet expectations, 3 = meets expectations, 5 = exceeds expectations). This helps ground your evaluation in objective criteria rather than personal impressions.

  o Behavioral descriptions are provided for the 1, 3, and 5 anchor points on the rating scale, but the full range of the scale should be used (2 and 4 ratings).

  o Interviewers should leverage the behavioral descriptions and their best judgment when differentiating between 1 and 3 and 3 and 5 ratings for competencies.

- **Mid-point emphasis (3):** Remember that a score of 3 represents meeting expectations for the role. It is not a sign of underperformance, but rather a baseline for adequate capability.

- **Compare evidence to descriptors:** Match the candidate's demonstrated behaviors and outcomes with the corresponding descriptors for each rating level.

16

Creating Candidate Trust

Now that you have your interview guide ready to go, it's time to actually conduct the interview.

One of our favorite ways to avoid any legal complaint or claim from ever being launched is to help candidates feel that your hiring process, regardless of whether or not they got the job, is fair. Even if you are dealing with thousands of unqualified candidates per day, our advice is to treat each of them like your favorite customers. Actually, many of you may be hiring for consumer-facing companies, so they *are* actually your customer as well as a candidate.

Start by putting yourself in the candidate's shoes. Reflect on your own job application experiences—when the focus felt more on screening people out than welcoming the right ones in. This mindset can lead to a negative experience for candidates, even if unintended. Remember, if you've set clear minimum qualifications and screened out those who don't meet them, you're now focused on engaging qualified candidates with a positive and respectful approach.

Prepare Candidates

Preparing a candidate to perform their best is essential to creating a fair selection process that allows candidates to fully showcase their skills. For any selection process, we encourage recruiters or hiring managers to provide clear information describing all aspects of the process and what each stage is designed to assess.

"But wait—should we really share what we're measuring with the candidate?"

Yes!

"What if a candidate uses this information to 'cheat' and prepare in advance?"

Here's what we've learned over years of assessing candidates: It's virtually impossible for someone to fabricate a complete profile of competence during an interview with a skilled interviewer. Even candidates with inflated self-images struggle to maintain a misleading narrative if you ask focused, probing questions that align with the competencies you're evaluating.

Imagine you ask a candidate to describe a time they solved a challenging problem, and they try to pass off someone else's experience as their own. If you follow up by asking about specific actions they took, their reasoning, and how they applied their knowledge in that scenario, any fabrication will likely become apparent as their responses grow vague.

Below are some examples of vague responses to probing questions, which may indicate a candidate is exaggerating or cannot recall key specifics about a situation. In either case, if a candidate cannot provide sufficient detail about their actions, reasoning, and the context, it becomes difficult to accurately assess their behavior against the criteria. As one of Mollie's former assessment leaders put it, "The lack of data is data."

EXAMPLES OF VAGUE RESPONSES TO FOLLOW-UP PROBES

"I generally would try to have a conversation with the person about what happened and see if we could xyz…"

"It was a complicated situation, but in the end, we worked through it."

"I don't remember all the details but I do feel like it turned out well."

This is exactly why strong, probing questions set excellent interviewers apart from poor ones. Well-crafted questions help you not only determine if a candidate arrived at the correct solution (in a knowledge-based question) but also understand *how* they achieved that outcome. And if a candidate studied in advance based on the topics we shared? Great! If they genuinely learned and performed well, we can consider them qualified in that area.

Today, hundreds of prep resources, websites, books, and tools—including GenAI—are available for coding interviews and other technical topics. However, not everyone has equal access or knows how to use them. This creates an unfair advantage for those with insider knowledge. We don't want some candidates to have an edge while others don't. By giving all candidates an overview of the areas we'll cover in advance, everyone has a fair chance to prepare using the resources available.

Another perk to using behavioral interviews: Using behavioral questions ("tell me about a time when") allows your hiring team to present an organized, structured, and credible process to candidates. This approach also allows you to reference specific skills when asking questions, helping candidates respond with relevant examples that are easier to assess.

For instance, if you say, "This next question focuses on strategic thinking and long-term planning. Tell me about a time when you designed something that needed to last more than three years," it clarifies what you're looking for. Now, if Paolo starts talking about aesthetic design rather than future-oriented planning, it's easier to steer him back toward the intended focus of the question.

Make it Natural

Earlier, we discussed the misconception that structured interviews have to feel "robotic." Our goal is to help you maintain a natural, conversational tone while still following a consistent interview structure and question format. We know it can be challenging to keep a conversational flow within a structured process.

To create a comfortable atmosphere, use open, friendly body language and make natural eye contact—even if it's tricky while taking notes, try to connect visually throughout. Also, remember that you don't need to read each question word-for-word. Think of each question as a prompt, a topic to explore. Use conversational language to guide the discussion naturally around that topic.

Let's say you just asked the candidate to tell you about a time when they had a conflict with a coworker.

Prompt: "Tell me about a time when you experienced a conflict with a coworker."

You: "Have you been in a situation where you've had to navigate a conflict with someone you worked with? Earlier, you mentioned being part of the design team and partnering with program management. This kind of an example, with more detail, may be helpful to explore here. Was there a time when you and one of the other team members didn't agree? Feel free to leverage another example, too, if a better one comes to mind."

Candidate: (Laughs) "It seems like you've worked at my company. Yes. Absolutely. So this is pretty common. We run into conflicts all the time. In one specific instance…"

Tips for Rapport Building

1   **Be grateful.** When the candidate responds to your question, even if you know it's *not* the best answer, always show gratitude for their effort. There is no need to be dishonest and tell them that their answer was great. But you can always be sincerely grateful that they answered your question and showed up in whatever way they could show up. At the end of the question, when we have collected enough data to move on to the next question, we say one of these things:

"Thank you."

"This is helpful, I appreciate you digging into this question a bit more."

"I have what I need on this topic, and I appreciate that."

"I am happy to move on with the information you gave me; thanks again for going into this situation a bit more with me."

2   **Interruption is kindness.** To help a candidate succeed in demonstrating their best self, sometimes we need to help them give us the information we are seeking and reduce the information-sharing of context and details of less significance. Candidates don't have a playbook on the skills and types of responses that are meeting those skills. Even if they did, and the recruiter let them know what you're measuring, it's very hard to link these to their actual experience at the moment of the interview (because… nerves). When a candidate goes off track, and starts telling you all about their global experience when you asked them to describe building relationships with people who were different from themselves, do them a huge favor and interrupt them. "Hey, Paolo. I am sorry to interrupt, but I want to make sure that you have a chance to give me all the information in the short time we have. The information you're sharing is interesting, but with this question, I am hoping to understand more about how you…" If you just let Paolo keep going, take notes, and then go back to determine if he got the answer right, you would likely give him a low mark on that skill because he didn't provide the example or evidence you

needed. Is that fair? We don't think it is. You also will run out of time to properly assess other key skills, so you're doing the candidate a disservice by not interrupting them.

3 **Rate the right thing and rate what you can.** Evaluate the relevant aspects, and focus on what you can actually assess. If a candidate provides information that doesn't directly answer your question, it might indicate a gap in listening or following instructions, but it doesn't necessarily mean they lack the skill you're assessing—such as working effectively with people who are different from themselves. In this case, there simply isn't enough information to judge that skill based on the data you've gathered. Your responsibility is to ask questions that capture all the relevant data needed for assessment, rather than expecting the candidate to anticipate exactly what information you're looking for.

PRO TIP

If during a question that was supposed to target *Collaboration* you ended up also gathering data about the candidate's *Strategic Thinking* abilities, you should absolutely use that data to evaluate *Strategic Thinking*, assuming that is a skill that is also being assessed.

---

4 **Reference the evaluation criteria during the interview.** During the interview, use the evaluation criteria as a guide. Before moving to the next question, check if you have enough information to confidently rate the candidate on the job profile attribute you were assessing. Encourage the candidate to provide detailed responses and ask follow-up questions to ensure they have a chance to showcase their strengths. Continuously refer to the evaluation criteria to confirm whether you've gathered sufficient insight or need to explore certain areas further with probing questions.

This section covered ways to ensure that you collected all the needed data from your candidate in the short time you had with them, in order to give them a full chance to show their most qualified self.

17

Conducting Your Interview

Question Framing and Follow-up Probes

For our novice interviewer, here are just a few questions you should ask yourself when conducting a behavioral interview. By considering these questions, you'll realize where you need to probe more to really understand the candidate's thinking and impact during shared situations.

Who Demonstrated the Behavior Shared?

Did the interviewee share "I did xyz" statements, or was it "we did xyz" or "the team did xyz" statements? This is the candidate's chance to be proud, bold, and showcase their personal talent. We are not interested in what the team accomplished, we need to know specifically what this candidate did by themselves. So, if you're hearing a lot of "we" statements, make sure to ask the candidate to distinguish between individual or team ownership.

Is It Clear?

To check your candidate responses, evaluate whether the description of the candidate's actions was sufficiently clear and specific. Can you see what the interviewee is doing, saying, and to whom the action is being performed on or towards, almost like watching a film of them? Second, does the information shared reflect the interviewee's thoughts or feelings about the situation or behaviors taken during that time?

Does It Tell Me the Future?

Can you use this to determine how much they learned or how they would handle the situation in the future, but in slightly different circumstances?

Sometimes, a candidate provides an example that is so specific, you realize this is not something they will ever need to do in your job. Ensure that your questions pull back from the situation enough to see their rationale and methodology, since they would likely apply those again. We always recommend before moving on from a behavioral question to ask the candidate, "What did you learn from that situation and how have you applied that since?"

PRO TIP

When conducting behavioral interviews, it's helpful to set clear expectations with candidates upfront about the level of detail you'll be seeking. This ensures they understand what you're looking for and can structure their responses accordingly.

Here's a way that both Kasey and Mollie have effectively communicated this to candidates:

> I'll be asking you about specific situations you've experienced and how you handled them. For each question, I'm looking for detailed responses. This includes what you were thinking during the situation, what you said, the actions you took, any important interactions with others, your reactions, and the outcome. To help you visualize this, think of it as if I'm following you with a video camera during the event you're describing. I want to be able to create a documentary about that moment based on the details you provide.

This approach not only clarifies expectations but also encourages candidates to reflect deeply on their experiences, allowing you to gather the nuanced, specific insights needed for a thorough assessment.

Standard Probing Questions: STAR framework

In a behavioral interview, a candidate describes a time when they did something at work. There are four standard probes we like to use to ensure we get the full story. To help the candidate help you, it's totally reasonable to ask them to give you all these additional pieces of information up front, and then continue to prompt them as they go through the interview.

The STAR framework[1] is a widely used method for structuring behavioral interview responses. It helps candidates provide clear, concise, and relevant answers that demonstrate their competencies and experience. STAR stands for Situation, Task, Action, and Result:

- **Situation:** What was the situation or circumstance?
  - o Describe the context or background of a specific situation where you faced a challenge or opportunity. Here, try to understand:
    - – Why was the candidate in this situation?
    - – What were they asked to do?
    - – What was the problem?
    - – What circumstances were they faced with?
    - – Why is this an interesting story to share as an example of them being effective at whatever you want to measure?
- **Task:** Explain what your responsibility or goal was in that situation.
  - o What task were you trying to achieve and what role did you play in this situation?
  - o What were the expectations?
  - o **Note:** The task is often a critical component that helps interviewers understand the scope and challenge of the situation they faced.
- **Action:** What did you do? Detail the steps you took to address the task or challenge.
  - o Focus on your specific contributions.
  - o Not what did "we" do? What did "you" do?
  - o What was your role in this situation?
  - o What actions did you take to resolve the situation, and why did you choose those specific actions?
- **Result:** In the end, what was the final result?
  - o How did you contribute to this result?
  - o What metrics did you leverage to understand how well it all went?
  - o Share the outcome of your actions, emphasizing the positive impact or learning gained.

We always recommend adding in a final probing question outside of the STAR framework which is focused on continuous learning and improvement as well as self-awareness.

- **Learning?** What did you learn from this situation?
  - What would you change if you had to do it again?
  - What feedback did you receive?
  - Did the situation come up again? How was it different the second time?

If a candidate listens carefully and responds to each of these standard probes, you should have a wealth of information. Unfortunately, candidates can get caught up in the story they want to tell, not always the story you want to hear, so they leave things out. This brings us to the next section.

Probing for Deeper Insight

How do you know that you gathered enough data from the candidate during your interview? Do you feel like you could almost see the candidate handling similar situations in the job you're hiring them for by the end of your interview? Sometimes our interviewers find this to be a challenge. We've had the uncomfortable experience of starting to rate the skills after the interview, but not feeling like we captured enough data to give a fair evaluation. We may realize that the candidate answered all the questions like, "I typically like to…" or "I do this all the time, and I do it well" or "We had a tough situation where I needed to do this, and then I did it, and it was resolved." In all of these examples, we're missing the deeper *how* behind what the candidate did. More than knowing that the candidate did this, as if it was a checkbox on a form, we want to know exactly how they handled the situation in the prompt—what specific behaviors and actions they took and their rationale.

Probing questions are intended to give you the full scope of the candidate's knowledge, behavior, or ability. These questions are used to dig deeper into a candidate's response to a behavioral question or to seek additional clarification for any of the above question types. They can be especially useful to help encourage candidates to provide more details or examples, without "leading the witness" of course. For example: "Can you elaborate on the steps you took to achieve that result?" "Who was involved in this activity?" "Who was driving this conversation with the key stakeholder?"

Probing is the means to avoid having too little data at the end of the interview. We recommend that you probe on every single question. Yet, even after attending interview training courses, we've noticed that our trainees still don't probe enough. What makes probing a challenge?

For one, most interviewees don't realize how few details they provide. Communicating with the level of detail that we're looking for is actually uncommon in a typical conversation. Imagine that you're talking with your coworker about challenges they faced during a new customer relationship management (CRM) system implementation. Perhaps it would look something like this:

You: "I heard that the new CRM's been a killer on your team. How's that been going?"

Your coworker: "It's been a mess. We uploaded the old data last Tuesday and the system still hasn't completed the transfer. Now we're updating two systems. It's taking me forever."

You: "That's painful. I went through something like that with our reporting system a year ago. I feel for you. What's your plan?"

Your coworker: "I don't even know. My best plan is to go hide in my office so the team stops yelling at me about it. Any ideas?"

If this information was presented in an interview by your coworker, we feel pretty certain they would not do well. Transitioning from speaking about situations in the casual way above to explaining what we, as interviewers, need to know, however, is more challenging than removing negativity or presenting oneself positively. In an interview, the coworker might say:

> We implemented a new CRM, and experienced technical difficulties around the data transfer. This meant that we had to double enter information for a month while it was resolved and audited, and probably cost us about 30 lost hours across the team in that time. In the end, I pushed the data team to move faster, and probably saved another 30 hours of lost time.

This is more professional, but it's still not enough detail to give your coworker a score on how they manage system changes. That's why, even with a pretty decent explanation, we need to continue to probe.

Here are some probes you could use for the situation above to help them give you the full STAR answers:

1 Tell me more about why implementing this CRM was important.

2 Who did you speak to about expediting the data transfer?

3 What were the risks and benefits of the expedited data transfer?

4 When you planned for the new system implementation, how did you address these issues?

5 How did you keep your team engaged during the process?

6 If I was on your team, how would you explain the need for this change to me?

7 How did you evaluate the ROI of this change?

8 A quarter later, how is the implementation going?

Only our candidates seem to feel that we are asking for a tedious amount of detail; we know we're getting the *right* amount to make a sound decision. If the candidate seems hesitant, you can add some further explanation such as:

- I know I'm asking for a lot of detail. This helps me to understand the full scope of your strength in this area.

- I am hoping to get a sense of what it's like to go through this type of project with you. Can you tell me how you handled each aspect that came up, and what you said to your stakeholders, so that I can see it like I'm watching a film?

Call Center Example: Contact Center Representative

Let's say you asked your contact center representative candidate, "Tell me about a time when you resolved a tough conflict with a customer," and they respond, "I do this every day. I did it yesterday. I am comfortable doing this."

The candidate is now under the impression that they gave you everything you needed, but this is not enough to give them a rating on the skill. Ideally, you'll want to almost see the candidate as if you were there with them. As we recommended, sometimes we suggest that our candidates give us a really detailed view of how they handled their situation as if they were showing us a film. When someone cannot do this, it may mean that they chose an example without enough action to portray a whole situation, or that they are making up a scenario. In fact, one of the ways we avoid any form of "cheating" with candidates is to ask for a lot of details on what happened. The more detail they need to convey about their story, the harder it is for them to invent something. We also don't worry as much about candidates inventing stories, since knowledge of how to handle whatever situation they are describing is almost as important as having actually done it. Usually, if a candidate is fabricating a story about an accomplishment, they don't provide great examples of why they did what they did or clear information about their decision-making.

Here are some responses to combat a lack of specific examples, which helps you differentiate the candidate's contribution in a situation from those of others involved:

- I will need to understand how you specifically handled a situation that came up in the last year or two.
- Could you tell me what the situation was, what actions you took, and how it was resolved?
- Please provide additional details on the actual situation that occurred.
- Focus on what you did, said, thought, and felt in that situation.
- Tell me about a specific time you did that in this situation.
- What did you specifically do?
- What was it about that situation that ended up causing the issue?

Sometimes you'll find yourself reminding the candidate to provide specifics for each and every question. This makes for an exhausting interview. Unfortunately, candidates simply aren't skilled at giving interviewers the exact information that is being targeted. We often must probe to uncover sufficient levels of detail so we can more properly assess the qualities we are seeking.

Here are a few other common reasons why interviewers find it challenging to ask sufficient probing questions:

1 **Overreliance on prepared questions**
   Interviewers may focus too heavily on sticking to a structured guide, fearing that deviating from the script could lead to inconsistency or risk missing key topics.

2 **Fear of interrupting or overstepping boundaries**
   Concerns about interrupting candidates, making candidates uncomfortable, or appearing too intrusive can lead interviewers to avoid asking follow-up questions.

3 **Lack of confidence in probing**
   Some interviewers are unsure how to ask effective follow-ups or how to evaluate complex, open-ended responses, leading to hesitation.

4 **Time constraints**
   The pressure to cover all planned questions within a limited timeframe can prevent interviewers from exploring deeper insights.

5 **Cognitive overload**

Balancing multiple tasks, such as note-taking, observing behavior, and managing time, can make it challenging to identify and pursue opportunities for deeper questioning.

Here are a few strategies to help tackle some of these additional challenges.

OVERRELIANCE ON PREPARED QUESTIONS

Strategy: Train interviewers to see the guide as a foundation, not a constraint.

- Introduce the concept of "flexible structure," where follow-ups enrich rather than disrupt the process.
- Provide examples of how to seamlessly transition from a prepared question to a probing one, e.g. "You mentioned X—can you tell me more about how that played out?"

FEAR OF INTERRUPTING OR OVERSTEPPING BOUNDARIES

Strategy: Set expectations with candidates upfront and emphasize respectful probing techniques.

- First, ensure interviewers set expectations appropriately with candidates upfront before beginning their interviews; this includes "setting the stage" and tackling any housekeeping items, including something like "I apologize in advance but I may interrupt you at times. This is just to ensure I get as much detailed information from you as possible, so I can represent you in the best light against what I'm assessing."
- Teach interviewers to frame probing questions as curiosity-driven rather than interrogative, e.g. "I'm curious to understand your thought process there—can you elaborate?"
- Reinforce psychological safety by clarifying that follow-up questions are meant to give candidates more opportunities to shine.

LACK OF CONFIDENCE IN PROBING

Strategy: Build confidence through practice and frameworks.

- Use role-playing exercises where interviewers practice following up on vague or incomplete answers.
- Introduce the **STAR + Why/How** technique: Encourage interviewers to ask questions about the **Why** and **How** behind **Situation, Task, Action,** and **Result.**

- Example:
  - "Why did you choose to approach the situation in that particular way?"
  - "Can you explain the thought process behind your decision to take those specific actions?"
  - "How did you manage to overcome the challenges you faced during this task?"

TIME CONSTRAINTS
Strategy: Train for balance and prioritization.

- Provide interviewers with time-management tips, such as limiting initial answers and leaving time for follow-ups. This includes practicing how to interrupt and redirect candidate's responses when you realize they are going off track. The interviewer is the timekeeper and it is their responsibility to ensure they do their best to capture the necessary data.
- Teach them to prioritize depth over breadth for critical competencies. For example, if a candidate's leadership style is a priority, allocate more time to that area, even if it means skipping less relevant questions.

COGNITIVE OVERLOAD
Strategy: Simplify note-taking and observation.

- Equip interviewers with tools like pre-written templates that highlight areas for probing (e.g. "What was your specific role in this example?").
- Encourage interviewers to pause and ask clarifying questions immediately rather than trying to document everything in the moment.

GENERAL BEST PRACTICES

- Encourage post-interview reflection, where interviewers can identify missed probing opportunities and learn from them.
- Provide real-time feedback during mock interviews to help interviewers fine-tune their approach.

PRO TIP

When speaking with Ruth Cochran, a leadership assessment expert and executive coach—and a close colleague of Mollie—she offered insightful advice on effective interviewing:

> Approach each interview with genuine curiosity about the candidate. This mindset not only helps you stay engaged but also ensures you're digging deeper to uncover meaningful insights. In my own preparation, I rely on the mantra, *Ask the next question*. It's a reminder to keep probing for details. Without this, I find that as a big-picture thinker, I can fall into the trap of letting candidates share broad, high-level stories. While these narratives can be compelling, they often lack the specificity needed to assess key capabilities. By asking that next question, you get to the substance of what truly matters for the role.

This advice underscores the importance of balancing curiosity with intentional probing to extract detailed and actionable information during interviews.

Note

1   Development Dimensions International (2020) Targeted Selection®: A comprehensive guide, www.ddiworld.com/solutions/targeted-selection (archived at https://perma.cc/PTC6-VYSB)

18

Including Multiple Interviewers

Many of our clients organize their interview processes into "rounds" or "loops," where candidates typically go through four to six interviews, each conducted by a different team member. However, in some cases, this process can spiral out of control, with candidates enduring as many as 15 interviews. This often happens when interviewers are not properly trained or fail to gather sufficient information during earlier rounds, prompting the team to schedule additional interviews to cover missed topics. To avoid this, it's crucial to invest in interviewer training and establish strong, structured interviewing processes.

For many of our software engineering clients, the hiring manager performs the screen and relies on other trained interviewers to cover the KSAs deemed critical for success on the job on day one. The approach works fantastically if you are well-calibrated and coordinated. In those situations, you've potentially amplified your prediction power as well as lowered your risk of a poor hire. On the other hand, it's a complete disaster without clear interviewer roles, understanding of evaluation guidelines, and potentially a significantly worse prediction than a single interviewer. Adding more people into your interview process does not guarantee that you reduce cognitive error, and may actually increase the likelihood of faulty assessments or selection decisions if there is not a solid structure and sufficient criteria in place.

Why do our clients choose the multiple-interviewer approach? There are plenty of good reasons. In technical jobs, the hiring manager may not be the technical expert. Therefore, getting perspectives on candidates from people who actually do the job each day is helpful in collecting better data. In other situations, an employee may need to work with other people outside of their own group or department. This helps ensure that your candidate is vetted by cross-functional team members as well.

Here's an example from a client we worked with in the past. Before we built the job profiles for this organization, a client shared their typical interviewing process for front-end web developers. First, the designated recruiter combed through LinkedIn profiles and applications in the system. Then, he noted certain profiles that contained the appropriate qualifications, conducted a recruiter screen by phone, and sent these resumes to the hiring manager. The hiring manager would provide a "thumbs up" or "thumbs down" for each resume, and those with a "thumbs up" were invited to a screening interview with the hiring manager. The hiring manager asked a standard list of screening questions that included about five or six knowledge questions.

A couple of those questions were: "How would you approach fixing a rendering issue where a webpage looks correct in one browser but not in another?" or "Describe a project where you implemented a feature that significantly improved user experience."

She did not have a list of correct answers or scoring guidelines, explaining to us that she knew from their answers whether or not they had given a correct response. She typically screened about eight candidates and recommended two or three for an onsite interview.

During the onsite, the candidates would be interviewed on three different technical topics and two behavioral topics. Each interview was 30 minutes. Although no "right" or "strong" answers or scoring guides had been created for any of these interviews, interviewers had workshopped loose guidance on "things to look for." After each interview, the interviewer was tasked with giving a "thumbs up" or "thumbs down" for hiring or not hiring the candidate. So far, we felt optimistic with the structure and diligence of the process, minus the fact that the hiring manager did not have criteria documented for what was assessed during the hiring manager screen (but we'd fix that). The problem arose when a candidate performed beautifully on four interviews, but less well on the fifth, thus receiving a "no hire/thumbs down" recommendation from one single interviewer. When this occurred, the recruiter would assemble the team of interviewers to discuss the candidate. In many cases, the interviewer with the "no hire"/"thumbs down" recommendation felt compelled to justify the assessment and did so with such passion that they convinced the rest of the interviewers to reject the candidate. Going against the grain in a group like this felt akin to Henry Fonda's Juror #8 in *12 Angry Men*.[1] When one of the interviewers, the hapless recruiter, or the hiring manager felt strongly enough about the candidate, they would be offered to repeat the interview again with a different interviewer. You may be curious how often the second interview results matched the first. Looking through the recruiting analytics data, we found the match to be about 50 percent, meaning that it was about as good as flipping a coin. Our optimism with the process dissolved completely at this point, because we knew that the hiring decision was fraught with subjective decision-making.

The cognitive errors were not necessarily manifested in terms of excluding people based on gender, background, ethnicity, or socioeconomic status, although that certainly happened too. It turned out that each interviewer had their own strong opinions about how to solve problems in their area of expertise, and they did not agree with one another. In the times when someone reviewed the code submitted during the interview, they were not fully calibrated on the correct answer or methodology. The work done by these engineers was complicated and multifaceted, and the interview process had not sufficiently taken those different facets into account.

The team was open to rebuilding their process. Experienced software engineers, especially in some startups, have set up interviewing teams for optimal, error-mitigating interview processes. They begin with conducting a job analysis to clearly document the activities, KSAs, and minimum qualifications for the role. These provide the recruiting team with workable criteria for screening and the engineering interviewers with skills to assess. Next, the recruiting team lead the engineering teams in building a bank of interview questions aligned with each specific skill being assessed. Reaching agreement on the topics and questions is understandably complex.

Our recommendation: Choose your interviewers wisely. They should be people who are not only willing but eager to go through training and calibration to contribute meaningfully to your hiring goals. If your team is small and you don't have the resources to rotate in fresh interviewers for every step of the process, don't worry—it's fine to rely on the same core group of people. What matters most is that whoever conducts interviews is fully prepared and aligned with your structured process. This means they've completed the necessary training, understand how to use the interview guides and evaluation criteria, and are committed to reviewing and improving their approach over time. Structured interviewing works best when interviewers are calibrated, consistent, and focused on fair, objective evaluation. So, whether it's one person, a few, or many, the key is preparation and dedication.

One of our clients shared their approach to improving their interview process:

> Collaborating with other engineers—especially those committed to reducing bias in our process—is critical when writing interview questions. It ensures the questions reflect diverse perspectives and real-world challenges. When

engineers from different teams contribute, we get a balanced set of questions that test not only technical skills but also creativity and the ability to work in cross-functional environments. This collaboration helps create a process that evaluates both depth of knowledge and practical teamwork.

After agreeing on a set of criteria and questions, the interviewers worked together to create clear answer options for each question. Individual engineers volunteered to build initial answer guides, address ambiguous solutions, and document acceptable response variations for consistent scoring.

To improve decision-making, the team removed the responsibility of making overall hiring decisions from individual interviewers. Instead, they recommended that either the hiring manager or a hiring committee review the scored interview packets to make final hire/no-hire and leveling decisions.

Additionally, a few interviewers volunteered to spot-check scoring calibration across interviews. When inconsistencies were found, the team either removed problematic questions from the question bank or provided coaching to interviewers to improve their approach.

As a result, the client reported greater confidence in the accuracy and fairness of their assessment process.

Next, we'll share some tips for making your interview rounds a success.

Take Charge

A successful interview process requires strong leadership to guide and oversee the team. While a recruiter might take on this role, recruiters are often overextended. We recommend that, if you are the hiring manager, you either personally lead the interview process or designate someone from HR to take charge.

Leading the process involves:

1 **Forming an official interview team:** For each hiring requisition, establish a dedicated team. This includes setting up regular meetings, creating a communication channel (e.g. email or messaging platform), and holding team members accountable for their specific roles.

2 **Assigning clear roles:** Ensure each team member knows their responsibilities in the interview process and has the tools and resources needed to contribute effectively.

3 **Providing structure:** Create a process that emphasizes objective, evidence-based data sharing during candidate debriefs. Ensure interviewers report on the specific competencies or criteria they were responsible for assessing.

4 **Holding team members accountable:** Actively manage the team by challenging discrepancies between interviewers' data and ratings and addressing inconsistencies in their evaluations.

Finally, as the leader, you hold the ultimate responsibility for making the final hiring decision, based on the evidence and input gathered throughout the process.

Roles and Responsibilities

Treat the hiring process like any other project by clearly mapping out the goals, the team members involved, and their unique contributions. Document each team member's commitments, including specific deadlines.

Key Steps

1 **Identify your interview team:**
   - o Decide who to include. A typical group might consist of a technical expert, a higher-level leader, a peer, and a cross-functional partner from another team.
   - o Use the KSAs from your job analysis to determine which roles, positions, or individuals are best suited to assess specific qualities.
2 **Set clear expectations:**
   - o Define each person's responsibilities, such as attending regular progress meetings, providing input on the interview guides, and submitting ratings and evaluations on time.
   - o Ensure everyone understands their role in creating a thorough and structured interview process.

By setting these expectations upfront, you'll create a well-coordinated team that contributes effectively to the hiring process.

Gather Results and Decide

We've seen too many hiring meetings where interviewers spend time debating candidates, only to end in stalemates or "no hire" decisions due to unclear criteria and a lack of a clear decision-maker. As the hiring manager, you are in charge and should own the final decision. However, this decision should be informed by data-driven input from your interview team.

Key Recommendations

1 **Collect individual evaluations:**
   - o After each interview, ask all interviewers to submit their evaluations and ratings independently.
   - o Use this data to make your decision, ensuring it's based on objective evidence rather than group dynamics.

2 **Use meetings thoughtfully:**
   - o For senior-level or complex roles, a meeting may be helpful to discuss the interviewer's findings or to ask any questions about ratings/notes submitted.
   - o If a meeting is necessary, schedule it only after all interviews are complete and evaluations have been submitted.
   - o If a meeting is organized with all interviewers and the hiring manager, assign the hiring manager or the recruiter/HR partner as the facilitator of the conversation to keep the group on track.

3 **Reduce likelihood of cognitive errors:**
   - o To reduce flawed judgments or subjective decision-making (e.g. cognitive errors), interviewers should not see each other's notes or ratings or discuss their impressions of the candidate before submitting their evaluations.

4 **Score immediately:**
   - o Block 30 minutes on your calendar after each interview to review your notes and complete the scoring guide while the information is still fresh.
   - o This step is critical, as even with good notes, important details can fade within 24 hours. We've learned this the hard way.

By following these practices, you'll ensure a structured, accurate, and fair process that leads to better hiring decisions.

How Many Is Too Many?

A group of product engineers had built a highly inclusive interview process where each candidate went through eight interviews, spanning technical, cross-functional, and peer discussions. While candidates appreciated the insight they gained into the company and role, the process was exhaustively costly in terms of time and energy for everyone involved. Worse, candidates who weren't hired after such a significant investment of time felt disheartened, leading to a loss of trust and damaging the company's employer brand. On top of that, the sheer size of the interviewing team made it nearly impossible to align on what "good" looked like for a candidate, resulting in inconsistent decisions.

The team asked us how many interviews were appropriate for their hiring goals. Based on the KSAs identified through our job analysis, we recommended four to five interviews. For individual contributors, four interviews would cover the necessary skills, while a fifth interview would focus on people management competencies if hiring for a leadership role. While there's no scientific consensus on a "magic number" of interview rounds, what's clear is that more interviews don't always lead to better hiring decisions—in fact, they often dilute alignment and increase the risk of overburdening your team.

Let's break it down. Say your interview process targets the skills shown in Figure 18.1.

A well-structured process allows each interviewer to assess three to four skills in a 45-minute interview, more if the interview is 60 minutes. Some skills, like communication, can be evaluated throughout the interview without necessarily adding questions to your interview guide. Depending on how you distribute the skills and whether you choose to evaluate critical ones more than once (to boost reliability), four to five interviews were sufficient in this example. For highly technical roles, you may opt to evaluate all technical skills twice, ensuring depth and rigor.

FIGURE 18.1 Example: Skills Assessed in All Candidates and Additional People Manager Requirements

FOR ALL CANDIDATES	ADDITIONAL SKILLS FOR PEOPLE MANAGER CANDIDATES
• Problem Solving • Collaboration • Communication • Adapts to Change • Thinks Strategically • Technical Skill1 • Technical Skill 2 • Technical Skill 3	• Manages Performance • Inspires Others • Drives Results • Builds Effective Teams

Here's how this could look in practice:

- **Option 1:** Each interviewer focuses on three or four distinct skills, with little or no overlap.
- **Option 2:** Select a few critical skills (e.g. problem solving, collaboration, and/or technical skills) to assess more than once, ensuring diverse perspectives on key skills.

Ultimately, the goal is balance: Enough interviews to gather reliable data, but not so many that candidates or your team burn out. With the right structure and calibration, you can evaluate all critical skills efficiently while maintaining a positive candidate experience.

Putting together these interview rounds will ensure complete coverage, and every stakeholder will have a chance to set their eyes on the candidate.

FIGURE 18.2 Example Approaches to Structuring Interviews by Skills

	OPTION 1	OPTION 2
INTERVIEW 1	• Problem Solving • Collaboration • Communication • Thinks Strategically	• Problem Solving • Collaboration • Communication
INTERVIEW 2	• Thinks Strategically • Adapts to Change • Communication	• Thinks Strategically • Adapts to Change • Collaboration
INTERVIEW 3	• Technical Skill 1 • Technical Skill 2 • Technical Skill 3	• Technical Skill 1 • Technical Skill 2 • Technical Skill 3 • Communication
INTERVIEW 4	Add on for People Manager candidates: • Manages Performance • Builds Effective Teams • Inspires Others • Drives Results	• Technical Skill 1 • Technical Skill 2 • Technical Skill 3 • Problem Solving
INTERVIEW 5	N/A	Add on for People Manager candidates: • Manages Performance • Builds Effective Teams • Inspires Others • Drives Results

Make It a Program

Some of you may be designing systems to hire large groups or batches of employees all at once. This happens when rapid-growth startups hire software engineers, for example. It's also common among manufacturing, retail, nursing, construction, logistics, and, of course, call centers, among others.

Often, large batch hiring includes a comprehensive screening measure that doesn't require human time. An example is an online customer service assessment meant to screen out those who don't have the minimum requirements. For software engineering or data science, options exist to use online coding assessments or other technical knowledge tests (assuming a good test publisher) to narrow down your pool of applicants. However, if you're reading this book, you may not have the budget or the time to evaluate, select, and purchase a tool for screening. Or, as many of our software engineering managers and leaders have noticed in their experience, good engineers may do a better job evaluating candidates with a solid job profile and interviewing guidelines. As a result, you might be in a situation where you have to interview a large volume of candidates.

Our first recommendation is to leverage interviewers from around the organization. If your HR policy allows it, why not use high-performing incumbents to volunteer as interviewers? One of our clients worked with a team of directors and VPs to identify engineers who showed dedication to using processes and eradicating subjective decision-making and cognitive errors in the selection process. Many of our clients have successfully built programs that involve incumbents in the selection process.

Airbnb effectively integrated their Core Values into their standard interview process by:

- **Developing a set of core questions**
  They created behavior-based questions designed to assess key behaviors they wanted in all employees, regardless of role.

- **Building and training a global team**
  They assembled a team of interviewers from around the world, providing training to ensure consistency in how the interviews were conducted.

- **Using consistent standards**
  They implemented a structured process with standardized questions and scoring, ensuring the same level of rigor and quality across all interviews.

This approach not only elevated their interview process but also reinforced their culture and values through every candidate interaction.[2]

Here are the steps, in a nutshell, to build such a program:

1 **Gain buy-in** for an interviewing program from talent acquisition, HR, and the team's leadership

2 **Give your interviewer program a name.** While it might seem trivial, a well-named program can foster pride and a sense of honor among participants.

3 **Recruit volunteers** to conduct the interviews. If the interviews are technical or job-specific, the interviewers should be experts in that area. Send call-outs to managers to nominate folks to join the team, and offer incentives such as company swag, public recognition, or even notes on their annual performance reviews regarding corporate contribution.

4 **Design a training program** and identify individuals to lead the program (that person might be you). Such training can be about two hours online and delivered remotely. The content would include:

   a. overview of common interviewer cognitive errors

   b. the purpose of the interview

   c. overview of the questions

   d. how to score the responses

   e. where to score the response

   f. dos and don'ts

When building a training, ensure that you have some means of checking knowledge post-training, such as with a short quiz. In the past, we've created quizzes and stored the data using Google or Microsoft forms.

1 **Identify someone to manage the program logistics** if that cannot be done through your recruiting team. This includes scheduling interviews, matching interviewers with candidates, tracking the evaluation criteria across interviews, and keeping the information organized.

2 **Audit the results** of the interviews regularly, including reading through notes from the interview, to ensure that you see consistency and good processes. Share the results of the audit with your fellow interviewers. When our engineering interviewers found strange or faulty evaluation criteria in the applicant tracking system records, they quickly addressed the issue with the committee and provided training to fix the problem.

This will be a learning journey, so set the interviewing team up to expect feedback and continuous, collective improvement.

Since employees may come and go, ensure you can regularly add new interviews every half-year or so, depending on the volume of interviews in your team or organization.

There is always a way to create efficiency in your interview process, so there is no need to feel discouraged when you are overwhelmed with requisitions and candidates.

In Part 4, we outline tips and guidance in scoring interviews from multiple interviewers.

Part 3 Summary: Key learnings

Congratulations! You've gained a comprehensive understanding of designing and conducting structured interviews that provide an outstanding candidate experience while gathering complete, job-relevant data. Your candidates will leave feeling like their qualifications were thoroughly explored, and you'll have a clear sense of how they might perform in the role based on your 45-minute conversations.

Interview Questions

- **Types of questions:**
  - Behavioral, situational, and biographical questions were covered, each with its pros, cons, and considerations.
  - Behavioral questions help assess how candidates have handled specific challenges in the past, offering insights into how they might perform in similar scenarios.
  - Situational questions, role plays, and presentation assessments focus on how candidates would respond to hypothetical job-related situations.
  - Biographical questions allow candidates to share their career history and motivations, which can be useful depending on the role and seniority.

- **Creating effective questions:**
  - o You learned to craft questions by rewording key job behaviors into direct questions based on the role's critical skills.
  - o Creative approaches, like asking candidates to demonstrate skills through realistic scenarios, can provide deeper insights.
- **Probing and STAR framework:**
  - o Probing questions clarify and elicit specific details from candidates.
  - o The STAR framework (Situation, Task, Action, Result) helps candidates structure answers for more complete insights as well as help interviewers probe candidates to provide necessary detail about the situation, tasks, actions, and result.

Structured Interviews

- **Importance of structure:**
  - o Structured interviews with consistent questions and evaluation criteria lead to more fair and accurate assessments. Structure increases the reliability of interviews and their ability to predict job performance.
  - o In contrast, unstructured interviews can introduce flawed judgments, subjective decision-making, and inconsistency.
- **Efficiency and fairness:**
  - o Myths about structured interviews being robotic or time consuming were dispelled. They are efficient and effective for reducing cognitive errors and improving selection quality.

Measurement and Evaluation

- **Evaluation criteria:**
  - o Establishing clear criteria before interviews is crucial for objective assessment.
  - o Rating candidates immediately after the interview ensures accuracy and reduces the likelihood of cognitive errors.
- **Role of ratings:**
  - o Avoid rushing to judgment based solely on gut feelings. Comparing evidence against the job profile can transform how you view a candidate's suitability.

Screening and Candidate Experience

- **Screening interviews:**
    - o Screening interviews should also be structured, with time allocated for introductions, career history, interest in the role, and behavior-based questions.
- **Building trust:**
    - o Treat candidates like valued customers. Prepare them for the interview and provide transparency about the selection process to build trust.

By mastering these elements, you're equipped to create a structured, efficient, and fair interview process that identifies the best candidates while ensuring a positive experience for everyone involved.

Part 3 Key terms

Adverse impact: Adverse impact, also known as disparate impact, is an employment or hiring practice that, while seemingly neutral, disproportionately affects members of a protected group (e.g. based on race, gender, age, or disability) in a negative way. This impact often arises unintentionally when certain policies, tests, or selection criteria result in a lower selection rate for members of these groups, even though they may not explicitly discriminate.

Applicant tracking system (ATS): Software used to screen and manage job applications, often through predefined questions and criteria.

Behavioral interviews: Interview question methodology that asks a candidate to describe how they handled a situation in the past, which is strongly predictive of how they might handle that situation in the future.

Biographical interviews: Asking candidates to describe their work experience in order of events, versus in order of competencies.

Candidate trust: Candidate trust is the confidence candidates have in the fairness, transparency, and professionalism of the hiring process, fostered through clear communication, respect, and consistent treatment.

Measurement and evaluation criteria: Measurement and evaluation criteria are the predefined standards and benchmarks used to objectively assess candidates' responses and performance against the requirements of the role.

Probing questions: Follow-up questions in an interview to achieve more details on a scenario the candidate is describing.

Role plays: An interview where the candidate pretends to do something they would need to do on the job, like make a presentation or coach a direct report.

Screening interview: A short 30–45-minute interview designed to narrow down your pool of candidates before they come onsite and interview with hiring manager and subject matter experts.

Situational interviews: Interviews where candidates describe how they would handle a hypothetical situation.

STAR framework: A technique for answering behavioral interview questions by explaining the Situation, Task, Action, and Result.

Technical interview questions: Questions designed to explore someone's technical knowledge and skills on a job-related topic.

Notes

1 Lumet, Sidney, director, *12 Angry Men*, Orion-Nova Productions, 1957

2 Lattice Team (2017) How defining values and culture helped Airbnb achieve worldwide success, Lattice, https://lattice.com/articles/how-defining-values-and-culture-helped-airbnb-achie (archived at https://perma.cc/3RDW-UESP)

PART FOUR

WHO to Select

In this section, we'll discuss how to transform the outputs from your interview into a meaningful decision about your candidate(s). Before we get into this, however, let's talk about recording your interview data (meaning, taking notes).

19

Taking Outstanding Notes

Throughout your interview, ensure you collect great data (notes) on the candidate. Notes help you remember and objectively evaluate the candidate against the criteria. Let's pause on this topic, because many people end up taking terrible interview notes in spite of good intentions.

Each of us has our own unique style of note-taking, so all of these methods work well. It's important to have notes that conform to best practices. One of the most obvious ones is that they give you a really solid and accurate record of what the candidate actually said and did in a situation, if they were describing a past situation. In addition, you'll want to record any information about the candidate in a way that you'd be comfortable with the candidate actually reading it. Not just by avoiding judgmental language, but also in a way that could be easily traced back to what they actually said. Why is this important? Because in some countries and states, your candidates have the legal right to see your notes. It always comes as a surprise when we disclose this information during our training sessions, so we like to state it boldly and plainly. **Candidates have the right to request access to all the data you collected about them in the interview process, in countries or states where privacy laws dictate.** Privacy laws such as the California Consumer Privacy Act (CCPA)[1] or General Data Protection Regulation (GDPR)[2] describe a candidate's rights to see the information you gathered, which includes any assessment results, notes, or the contents of the applicant tracking system (ATS) that relate to them. Based on our experience, it's not common for candidates to go to the lengths required to make such a request, but our motto is to record any information about candidates with the thought that they may potentially read the information. Although we encourage you to read the legislation itself, the implications are not always clear, so we recommend a conversation with a local employment lawyer who understands privacy legislation, or speak with your in-house expert. We cover more about this in Part 5.

Verbatim or Transcript Notes

What kinds of notes are best? Should you record everything the candidate says, or summarize the information instead?

Both of us tend to write down everything the candidate says in a file separate from the ATS, and later go through and leverage the notes like a transcript for scoring the interview. We can do this because we type fast, and never conduct an interview without a laptop, even in person. Also, our handwriting is slow and not easily legible. When the interview is in person, we recommend pushing the screen down so that it's not blocking the candidate's view of us—as flat as possible. This does mean that we type without looking at our screens. Then, the interviewer can make eye contact with us while we are typing without the distraction of the screen. Although there may be typos in the interview notes, we carefully read through them after the interview to make sure they are legible. We and other transcribers believe that we can capture a most accurate account of the interview, but it's likely that we still inadvertently miss a few sentences or words, so we remain open to the fact that we're not always aware of what we're missing.

Summarized Notes

Other interviewers like to listen to the candidate first, before writing down the notes. Then, towards the end of the candidate's summary of a given topic, they write the main themes of what they heard, relating these back to the job profile in their notes. For example, if the candidate tells a story about a conflict with a coworker, the interviewer will make eye contact, nod, appear to be in a conversation with the candidate, and then make a few notes by hand or by computer as the candidate is wrapping up. The notes might say something like this, in the same familiar format as how we asked the probes:

> **Situation:** Jimmy had a conflict with a coworker about leveraging another team member for a project.
>
> **Action:** Jimmy set up a meeting with the coworker to discuss it, and pre-empted the meeting with a friendly email.

Result: Discussion went well, the team member was taken off the project, and they agreed on a different way to work on borrowing resources in the future.

Communication: Jimmy clearly outlined what he observed in the other coworker and directly asked for a correction to the situation. He came back to follow up three weeks later and ensure a resolution.

Collaboration: Asked the team member how they could help in future situations with shortage of staff.

Here's what we like about this approach. It can help an interviewer focus on really deeply listening, in the moment, rather than recording information diligently, especially if the interviewer finds it difficult to listen and write all at once (if you do, that doesn't mean you're not a good interviewer, it just takes practice). Also, this method gives you the summary right away. With a transcript, we're going to need to write up a summary from our notes later. This means we are taking an extra step.

Here's what we like less about this approach. It's easy to forget to notice or record information or pieces of the candidate's story, without ever realizing that you missed them. Our brains really like to streamline and sometimes literally hide information that doesn't fit into the pattern it wants to see. If you miss 10 percent of the information, and 2 percent of that missed information is important in evaluating the candidate, it could make the difference in how you see them in an entire area, such as collaboration. Our brains tend to do this even more when we're distracted by something about the candidate, such as thinking that they are a great communicator. If we subconsciously think that the candidate is a great communicator, then we could miss signals that suggest they are lacking in another area.[3]

What do we recommend? Ultimately, we recommend trying to get close to verbatim notes.

How About I Just Record the Interview?

What if you just use your smartphone to record a transcript of the interview, and then have an automatic transcript made through a web app? Wouldn't that save a lot of time and effort in taking notes? Plus, it would give you an exact record of what happened. Why are we waiting so long to talk about this?

We're not going to say you should never do it, but we personally don't record our interviews. If you are interested in recording your candidates, check the laws in the country and state that where will be doing this. We go by the assumption that any time you record another person, their documented consent is required.

First of all, it's awkward to ask candidates if they can be recorded. A statement such as the following may help, assuming this is legal in your state or country and you abide by the requirements outlined in any related country or state policy or regulations.

> "Before we get started, may I get your consent to record the interview? I record these so that I can better remember what we discussed."

Even if you pose your request in a clear and non-threatening way, a request to record can erode trust. Some people are easily triggered by any hint of surveillance, even if you give them a good reason for the recording. Furthermore, recording conversations is usually associated with legal events, insurance companies, and customer service calls. None of those should feel similar to a candidate interview.[4]

Disclaimer: Below are some of the primary considerations for recording audio from an interview as it relates to General Data Protection Regulation (GDPR) standards. We advise you to consult with your in-house expert or legal counsel before recording audio for any candidate interviews.

Recording audio from a candidate interview is permissible under GDPR standards, but it must comply with specific requirements to protect the candidate's personal data and ensure their rights. Here are the key considerations:

1 Obtain explicit consent

Inform the candidate that the interview will be recorded, explain the purpose of the recording, and obtain their explicit consent before recording. Consent must be freely given, specific, informed, and unambiguous.

2 Purpose limitation

Clearly define and communicate why the recording is necessary, such as for evaluation, training, or record-keeping purposes. The recording should only be used for the stated purposes.

3 Data minimization

Record only what is necessary. Avoid collecting excessive information unrelated to the interview's purpose.

4   **Secure storage**
    Store the recordings securely to protect them from unauthorized access, loss, or misuse. Implement encryption and access controls as needed.

5   **Retention period**
    Define a clear retention period for the recordings and delete them when they are no longer needed.

6   **Access rights**
    Inform candidates of their rights under GDPR, including the right to access, correct, or request deletion of their data, including the recording.

7   **Data protection policies**
    Ensure that your organization's data protection policies align with GDPR requirements and that staff handling the recordings are trained in compliance.

Failure to adhere to these principles can result in legal repercussions and damage to your employer brand. Always consult with a legal or compliance expert to ensure full adherence to GDPR and local regulations.

Writing Up Evidence

The minimally viable product in your notes includes a description of each of the scenarios the candidate described in terms of the *Situation*, *Action*, and *Result*, and a brief summary of their KSAs evidence, per the notes in the summary above. Based on this information, you have what you need to make a decision.

The documentation from an interview is actual admissible evidence in a courtroom in the United States. It's also subject to candidate review in Europe and in some states in the United States due to privacy laws, should the candidate go through a formal process to request access. We strongly recommend you write up your notes according to clear guidelines. All the evidence you keep should have the following properties in your write-up.[5]

Holistic

Document evidence for every KSA you are assessing to ensure a thorough and fair evaluation. Your goal is to gather as much relevant information as possible during the interview, so you can confidently demonstrate that you explored each KSA in depth.

KEY GUIDELINES

1 **Comprehensive coverage**

Ensure your notes address all the KSAs outlined in the interview plan. If a candidate provides relevant examples or behaviors, capture those details accurately to reflect their qualifications for each area.

2 **Active exploration**

Use probing and follow-up questions to uncover evidence for each KSA. If a candidate's initial response is unclear or incomplete, dig deeper to clarify and gather specific examples.

3 **Evidence-based notes**

Focus on concrete behaviors, examples, and statements that demonstrate the candidate's proficiency in the KSAs. Avoid vague or generalized comments that lack supporting evidence.

4 **Balanced assessment**

Record both strengths and gaps in each KSA to provide a complete picture of the candidate's capabilities. If evidence for a particular KSA is limited, note that as well—it's just as important to document areas where clarity was lacking.

5 **Consistency across candidates**

Apply the same level of rigor to all interviews, ensuring that each candidate has the opportunity to demonstrate their abilities in every KSA.

Complete

Your questions focus on each of the KSAs being assessed in your interview and your notes reflect this. Further, the evaluation criteria or scorecard also cover each of the KSAs being assessed.

Justified

When documenting interview notes, think like a scientist collecting and analyzing evidence. Your role is to observe and report facts that support your conclusions, just as a researcher would when investigating a hypothesis. Imagine trying to prove the existence of craters on the moon without traveling there. What would you rely on? Perhaps detailed photographs, soil samples from prior missions, or geological theories about the moon's formation. Similarly, in interviews, you gather evidence—specific examples from the candidate's responses, behaviors, or skills demonstrated during the discussion—that supports your assessment of their KSAs.

To ensure your notes are meaningful:

1 **Be specific and objective**
   Record what the candidate said or did, not just your interpretation or feelings about it. For example, instead of writing "seemed confident," note "spoke clearly and answered follow-up questions with detailed examples."

2 **Tie evidence to KSAs**
   Clearly connect the evidence you observed to the specific KSAs being assessed. If evaluating problem-solving skills, describe the candidate's approach to a scenario or task you discussed.

3 **Avoid assumptions**
   Stick to what you can observe or verify. Avoid making judgments based on tone, body language, or vague impressions unless directly tied to the KSAs being assessed.

4 **Be consistent**
   Use the same level of detail and rigor for all candidates to avoid cognitive errors and ensure a fair comparison.

5 **Clarify your reasoning**
   Explain why the evidence supports your assessment. For instance, if a candidate provided a specific example of leading a project, outline how their actions aligned with leadership skills outlined in your criteria.

By documenting your observations with this level of rigor, you ensure that your assessments are fair, transparent, and defensible. Your notes should provide a clear, evidence-based foundation for hiring decisions.

Clear

Ensure your interview notes are clear, concise, and focused on the relevant evidence tied to the KSAs being assessed. While a verbatim transcript of the interview may sometimes be requested or useful, it's often unnecessary and can include irrelevant details. Candidates may provide information that isn't pertinent to the role, so your job is to distill the conversation into a meaningful summary.

After the interview concludes and you have your close-to-verbatim notes:

1 **Summarize the key points**
   Focus on the candidate's responses that directly address the KSAs you're assessing. Highlight specific examples, actions, or statements that demonstrate their skills or qualifications.

2 **Organize notes by KSAs**

   Structure your summary around the KSAs to make it easy for others to follow. For each KSA, provide evidence from the interview that supports your assessment, such as direct quotes, actions, or behaviors observed.

3 **Exclude irrelevant information**

   Filter out any details that don't add value to the assessment. For instance, avoid including tangents or off-topic remarks unless they provide critical context.

4 **Provide context for ratings**

   Explain how the evidence supports your evaluation. If you rate a candidate highly on problem solving, include a summary of the scenario they described and how their approach aligned with the job requirements.

5 **Make it easy to review**

   Use a clean, organized format for your notes. This ensures hiring managers or other stakeholders can quickly understand the evidence and how it relates to the decision-making process.

By summarizing and organizing your notes effectively, you not only streamline the hiring process but also ensure transparency and fairness in how candidates are evaluated.

Focused

Focus your notes strictly on the KSAs you are assessing. Think of it like panning for gold—stick to what you're looking for and avoid distractions. If you're tasked with evaluating the moon's craters, don't start writing about Mars. Similarly, in an interview, you may come across evidence of skills outside the scope of the assessment or personal information unrelated to the job.

   Here are some key principles to guide your focus:

1 **Stick to the assessment goals**

   Keep your notes centered on the job-related KSAs outlined in the interview plan. Avoid veering into unrelated areas, even if they seem interesting or impressive.

2 **Avoid personal information**

   If a candidate shares personal details not relevant to the role, don't include these in your notes. Documenting non-work-related topics can introduce potential for subjective decision-making and cognitive errors or create privacy concerns.

3 Focus on evidence-based insights
Only document observations that directly support or challenge the criteria you're evaluating. For example, if you're assessing design skills, note specific examples of how the candidate demonstrated creativity, problem-solving, or technical proficiency during the interview.

4 Stay consistent
Ensure all candidates are evaluated against the same criteria. This helps maintain fairness and creates a clear basis for comparison.

By keeping your notes targeted and work-related, you ensure the interview process remains focused, professional, and aligned with the role's requirements.

Maintaining Records

Our clients often track evidence in their own notes, and then transfer them to an ATS, software that collects recruitment and hiring data. You can ask your HR representative or employment lawyer how to best store your notes and how long they should be stored. We have advised our clients that seven years is about the maximum for assessment data. We always recommend consulting with your legal teams to tailor data retention policies to your specific context and jurisdiction.

Notes

1 California Consumer Privacy Act (CCPA): California Consumer Privacy Act of 2018, Cal. Civ. Code 1798.100-1798.199 (2022), State of California—Department of Justice

2 General Data Protection Regulation (GDPR): Regulation (EU) 2016/679 of the European Parliament and of the Council of 27 April 2016 on the protection of natural persons with regard to the processing of personal data and on the free movement of such data, and repealing Directive 95/46/EC (General Data Protection Regulation), GDPR.eu

3 Lv, J., Sun, Z., Li, H., and Hou, Y. (2023) The role of negative perfectionism and the relationship between critical thinking and the halo effect: Insights from corporate managers in human resources, *Behavioural Science (Basel)*, June 26, 13(7), p. 533, doi : 10.3390/bs13070533, PMID: 37503980, PMCID: PMC10376162 (archived at https://perma.cc/L27Y-S7MW)

4 Jain, M (2025) Interview recording compliances – 6 things to consider, BarRaiser, www.barraiser.com /blogs/compliances-to-consider-while-recording-job-interviews#:~:text=Obtaining%20the%20consent%20of%20all,and%20self%2Dconsciousness%20in%20individuals (archived at https://perma.cc/P4AV-CDWE)

5 Butt, P. and Ritchie, J. (1978) Admissibility of Records of Interview, *Criminal Law Journal*, 2(3), pp. 136–57

20

It's All About Metrics

Let's break down the three key steps of our analysis process, which we consistently use to make data-driven decisions:

- **Step 1: Observe and record**

  Imagine you're in an interview, notebook or laptop in hand, listening closely to the candidate. Your job here is to act like a detective, gathering facts. Pay attention to what the candidate says, how they say it, and any examples they share to illustrate their skills. Take detailed notes, capturing as close to verbatim notes as you can.

- **Step 2: Analyze**

  Now that you've collected your raw data, it's time to make sense of it. Revisit your notes and ask yourself: How do the candidate's answers connect to the KSAs we're evaluating? Look for patterns and evidence—are there consistent examples that align with the job requirements? Pay attention to how the candidate's responses demonstrate their ability to succeed in the role based on the KSAs you are measuring. If their examples are vague or lack substance, that might signal a gap. This step is about making connections between the evidence collected and starting to form a holistic view of the candidate's qualifications.

- **Step 3: Decide**

  Finally, the moment of truth: Deciding whether the candidate meets the mark. Using the evaluation criteria established before the interview, compare the evidence you've gathered against that criteria and see how the candidate's performance on each KSA compares to the standards outlined on the rating scale. Based on the evidence gathered, assign a numerical rating to each KSA, and be sure to provide a specific rationale for each score. For example, if the candidate excelled in teamwork but struggled with strategic thinking, make this clear in your evaluation. This step demands objectivity—rely on the data and avoid letting gut feelings influence your conclusion. The goal is a fair, evidence-based decision that aligns with the role's needs.

FIGURE 20.1 Three Key Steps to Make Data-Driven Decisions

OBSERVE AND RECORD

- During the interview, document the candidate's responses, behaviors, and examples.
- Focus your notes on how these reflect the key skills and attributes (KSAs) being assessed.
- Take detailed, clear notes to ensure an accurate analysis later.

ANALYZE

- Review your notes and link the candidate's responses to the specific KSAs.
- Look for patterns, consistency, and specific examples that align with the evaluation criteria.
- Assess whether the candidate has demonstrated the qualifications needed for success in the role.

DECIDE

- Compare the evidence gathered against the predetermined evaluation criteria.
- Assign a numerical rating for each KSA based on the evidence and provide rationale to support each rating.
- Base your conclusions on objective data, avoiding gut feelings or bias in your decision-making.

By following these steps consistently, you ensure that your hiring decisions are thoughtful and informed by concrete evidence.

This methodology is what we call the "minimally viable product" for evaluating candidates, and it's something we've implemented across diverse organizations—from big tech companies and Fortune 500s to small teams hiring fewer than 10 people and founder-led small companies with less than 20 employees.

In Part 3, we discussed how to screen candidates before moving them through the full interview process. During the screening phase, in addition to rating the KSAs included, you'll also want to assign a binary score: Either "continue" or "stop." For the full interview process, after the screening, it's essential to evaluate how each candidate performed on all of the KSAs you're assessing across **each** interview before making a final hire/no-hire decision. This means that once candidates "pass" the screen, they should go through **all remaining interviews** in the hiring process **before** a hiring decision is made.

As we learned in Part 3, having good questions is just one piece of your interview success; the real game-changer is having outstanding evaluation criteria. Even if we are forced to ask less-than-ideal interview questions, we are confident that we can craft solid measurement criteria based on a thorough job analysis. Let's be clear, we're not advocating for odd questions that ask candidates to compare Starbucks to Dunkin' Donuts coffee and then present on which is best. However, if that were the case, with good probing, we could still likely glean insights into strategic thinking, attention to detail, and market knowledge. Our point? Perfect questions are nice, but they aren't the be-all-end-all; the key is robust evaluation guidelines. Think of having good questions as laying the groundwork for your interview, much like having a solid foundation for a building. But just as a building's strength comes from its design and architecture, it's like having the blueprint that guides every decision, ensuring that you not only ask the right questions but also know exactly what to look for in deciding how they performed.

The Scale

Scales are all over the place. Considering which restaurant, hotel, or short-term rental to book? Which item to purchase on Amazon? You'll likely be looking at a five-star rating to make your decision. The "scale" is the five stars. When you give the rating on a single item or experience, you're submitting a rating on a scale.

The scales for Amazon, TripAdvisor, and other sites were developed using marketing research.[1] As part of their development, the researchers assigned an associated value with each scale point. For example, on Yelp.com, the scales are "Not Good," "Could Have Been Better," "OK," "Good," and "Great." These words defining each scale point are generally representative of consumer scales. They are easy and simple to understand, to the point that Amazon doesn't even provide words to define each scale point. We all know that a rating lower than 4 indicates an issue. A rating of 1 or 2 could mean that the business committed a serious infringement on a consumer in some way.

The ubiquitous nature of these consumer scales causes problems when we evaluate candidates for a job. At one company, a manager explained how they evaluate a candidate to be aligned to their own company's 3-point consumer scale. The manager felt good about their consistency of process and adherence to existing research on the consumer scale. However, we also happened to know that this particular company's scale had been developed by an engineer who felt frustrated by a perceived lack of democracy in the customer/business relationship. From our experience working with a variety of tech companies, we were told that the scale was created by someone who was not at all an expert in evaluating or rating people or rating things. The founder of that particular company wanted to provide a 5-point rating system, but we really ended up with a 2-point rating system. The ratings are separated by two points: 4 and above, or 3 or lower. If the rating was lower than a 4, nobody wants to eat at that restaurant. If the ratings are higher than a 4, people are happy to eat there.

Here are some good facts to keep in mind about a rating scale and its components.

Each level proceeds along an axis of difficulty, proficiency, or sophistication, where level 1 would be a very basic capability, and level 5 would be highly advanced (or if you prefer colors, you could say red is very basic and green is highly advanced, with shades in between). Based on how we train our clients, and unlike a consumer scale, a score of 3 is really good! That means that they did what they needed to do in order to show proficiency. A rating above 3 means that they met the proficiency expectations, and a rating of 2 means that they had some of the proficiency, but not all.

This is very unlike a rating of 2 for a restaurant, which could mean they gave you food poisoning or flat-out refused to serve you. If we used the proper rating scale for a restaurant, just as a fun example, a 3 might indicate that you thought the food was good, and the service was prompt and adequate. You didn't have to wait longer than you felt was reasonable, and you got what you expected. A rating of 4 would mean that the food was somewhat better than other restaurants, the server was more intuitive or attentive than usual, or that you felt the price was particularly low for the quality. If you rated the restaurant a 2, that would mean that the food was sub-par, or the service was slow (or rude), or that the price was too high for the quality or quantity. If all of those were true, maybe then you would rate it a 1. Or the rating of 1 could mean that one terrible thing happened, like food poisoning or completely neglectful service. Conversely, a 5 would mean that you could not think of more than one smallish thing to slightly improve the experience.

That brings us to another point. When someone quickly fills out a restaurant rating that wasn't at least 4 stars, we have no idea what specific thing was wrong with the restaurant unless they tell us. Yelp provides additional checkboxes, but many diners don't bother to complete them. It's like interviewing a candidate and giving them a 2, but not explaining what the issue was. It could have been poor communication, lack of knowledge, lack of experience, or something completely different. We strive to be much more precise when we give ratings for job candidates, and that includes using the whole 5-point scale as well as providing detailed, evidence-based data to support and justify the ratings made.

How Many Points Do You Want on Your Scale?

As a side note, an I-O psychologist at a large retail company once told us that his company trialed a performance management scale with 100 points. The HR team struggled with all the "in-betweens" on performance, so to be as detailed in differentiating employees as they could, they expanded their 5-point scale to 100. Holy moly.

Obviously, while we are all in favor of scales, 100 points is *way too many points* to measure someone's performance. Managers ended up bucketing ratings into 10-point ranges. The client abandoned the program within the first quarter because it was too complicated.

We felt this was certainly extreme, but you may actually have empathy for them when you rate your candidates. Sometimes there are not enough points on a scale to capture nuances, and we have to just pick a score anyhow without inventing half scores.

If you and/or your interviewing team are finding the 5-point rating scale system distracting and too similar to the restaurant reviews, you can use a 4-point or a 3-point scale instead.

When you use a 3-point scale, the middle point (a 2) is still solid or "passing," but not perfection. A 3 does "better than expectations," and a 1 does "worse than expectations." In other words, a 1 is a "fail" and 2 is a "pass."

With a 4-point scale, someone has two ways of being recommended as a "hire" or "no hire" decision. If someone scores a 2, the candidate missed things that were important for the job. A rating of 1 means they missed **most** things important to the job. With a 3, they did well. With a 4, they did **everything** that the KSAs required.

Table 20.1 shows an overview of scales with some primary considerations.

TABLE 20.1 How Many Points Do You Really Need? A Practical Guide to Rating Scales

Type of scale	Pro	Con
Even number of points, e.g. (1) Does not meet expectations (2) Meets some expectations (3) Meets expectations (4) Meets all expectations	You'll have a clear sense of candidate strength with no middle point	Raters feel uncomfortable rating on just one side or the other when the candidate "meets expectations" but does not exceed them

(continued)

TABLE 20.1 (Continued)

Type of scale	Pro	Con
Odd number of scale points, e.g. 1. Does not meet expectations 2. Meets expectations 3. Exceeds expectations Or 1. Poor 2. Moderate 3. Solid 4. Strong 5. Exceptional	It feels more natural to rate people on odd-numbered scales	Too many candidates will have "middle" scores (i.e. 3 out of 5), which makes differentiating performance and decision-making more difficult if sufficient evidence-based supporting data is lacking
Short, 3-point rating scale, e.g. 1. Does not meet expectations 2. Meets expectations 3. Exceeds expectations	It forces a clear decision and can be faster to create a rating The top score gets used more frequently than when there are more scale points	Central tendency error, i.e. interviewers will rate more frequently in the middle of the scale, "meets expectations" Raters often start using decimals, expanding the score range
5 points (preferred) 1. Poor 2. Moderate 3. Solid 4. Strong 5. Exceptional	Most available ranges of performance exist in 5 points, with less complexity	Central tendency error. Often, the rating of 3 is used more than it is warranted to avoid committing on either side of the scale.
7 points	For complex assessments with a wider range of performance, this can more accurately differentiate	Raters tend to avoid using the top score, truncating the scale There may not be meaningful differences between scale points

Using the Data

To evaluate candidates effectively, each KSA from your job profile must be assessed using a consistent rating scale. In Chapter 7, we covered how to create evaluation criteria and suggested involving SMEs (subject matter experts) for detailed input when needed. Here, we'll dive deeper into considerations for designing rating scales.

A single, well-crafted rating scale can work across all KSAs if it uses the right wording—like the "light and generic" option from Chapter 7. Whether you build your scale from scratch or use GenAI to help refine it, the goal is the same: A scale that fits your KSAs and ensures clarity and consistency.

If you're using generative AI, be clear in your prompts. For example: "Write a single rating scale with three levels of proficiency for <insert specific KSAs>." This ensures the AI creates a scale that makes sense for your criteria. Always review and tailor the output to align with your specific needs—AI is a tool, but final responsibility rests with you.

For the financial analyst job, here is what we came up with when building the light and generic version of evaluation criteria.

3-Point Rating Scale

- **Basic proficiency (1):** Demonstrates basic understanding and ability in the specified area but requires significant guidance and supervision to perform tasks effectively. May struggle with complex tasks or situations. Evidence may be lacking for this specified area.

- **Competent proficiency (2):** Displays solid proficiency in the specified area, capable of performing tasks independently with minimal guidance. Meets expectations and can handle most routine tasks effectively.

- **Advanced proficiency (3):** Exhibits advanced proficiency in the specified area, capable of handling complex tasks and challenges with ease. Consistently exceeds expectations and demonstrates a high level of expertise and competency.

5-Point Rating Scale

- **Novice proficiency (1):** Demonstrates a basic understanding of the key concepts but struggles with most tasks. Requires constant supervision and guidance to perform work and is still learning this specified area. Or there is a lack of behavior or knowledge required for this specified area.

- **Basic proficiency (2):** Displays a basic understanding and ability in the specified area but requires regular guidance to complete tasks effectively.

May handle some routine tasks independently but overall struggles with this specified area and does not meet expectations.

- **Competent proficiency (3):** Displays solid proficiency, capable of performing most tasks independently and consistently meeting expectations. Demonstrates the ability to handle routine and moderately complex tasks related to this specified area with minimal guidance.

- **Advanced proficiency (4):** Exhibits strong proficiency and the ability to handle complex tasks related to this specified area with ease. Can perform high-level behaviors associated with this specified area with little to no supervision. Recognized as a subject matter expert within the team, consistently exceeding expectations, and contributing valuable insights and recommendations.

- **Expert proficiency (5):** Demonstrates exceptional proficiency and a deep understanding of this specified area. Capable of leading complex initiatives and solving the most challenging problems independently. Sets industry standards, mentors others, and continuously innovates. Recognized for consistently exceeding expectations and driving strategic decisions that impact the business at a high level.

Note: The rating labels used in the above examples are simply examples. You can use whatever labels resonate for you. Here are a few examples of rating labels for 3- and 5-point scales:

FIGURE 20.2 Rating Label Examples for 3- and 5-Point Scales

	3-POINT RATING SCALE	5-POINT RATING SCALE
OPTION 1	(1) Does not meet expectations (2) Meets expectations (3) Exceeds expectations	(1) Does not meet expectations (2) Meets some expectations (3) Meets expectations (4) Exceeds expectations (5) Far exceeds expectations
OPTION 2	(1) Poor (2) Moderate (3) Strong	(1) Poor (2) Moderate (3) Solid (4) Strong (5) Exceptional

TABLE 20.2 What a Well-Designed Rating Scale Looks Like: A Normal Distribution Example

(1)	(2)	(3)	(4)	(5)
10 people	20 people	40 people	20 people	10 people

TABLE 20.3 What a Well-Designed Rating Scale Looks Like: A Normal Distribution Example Following Candidate Screening

(1)	(2)	(3)	(4)	(5)
<5 people	10 people	40 people	30 people	15 people

Whatever scale you use, make sure you and your interviewers learn to use the full range of the scope points (i.e. not avoiding 1, 2, 4, or 5). Align upfront with your interviewers on what a 1, 2, 4, or 5 rating might look like for each KSA that will need to be rated so interviewers are prepared to use the full range of the rating scale. If you notice that interviewers are not rating candidates a 5 on anything, for instance, that may be a sign that your scale and the criteria associated with each rating may be designed poorly or that interviewers are not using the scale properly. There should be reasonable criteria associated with the top score. As an example of a good distribution, let's say you assess 100 candidates on a 5-point scale. Table 20.2 shows how we might expect the scores to be distributed in a "normal" population.[2,3]

Your population is not really "normal," though, because you screened candidates before they came to your onsite interview and therefore they are likely stronger than the typical candidate. Therefore, realistically, you might see something more like Table 20.3.

This distribution is helpful to keep in mind when you feel like you want to give everyone a 3 to avoid high or low scores.

Notes

1   Rita, P., Ramos, R., Borges-Tiago, M. T., and Rodrigues, D. (2022) Impact of the rating system on sentiment and tone of voice: A Booking.com and TripAdvisor comparison study, *International Journal of Hospitality Management*, 104, pp. 103245

2 Kell, H. J et al (2017) Exploring methods for developing behaviorally anchored rating scales for evaluating structured interview performance, *ETS Research Report Series*, (1), pp. 1–18, https://files.eric.ed.gov/fulltext/EJ1168380.pdf (archived at https://perma.cc/48DJ-37JL)

3 Adams, J. K. (1955) Normal distributions. In J. K. Adams (1955) *Basic Statistical Concepts* (pp. 96–122). McGraw-Hill Book Company, https://doi.org/10.1037/11777-009 (archived at https://perma.cc/899Q-RXK4)

21

Using Evidence to Make Ratings

When rating a candidate on "results drive" for instance, consider all relevant examples of their skills collected throughout the interview process. For example, you might have gathered insights into their presentation skills not just from direct questions about presenting, but also while they responded to other prompts, such as solving a tough problem. Similarly, a question about preparing a big presentation might also reveal how they solve problems or navigate challenging interpersonal dynamics. All of this data is valid and should be included in your evaluation, assuming the data collected is relevant for the other KSAs being assessed.

After completing the interview, follow these steps to evaluate the candidate effectively:

- **Review and organize your notes:** Clean up and summarize your interview notes to ensure they are clear and comprehensive.

- **Compare against evaluation criteria:** Assess the candidate's responses for each KSA by comparing your notes against the predefined evaluation criteria.

- **Provide ratings and evidence:** Assign a rating for each KSA you assessed, supported by specific examples or evidence gathered during the interview.[1]

For **screening interviews**, take an additional step:

- Along with evaluating the KSAs included in the screening process, the interviewer should also decide whether the candidate should move forward to the full interview process.

This ensures that your decisions are both well documented and aligned with the role's requirements.

To rate any skill effectively, review your interview notes thoroughly. Look for examples that demonstrate the candidate's strengths and areas for development in the KSAs you're assessing. We suggest organizing notes under each KSA being measured in your interview and include any relevant data points from the interview that help understand the candidate's proficiency in a given area. Here's an example of mock interview data organized into "positive examples" and "constructive examples" for the skill *Collaboration*. We have also included the evaluation criteria to rate the evidence against.

INTERVIEW EVIDENCE FOR "COLLABORATION"

Collaboration: Works effectively with others to achieve shared goals, demonstrating active listening, adaptability, and a commitment to team success.

Positive Examples

- **Facilitating team dynamics**
  Candidate described leading a team during a high-pressure product launch, where they noticed communication silos between engineering and marketing. They proposed and implemented a shared project tracker, which improved transparency and accountability.
  - **Evidence:** "I noticed that deadlines were being missed because each team didn't understand the other's priorities. I created a shared tracker, held a kickoff to align roles, and made sure everyone felt comfortable raising blockers early."

- **Building trust across teams**
  Candidate shared an example of mediating a conflict between two senior team members with differing viewpoints on a strategic direction. They facilitated a constructive discussion, ensuring both voices were heard, and helped the group arrive at a consensus.
  - **Evidence:** "I invited both to a private conversation to understand their perspectives, then organized a team meeting where we focused on aligning our decisions with company goals."

- **Adaptability in collaboration**
  Candidate highlighted adjusting their approach to collaboration when working with an international team in a different time zone. They accommodated time differences and cultural expectations by shifting meeting times and emphasizing asynchronous communication.
  - **Evidence**: "I realized that expecting immediate feedback wasn't practical, so I set clear deadlines and detailed written updates to keep everyone on track without constant meetings."

Constructive Examples

- **Over-dependence on familiar teams**
  Candidate admitted preferring to collaborate with their usual close-knit team rather than exploring partnerships with other departments. While this resulted in efficient work within their group, they acknowledged missed opportunities for cross-departmental collaboration.

  o **Evidence**: "I realized I was leaning too much on my team instead of looping in operations, which might have given us a broader perspective earlier on."

- **Missed opportunities for broader input**
  Candidate recounted an instance where they could have sought input from a wider range of stakeholders on a project. They acknowledged that this omission resulted in rework when overlooked requirements emerged late.

  o **Evidence:** "If I'd included finance earlier, we wouldn't have missed budget constraints that came up last minute. I'm more proactive about stakeholder mapping now."

Evaluation Criteria

Following the methodology outlined in Part 2 and outlining "what good looks like," i.e. a 3 rating on a 5-point scale, compare the evidence above against the criteria below:

- **Active listening and contribution:** Engages respectfully in team discussions, actively listens to others' perspectives, and provides thoughtful input. Occasionally requires prompting to seek input from quieter team members or to fully synthesize diverse viewpoints.

- **Adapts to team needs:** Demonstrates flexibility when team priorities shift or challenges arise. Generally adjusts their approach to align with team goals but may occasionally struggle to adapt in highly dynamic or ambiguous situations.

- **Commitment to shared goals:** Maintains focus on team objectives, putting collective success ahead of individual preferences. May sometimes need reminders to balance their contributions with those of others to ensure equitable collaboration.

Rating and Rationale

RATING FOR COLLABORATION: 3 (SOLID)

The candidate demonstrates solid collaboration skills, with evidence of effective teamwork, active listening, and adaptability. However, there are notable opportunities to expand their collaboration practices, particularly in engaging broader stakeholders and cross-departmental teams. While their examples show they meet expectations, they fall short of the proactive and consistently strong behaviors required for a higher rating.

RATIONALE

- **Strengths:**

  o Facilitating team dynamics: The candidate effectively addressed communication silos between engineering and marketing by implementing a shared tracker and fostering transparency. This reflects a solid ability to promote teamwork and solve immediate collaboration challenges.

  o Building trust across teams: Mediating a conflict between senior team members demonstrates their ability to manage interpersonal dynamics and align decisions with company goals. This is a good example of meeting expectations in team collaboration.

  o Adaptability in collaboration: Adjusting to international time zones and cultural norms shows they can adapt their approach when required, contributing to functional team success.

- **Areas for improvement:**

  o Over-dependence on familiar teams: The candidate tends to rely on their close-knit team, which limits opportunities for cross-departmental collaboration. This indicates a need for broader engagement practices to build diverse partnerships.

  o Missed broader input: Failing to involve key stakeholders early led to rework, highlighting an area where they could improve their proactive collaboration and stakeholder management skills.

  o While their examples illustrate competency in collaboration, the candidate's approach lacks the consistent breadth, proactivity, and strategic foresight needed for a higher rating. They demonstrate "good" performance, but there is clear room to grow.

Optional: This is going to sound tedious, but you might consider counting the frequency of behaviors or examples across the entire interview which relate to your KSAs: This would include organizing all positive examples as well as instances that suggest the candidate might be less proficient or sophisticated in the area. Think of each skill as a "bucket" you're filling with evidence. A bucket brimming with positive examples likely indicates a higher rating for that skill, while a less-full bucket or a bucket filled with more examples suggesting room for improvement or development may suggest a lower score is appropriate. This shouldn't be done in a vacuum, of course; you would still compare the evidence organized in your "buckets" against the predetermined evaluation criteria. However, it can be a helpful step to do before evaluating and rating each KSA. It's important to note that the absence of constructive data for a given KSA does not necessarily mean the candidate is highly proficient in a given area. That is why you must always compare the evidence you've gathered against the predetermined evaluation criteria. That is your guidepost! As you build skill in evaluating interview data against your evaluation criteria, your interviewing skills will actually improve—you'll realize where you need to probe further to be able to evaluate certain behaviors or constructs in greater detail. For newer interviewers, this method of categorizing evidence from your interview notes into strengths and developmental data can simplify the process and improve consistency in scoring. It encourages a structured approach to coding and assessing interview evidence, helping ensure fair and accurate ratings. This is a nice way to start building skill in evaluating KSAs against specific evaluation criteria.

What if you organize the interview notes and find that you're lacking in negative or constructive examples for a given KSA?

Let's look at this example for the skill, "collaboration":

Strengths

- Led a cross-functional team of five to implement a new project management tool, ensuring all team members had input on the rollout plan.
- Highlighted their approach to building alignment by hosting weekly check-ins to proactively address any team concerns.
- Gave an example of resolving a disagreement between marketing and product teams by mediating the discussion and finding a mutually beneficial solution.

Development Areas

- No direct examples of challenges related to collaboration were provided.

Analysis of the Absence of Development Data

Potential reasons for missing data:

1 **Candidate framing:** The candidate may have chosen to focus on their successes rather than discussing struggles or conflicts.

2 **Lack of self-awareness:** The candidate may not realize or acknowledge areas where collaboration didn't go smoothly.

3 **Discomfort with conflict:** The candidate might view conflict as a weakness or failure rather than a normal part of collaboration.

4 **Limited probing:** The interviewer may not have asked follow-up questions about challenges or disagreements in collaboration.

Identifying Room for Growth

Despite the absence of constructive examples, the candidate might still have areas to develop:

- **Handling difficult team dynamics:** The candidate did not describe how they manage situations where collaboration breaks down, leaving uncertainty about their ability to handle challenging interpersonal dynamics.

- **Receiving constructive feedback:** There were no examples of the candidate navigating situations where their ideas were not adopted or they had to adapt based on team input.

- **Cross-cultural or diverse team collaboration:** While examples were strong, they were all related to co-located teams, leaving a gap in understanding how they collaborate across remote or global teams.

These areas could be probed further in future interviews or addressed as opportunities for growth in a development plan.

Follow-up solution: To uncover missing constructive data, ask probing questions like:

- "Can you share a time when collaboration didn't go as planned? How did you handle it?"

- "What feedback have you received about your collaborative style? How did you respond to it?"

> • "Have you ever had to collaborate with someone whose working style was very different from yours? What was that experience like?"
>
> As you or your interviewers begin building more skill in interviewing and evaluating KSAs against predetermined criteria, you will be able to recognize in the moment during interviews when you are not gathering the data you need to sufficiently evaluate a given KSA. Then, you'll know how to adjust, what probing questions to ask, or how to best redirect the candidate.

You may consider using your job analysis spreadsheet or other document that we discussed building in Part 2. Use that document consistently for each candidate, adding inputs for each of the KSAs based on how they performed.

That's a lot of work, people often tell us. Why do we have to do all that? Can't I just give them a pass-fail on the whole interview after we're done? I mean, right after the interview, isn't it all pretty fresh in your mind?

Thinking of the dog walker example, you could easily end up conflating the data you collected if you don't stop and analyze and score the data. That's how bad hiring decisions get made. This slightly tedious but worthwhile process is precisely how we stop our brain from making those automatic assessments that could be faulty, by systematically going back to the detailed evidence and comparing it against the predetermined evaluation criteria. And by following this process *every single time*, you've made major leaps in mitigating your tendency toward cognitive errors.[2,3]

Evaluating the Screen

For your screening interview with the financial analyst, the following areas were assessed in the screen.

> • **Interest in the role:** Understands the scope of the role and shows interest in the role as it's presented.
> • **Financial acumen:** Understanding of financial principles, accounting standards, and financial modeling techniques to analyze data and trends
> • **Financial modeling:** Proficiency in building and using financial models to analyze and interpret data.

- **Data analysis:** Strong analytical skills to interpret financial data, identify trends, and draw meaningful insights.
- **Collaboration:** Ability to work collaboratively with other departments to align financial goals with overall organizational objectives.

Imagine you got the following responses to a few of the interview questions for the areas being assessed during the screen.

Document: Interview notes

Interview: Screen for financial analyst

Interest in the Role

Interviewer: I got a copy of your resume here, and I'd appreciate learning more about the role you're in now, and what brought you there.

Candidate: Thank you for taking the time to review my resume. Currently, I am working as a financial analyst at XYZ Corporation. My journey to this role has been shaped by a combination of education, experience, and a genuine passion for financial acumen. During my undergraduate studies in Finance, I developed a strong foundation in financial modeling, data analysis, and risk assessment. I also interned at ABC Investments, where I gained practical exposure to portfolio management and equity research. These experiences ignited my interest in the intricate world of financial markets and analysis. Upon graduation, I joined DEF Financial Services as an entry-level analyst. In this role, I honed my skills in financial statement analysis, budgeting, and forecasting. I collaborated closely with cross-functional teams, providing insights that informed strategic decisions. My ability to dissect complex financial data and communicate actionable recommendations led to my promotion to a senior analyst position.

Interviewer: Can you give me a couple of specific reasons that you find this role interesting?

Candidate: What truly excites me about financial acumen is the opportunity to unravel the story behind the numbers. Whether it's identifying cost-saving opportunities, evaluating investment proposals, or assessing risk exposure, I thrive on analytical challenges. Additionally, I'm particularly drawn to the prospect of working for your company because of [specific industry focus]. I've been following [specific company initiative or recent success], and I see this role as an opportunity to contribute to your continued growth. I'm especially impressed by [a unique aspect of the company, such as its emphasis on innovation or its data-driven approach to decision-making].

Knowledge: Financial Acumen

Interviewer: Tell me about a time when you had to analyze complex financial data to make a critical business decision. What was the situation, and how did you approach it?

Candidate: In my previous role, we were evaluating a potential merger with a healthcare tech competitor. The analysis was intricate due to the need to integrate data from both companies, including revenue streams, cost structures, and market overlap. I started by consolidating historical financial data and identifying key drivers of profitability. Then, I built a scenario analysis model to evaluate potential synergies and risks. For example, I quantified the potential cost savings from operational efficiencies and factored in the impact of regulatory changes on revenue streams. I also collaborated with the legal and strategy teams to understand the broader implications. Ultimately, the analysis provided a comprehensive view of the merger's financial impact, and we recommended proceeding. Post-merger, the combined portfolio generated a 15 percent increase in EBITDA within the first year, validating our projections.

Skill: Financial Modeling

Interviewer: Can you describe your experience with financial modeling and give an example of a model you've built?

Candidate: At DEF Financial Services, I built various models, such as DCF (Discounted Cash Flow) and sensitivity analysis models, to support investment decisions. For instance, I created a DCF model to assess the valuation of a potential acquisition target. I incorporated projections for cash flows over a five-year period and adjusted for potential risks like fluctuating interest rates. However, I recognize that there's room for improvement. While my models are effective for routine analyses, I'm eager to enhance my skills with advanced techniques, such as Monte Carlo simulations, and tools like Python for more complex predictive modeling.

Skill: Data Analysis

Interviewer: What's an example of how you've used data analysis to uncover insights and drive business decisions?

Candidate: In my current role, I analyzed sales and expense data to identify patterns impacting profitability. One insight revealed that certain regions were consistently underperforming due to higher logistics costs. Using this data, I developed a recommendation to streamline distribution channels and renegotiate supplier contracts. As a result, we reduced logistics costs by 12 percent, directly improving the bottom line. While my analysis skills are strong, I'm continuously working on enhancing my ability to integrate external market data to add even more context to my findings.

Collaboration

Interviewer: Describe a situation where you had to collaborate with cross-functional teams (e.g. accounting, sales, or operations) to achieve a financial goal. How did you navigate any challenges, and what was the outcome?

Candidate: At DEF, I led a project to streamline our budgeting process, which required collaboration with accounting, sales, and operations teams. One challenge was aligning different priorities—sales wanted more aggressive growth assumptions, while operations were cautious due to supply chain constraints. To address this, I scheduled regular cross-functional meetings to ensure all voices were heard and facilitated discussions to resolve conflicts. By encouraging open communication and transparency, we developed a unified budget model that improved accuracy and alignment. The final product was adopted company-wide and significantly reduced budgeting cycle time. While I'm confident in my ability to collaborate effectively, I realize that I can further improve by proactively seeking feedback and ensuring all stakeholders feel equally engaged throughout a project.

Let's evaluate the candidate on each KSA using the 5-point rating scale outlined below. This scale is the "light" and universal option, not specifically tailored to individual KSAs, making it applicable across different skills (aligned with Option 1 from Chapter 7). Below, we present the evaluation criteria along with our specific ratings for each KSA assessed during the screen.

Document: Evaluation guidelines

Interview: Screen for financial analyst

Instructions: Rate the candidate on the 5-point scale for each of the areas measured. Then, provide a recommendation for whether or not the candidate should move to the onsite process and go through the full interviewing process.

Evaluation Criteria

- **1 – Poor**
  - Displays minimal knowledge or experience with relevant principles, skills, or industry-specific standards and requirements.
  - Struggles to apply basic concepts effectively and lacks familiarity with foundational expectations.

- **2 – Needs improvement**
  - Displays limited knowledge or experience with relevant principles, skills, or industry-specific standards and requirements.
  - Can apply some basic concepts but requires significant guidance to meet expectations.

- **3 – Solid**
  - Demonstrates sufficient knowledge and experience with relevant principles, skills, and industry-specific standards and requirements.
  - Meets expectations consistently and can apply key concepts with moderate guidance.

- **4 – Strong**
  - Demonstrates strong understanding and extensive experience with relevant principles, skills, and industry-specific standards and requirements.
  - Consistently exceeds expectations, applying advanced concepts independently.

- **5 – Exceptional**
  - Demonstrates comprehensive mastery and significant experience with relevant principles, skills, and industry-specific standards and requirements.
  - Proactively innovates, advises others, and applies concepts at an expert level without supervision.

Interviewer's Ratings and Evidence for the Screen

- **Interest in the role (4):**
  - Candidate expressed clear enthusiasm for the role and demonstrated an understanding of its scope.
  - They provided specific reasons tied to their personal interests and the company's goals but lacked detailed questions or unique insights that would elevate the rating to a 5.

- **Financial acumen (5):**
  - The candidate provided a detailed, well-rounded example of a complex analysis project.
  - Their example highlighted technical expertise, business impact, and collaboration, leaving little room for improvement.

- **Financial modeling (3):**
  - The candidate demonstrated foundational modeling skills but admitted to limitations in advanced techniques.
  - Their willingness to improve is promising, but current proficiency aligns with a 3.

- **Data analysis (4):**
  - They provided a strong example with quantifiable results and showed a solid ability to interpret data.
  - Slight room for growth in integrating broader market data keeps this at a 4.

- **Collaboration (3):**
  - The candidate effectively worked with cross-functional teams to resolve conflicts and achieve outcomes.
  - However, they did not provide evidence of fostering deeper partnerships or preemptively addressing collaboration challenges.

Recommendation: Move the candidate forward from screen to full onsite interview.

As you can see from the interview notes above, we've clearly assigned a numerical rating for each KSA being measured, along with supporting evidence from the interview for each rating. Further, since this was a screen interview, we provided a recommendation on whether or not the candidate should proceed to the full interviewing process.

FIGURE 21.1 KSAs for the Financial Analyst Role

KNOWLEDGE (K)	SKILLS (S)	ABILITIES (A)
Financial Acumen	Communication	Analytical Reasoning
Investment Acumen	Collaboration	Numerical Reasoning
Risk Assessment	Financial Modeling	
	Data Analysis	
	Decision-Making	
	Budgeting and Forecasting	

If you complete this evaluation immediately after the interview, the process will be speedier and more efficient. Waiting a few hours or longer will slow things down significantly. When we delay our ratings, it often takes twice as long, as we need to re-read the notes and recall specific details from the interview.

Figure 21.1 shows our job profile for the financial analyst. Note how we organized the KSAs so that they naturally flow from the key activities on the job. We will simplify these to a list of core areas to rate.

Evaluating a Full Onsite Interview

Now that this candidate has moved past the screen, let's work through an example for the first onsite interview. Review the interview notes below and evaluate each KSA using the same 5-point scale we used in the screening interview. Then compare your ratings and rationale to ours.

Interview: Investment and financial planning interview

KSAs assessed: Investment acumen, budgeting and forecasting, decision-making

Document: Interview Notes

KSA: Investment acumen

Interviewer: "Describe a time when you evaluated an investment opportunity. What was your process, and what recommendations did you make?"

Candidate: "In my current role, I assessed a proposal to invest in a healthcare startup. I conducted an industry analysis, built sensitivity models, and made a recommendation to invest at a lower valuation."

Interviewer: "Can you elaborate on the industry analysis? What specific factors did you evaluate?"

Candidate: "I looked at key market trends, including the rise in telemedicine and shifts in consumer demand for digital healthcare solutions. I also analyzed regulatory dynamics, like potential impacts of changes in FDA approval timelines, as well as the competitive landscape to identify barriers to entry for the startup."

Interviewer: "How did you approach building the sensitivity models? Were there specific variables or risks you focused on?"

Candidate: "I incorporated variables such as projected revenue growth, customer acquisition rates, and operating costs. I also ran scenarios with different assumptions, like slower-than-expected product adoption or increased competition, to test the resilience of the investment under various conditions."

Interviewer: "What led you to recommend a lower valuation? Was that conclusion driven primarily by your analysis or external input?"

Candidate: "My analysis showed that the startup's financial projections were overly optimistic, particularly their assumptions about market penetration. I cross-referenced their numbers with benchmarks from similar companies in our portfolio. This supported my case for negotiating a lower valuation."

Interviewer: "Can you share the outcome of your recommendation and its broader impact?"

Candidate: "The negotiation saved the company 15 percent on the initial investment. Over two years, the startup achieved 20 percent annual growth, which aligned with the scenarios I predicted. This reinforced confidence in my approach to evaluating similar opportunities."

Interviewer: "Looking back, is there anything you would have done differently during this process?"

Candidate: "I could have engaged our operational team earlier to evaluate integration challenges. Their insights might have uncovered risks or opportunities that weren't as apparent in my financial models."

KSA: Budgeting and Forecasting

Interviewer: "Can you share an example of how you developed and monitored a budget for a major project? What challenges did you encounter, and how did you address them?"

Candidate: "Sure, I managed the budget for a regional marketing campaign. I created a forecast based on historical data and adjusted for inflation. Overall, it went pretty smoothly."

Interviewer: "That sounds straightforward. How did you ensure your budget accounted for unexpected costs or variables during the campaign?"

Candidate: "Well, I mainly relied on the historical data to guide the forecast. We did encounter some unexpected vendor costs halfway through the project that I managed pretty well."

Interviewer: "Interesting. When those unexpected costs came up, how did you handle them?"

Candidate: "I worked with the team to reallocate funds from other areas of the campaign. For instance, we trimmed some of the digital ad spend to cover the vendor costs. We managed to stay close to the original budget."

Interviewer: "Looking back, is there anything you would have done differently in the planning phase to avoid that kind of challenge?"

Candidate: "Definitely. I realize now that I should have built a buffer for unforeseen expenses. Without it, the reallocation caused some disruptions to our campaign priorities, which added stress to the team."

Interviewer: "Got it. Did the lack of a contingency plan impact the campaign results?"

Candidate: "The campaign still achieved its primary goals, but the process was more challenging than it needed to be. In hindsight, a more comprehensive approach would have made things smoother."

KSA: Decision-Making

Interviewer: "Describe a time when you had to make a high-stakes decision with incomplete information. What was your approach, and what was the outcome?"

Candidate: "In one instance, I needed to decide whether to continue funding a pilot project for a new product line. The initial data from the pilot was inconclusive, and there was pressure from stakeholders to either double down or cut our losses."

Interviewer: "How did you manage the incomplete data? What steps did you take to ensure the decision was as informed as possible?"

Candidate: "I focused on gathering additional insights within the time constraints. I consulted with our customer insights team to analyze preliminary feedback, examined sales trends for similar products, and collaborated with the operations team to evaluate scalability risks. While the data wasn't comprehensive, these perspectives provided enough context to weigh the potential upside against the risks."

Interviewer: "What specific factors weighed most heavily in your final decision?"

Candidate: "The scalability risks became a decisive factor. The operational review highlighted that significant infrastructure adjustments would be required to meet demand if the product succeeded. This added a level of risk we hadn't initially anticipated, which led me to recommend postponing further investment until those risks were addressed."

Interviewer: "What was the outcome of your decision?"

Candidate: "The decision to delay was initially met with resistance, but it allowed us to redesign aspects of the product and streamline the production process. When we relaunched six months later, the product exceeded revenue targets by 25 percent, and we avoided significant costs tied to the initial scalability challenges."

Interviewer: "Reflecting on that experience, is there anything you would have done differently?"

Candidate: "In hindsight, I could have built a more robust early-stage framework for pilot evaluations. That would have made it easier to identify potential roadblocks earlier and might have shortened the timeline to market."

Exercise: Evaluate the Interview

Review the evaluation criteria below, select a rating on the 1–5 scale for each KSA, and provide a few sentences of supporting evidence for your choice. You can use the space provided here or write your notes on a separate sheet of paper.

- **Investment acumen:** Rating _____

  _____

  _____

- **Budgeting and forecasting:** Rating _____
_____
_____

- **Decision-making:** Rating _____
_____
_____

EVALUATION CRITERIA

- **1 – Poor**
  - Displays minimal knowledge or experience with relevant principles, skills, or industry-specific standards and requirements.
  - Struggles to apply basic concepts effectively and lacks familiarity with foundational expectations.

- **2 – Needs improvement**
  - Displays limited knowledge or experience with relevant principles, skills, or industry-specific standards and requirements.
  - Can apply some basic concepts but requires significant guidance to meet expectations.

- **3 – Solid**
  - Demonstrates sufficient knowledge and experience with relevant principles, skills, and industry-specific standards and requirements.
  - Meets expectations consistently and can apply key concepts with moderate guidance.

- **4 – Strong**
  - Demonstrates strong understanding and extensive experience with relevant principles, skills, and industry-specific standards and requirements.
  - Consistently exceeds expectations, applying advanced concepts independently.

- **5 – Exceptional**
  - Demonstrates comprehensive mastery and significant experience with relevant principles, skills, and industry-specific standards and requirements.
  - Proactively innovates, advises others, and applies concepts at an expert level without supervision.

COMPARE: COMPARE YOUR RATINGS AND EVIDENCE WITH OURS

- **Investment acumen: Rating 4 (strong)**
  - o Clear process and competence: The candidate demonstrated a solid grasp of investment principles, outlining a methodical approach with industry analysis and scenario modeling.
  - o Proactive risk management: Identified inflated projections and recommended adjustments based on data-driven insights, leading to tangible business outcomes (15 percent cost savings and a successful investment).
  - o Reflection on improvement: Acknowledged a potential gap—earlier collaboration with operational teams—to refine risk assessment further, showing self-awareness and room for growth.
  - o Falls short of a 5: The process followed expected practices without showcasing innovative approaches or exceptional foresight beyond standard industry benchmarks.

- **Budgeting and forecasting: Rating = 3 (solid)**
  - o Demonstrates basic competence: The candidate effectively created a budget forecast using historical data and inflation adjustments, showing a solid understanding of fundamental budgeting techniques.
  - o Reactive problem solving: When faced with unexpected vendor costs, the candidate successfully reallocated funds from other campaign areas, ensuring the budget stayed on track and the campaign goals were met.
  - o Lack of proactive planning: The absence of contingency planning indicates a gap in foresight, which led to unnecessary disruptions and stress during project execution.
  - o Limited depth in execution: While the immediate issue was resolved, the reactive approach suggests the candidate relied on ad-hoc adjustments rather than strategic preparation, such as building financial buffers.
  - o Self-awareness and learning potential: The candidate's acknowledgment of what could have been improved demonstrates a willingness to reflect and grow, which is promising but does not elevate the example to a higher rating.

- **Decision-making: Rating = 4 (Strong)**
  - o Analytical approach: The candidate demonstrated a structured process for decision-making under uncertainty, leveraging multiple data sources and stakeholder input.

- o Effective risk assessment: Identified and prioritized key risks (scalability challenges) that influenced the decision, resulting in significant long-term benefits.

- o Impactful outcome: The decision not only mitigated potential risks but also set the stage for a highly successful product launch.

- o Reflection and growth: Showed self-awareness by identifying an area for improvement—developing a stronger framework for early pilot assessments.

- o Falls short of a 5: While competent and impactful, the approach does not showcase exceptional innovation or groundbreaking strategies that exceed strong performance expectations.

Deciding whether to rate a candidate a 4 or a 5 on a 5-point scale can be challenging, especially when a candidate performs really well. This is often where interviewers encounter a "strictness bias," where they hesitate to give the highest score because they feel there is always room for improvement. However, a 5 does not signify perfection—it signifies that the candidate has significantly exceeded the requirements for the role.

Here's how to distinguish between the "strong" ratings on a 5-point scale:

- **Score of 3 (meets expectations):** The candidate meets all the criteria outlined in the evaluation guide. They demonstrate the necessary skills and capabilities to perform the role effectively but do not provide evidence of going beyond what is required. For example, they successfully answer the question with relevant details but do not offer additional insights or innovative approaches.

- **Score of 4 (exceeds expectations):** The candidate goes above and beyond the baseline criteria in some way, showing a higher-than-expected level of proficiency or effort. For instance, they might give a thorough response that addresses the question fully while also demonstrating an extra layer of preparation, insight, or creativity in their approach.

- **Score of 5 (far exceeds expectations):** The candidate's performance goes well beyond expectations, showing outstanding capability or achievement. Their response not only meets all criteria but also demonstrates exceptional understanding, thought leadership, or innovative problem-solving. For example, they might offer a comprehensive, well-structured answer and propose a new perspective or solution that would add significant value to the organization. This score indicates that the candidate has far surpassed what is required for success in the role.

Addressing Strictness Bias

If you're hesitant to award a 5 even when the evidence strongly supports it, it's essential to revisit the evaluation criteria and remind yourself that a 5 does not mean "perfect." It means the candidate exceeded the role's requirements in a significant way. If you find yourself consistently reluctant to give the highest score, consider whether a 4-point scale might better align with your evaluation style, where the highest rating (4) indicates exceptional performance without requiring perfection.

This structured approach can help ensure consistency and fairness in your scoring decisions.

PRACTICAL TIP

When deciding between a 4 and a 5, review the evidence against the criteria and ask yourself:

- Did the candidate significantly exceed the expectations, or just slightly surpass them?

- Did their response show exceptional insight, creativity, or capability compared to what the role demands?

- If you had to explain the reasoning for your score to another evaluator, would your evidence clearly justify it?

Notes

1 Campion, M. A. et al (2011) Doing competencies well: Best practices in competency modeling, *Personnel Psychology*, 64(1), pp. 225–62

2 Bellach, A. (2019) Interviews are not designed for underrepresented groups, LinkedIn, August 2, www.linkedin.com/pulse/interviews-designed-underrepresented-groups-alison-bellach (archived at https://perma.cc/Y5WK-6M24)

3 Kessler, J. and Low, C. (2021) Research: How companies committed to diverse hiring still fail, *Harvard Business Review*, February 11, https://hbr.org/2021/02/research-how-companies-committed-to-diverse-hiring-still-fail (archived at https://perma.cc/2W2N-DV7G)

22

Making a Decision

Once all candidates have been interviewed and scored on each KSA across all interviews, it's time to make a hiring decision. The decision-maker(s) should use the ratings and evidence across all KSAs assessed throughout the hiring process in order to arrive at a final hire/no-hire decision. Even if you need to hire just one candidate, we recommend making a hire/no hire decision for each of them once all KSAs have been assessed. If there are multiple candidates for a given opening, this is where it could be helpful to have a meeting with the interviewers, reviewing their ratings, key strengths, and development areas per candidate, and creating space for any red flags to be shared that may not have been captured in the KSAs for each interview.

We always get asked at this point in the interviewer training: "Is there an algorithm to average the scores and make a decision?" You could decide to average the scores across the ratings and give anyone who got above a 3 a "hire." However, what if they somehow received two 2s and two 5s, which resulted in a moderate average? We often recommend not hiring candidates who have more than one area with a rating less than "capable," or 3, since that indicates there are significant portions of the job that they cannot perform at standard. Your decision tree may look like the following.

After all candidates have been interviewed and scored on each KSA across all interviews, the decision-making process should incorporate both quantitative ratings and qualitative insights from the interviewers.

1 **Review scores across all KSAs:** Start by reviewing the numerical ratings for each KSA. A candidate who consistently scores high (4s or 5s) across the board is likely a strong fit. However, a candidate who has multiple lower scores (e.g. two or more ratings of 2 or 3) should raise concern about their ability to perform critical aspects of the job.

2 **Look for consistency:** Consider the consistency of scores across the interviews. If a candidate scored highly on technical skills but low on collaboration or problem solving, it could indicate a gap in their overall capabilities, which might be critical for team-based roles.

3 **Identify key strengths and development areas:** Gather insights from the interviewers about the candidate's strengths and weaknesses. Did a candidate shine in areas that are essential to the role (e.g. technical proficiency for an engineer, leadership for a manager)? Were there clear development areas that would need further support or training?

4 **Discuss red flags:** Hold a meeting with the interview team to address any red flags that may not be fully captured in the ratings.

5 **Decision tree:**

   o **Hire:** If a candidate scores at least a 3 in all KSAs and demonstrates strong overall competencies (e.g. no areas of critical concern), they are a strong contender.

   o **No hire:** If a candidate has multiple ratings below "capable" (less than a 3) in critical areas (e.g. problem solving, communication), they likely lack the necessary skills for the role.

   o **Further discussion needed:** If the scores are mixed, for example, a candidate has strong technical scores but lower scores in collaboration or leadership, the hiring team should discuss whether these areas are trainable or if they pose a significant risk to the team's success.

By considering both the individual ratings and the overall interview feedback, the hiring team or appropriate decision-makers can make an informed, holistic decision. This approach ensures that the candidate's full potential is evaluated, not just a numerical score.

Whatever guideline you apply, however, must be applied the same across all candidates for the same role, otherwise (obviously) you are using different criteria for different candidates.

Selecting From Multiple Candidates

When hiring multiple candidates, it's essential to establish clear criteria for "pass" and "fail" in your interview process. If you're using a 5-point scale, a "pass" typically means scoring a minimum of 3 (meets expectations). If you're using a 4-point scale, passing remains a 3, but the standard is inherently stricter since there are fewer points on the scale, leaving less room for nuanced scoring.

Here's how to navigate situations where more candidates pass than you can hire.

EXAMPLE SCENARIO

You interview 40 candidates and 12 meet the passing criteria, but you can only hire six.

Alternatively, most candidates score reasonably well on average, but some have 1s or 2s in key areas.

In both cases, you'll need a more refined process to make final selections.

Step-by-Step Approach

1 Set baseline "pass" criteria

- o Require candidates to achieve at least a 3 out of 5 across the entire interview loop (i.e. the average of all assessed skills must meet or exceed a 3).

2 Introduce skill-specific minimums (if necessary)

- o If too many candidates pass the baseline, raise the bar by requiring a minimum score of 3 out of 5 for each individual skill being assessed.
- o Alternatively, identify specific "must-have" skills (e.g. technical expertise or communication) and require a minimum score of 3 in those areas.

3 Balance stringency with fairness

- o Be cautious when applying stricter requirements exclusively to technical skills. Research shows this approach can unintentionally disadvantage women or underrepresented minorities, as they may face systemic barriers that impact their preparation or performance in technical interviews.

4 Incorporate additional data points

- o Consider incorporating other relevant factors, such as overall interview feedback, work samples, or alignment with organizational values. These can help distinguish between similarly qualified candidates.

> *Practical Tip*
>
> To ensure fairness and consistency, document your scoring criteria and selection process. This transparency helps you make defensible hiring decisions while mitigating the risk of cognitive errors. By thoughtfully refining your approach, you can select the best candidates while maintaining fairness and clarity.

Multiple Qualified Candidates

What if you have more than one candidate in the "hire" category and you're in the tough situation of having to determine which one to hire out of the finalists?

First, check if any candidates scored higher on the KSAs than others. If so, then this candidate is likely the strongest. If not, however, you can determine the decision by these means:

Weighting: Are any of these KSAs more important than others? Pick the candidate who scored highest on the most important ones. Make sure you document your weighting decisions in your job profile.

Development: Are any of these KSAs harder to teach or learn? If so, pick the candidate who scored highest on the ones that are hardest to teach or learn.

When Too Few Candidates Meet Our Expectations

Occasionally, you may find that none of the candidates meet the established criteria for hire. This situation is common in highly specialized roles, such as software engineering, and it often prompts a critical evaluation of the process itself.

Step 1: Evaluate Your Criteria

Ask whether your expectations or rating criteria might be too stringent. For example:

- Was the job description realistic for the talent pool?
- Are the ratings aligned with what's truly required for success in the role?
- Did the interview process inadvertently set candidates up for failure?

A specific scenario might involve a coding interview that's overly complex, led by an exceptional software engineer whose standards are unreasonably high. If this happened, consider whether the problem or the scoring criteria need adjustment.

Step 2: Address Potential Calibration Issues

If interviewers were too strict, it could signal a need for interviewer training and calibration. Here's how to handle this:

- **Review the data:** Analyze how each interviewer scored across candidates. If one interviewer consistently rated all candidates lower than others, consider recalibrating those scores for fairness.
- **Document adjustments:** Any changes to scores must be applied consistently across all affected candidates and thoroughly documented to ensure transparency and fairness.
- **Recognize partial success:** In cases where candidates failed a difficult task but demonstrated strong problem-solving approaches, adjust scores to reflect effort and strategy, not just final outcomes.

Step 3: Adjust Priorities if Necessary

If no candidates meet the bar, consider re-evaluating the relative importance of the KSAs. For instance:

- Identify critical skills versus secondary skills for the role.
- Allow for slightly lower ratings in less critical areas to widen the pool of potential hires.
- Avoid prioritizing technical skills to the exclusion of behavioral ones, such as communication and collaboration. Research shows that while technical hires may succeed initially based on hard skills, they often fail in the long term due to deficiencies in interpersonal or behavioral competencies.[1,2]

Step 4: Consider Revising the Process

If candidates consistently struggle, it may be time to revise the interview process:

- Simplify overly complex interview tasks, such as coding challenges, to better reflect real-world job requirements.

- Introduce new questions or scenarios that are challenging but achievable for qualified candidates.

- Seek feedback from both candidates and interviewers to identify bottlenecks or unnecessary hurdles.

Step 5: Decide Whether to Continue or Adjust

If no suitable candidates emerge, you face two options:

- **Continue the search:** Stick with your current process if you're confident in the value of each assessment component and have the time to keep looking.

- **Adjust the process:** Redesign your evaluation criteria or interview structure to better align with the candidate pool while ensuring it still reflects the job's requirements.

Final Thoughts

While it's tempting to "wait for the perfect hire," an inflexible process can unnecessarily delay filling critical roles. Instead, focus on creating a balanced and fair evaluation system that ensures both technical and behavioral skills are considered in alignment with the role's needs. If no candidate meets the bar, the issue may lie in the process itself rather than the talent pool.

Multiple Interviewers

As is often the case in a corporate hire, you may have brought in your team or a cross-functional partner to conduct some of the interviews for your hire. To avoid repetition, make sure to ask each candidate *different* questions by each of those interviewers. Therefore, you offer them each a unique interview guide with their own KSAs and a sheet to submit their ratings (or instructions on how to submit these in the applicant tracking system).

Should we ask each of our interviewers for a hire/no hire decision? While this is something our clients have commonly done, our view is that a hire/no hire decision from too many stakeholders causes confusion when it comes time to make the decision. Logically speaking, it doesn't make sense for someone to make an entire hire/no hire decision based on just a part of the interview process. Instead, we would prefer that they submit their ratings on each of the KSAs and not an overall rating. Once all the ratings are together, the decision-maker(s) can use an approach to evaluate all of the quantitative and qualitative data for a final decision.

We have also seen situations where the interviewers become overly engaged in the final decision, even though they evaluated just one portion of the interview process. Back to our most brilliant engineer who enjoys giving the hardest coding challenge to all the candidates. That engineer is often also engaged in the overall decision, and likely to argue that "if this candidate cannot solve this problem, they absolutely cannot do the job because this particular problem is fundamental to the whole job."

This statement is a great example of halo/horns effect, or the horn effect.[3] Although we often see examples of this bias in terms of personal character-istics about a candidate ("Any candidate who shows up to an interview without a tie is simply not professional and has terrible credibility"). The horn effect is when hiring managers find *one negative thing* about the candi-date and then assume that if this thing "A" is true, then "B" must also be true. If a software engineer struggles with arrays during a timed interview, does that mean they can't code? No, that's not what it means. More infor-mation is always needed than a single coding problem.

Although having more input from your stakeholders is helpful, it's not helpful if they introduce flawed judgments or subjective decision-making into the process. Taking charge of bias risks amongst your stakeholders is critical. We've observed such stakeholders evaluate areas that they were not asked to evaluate, and sometimes refer to those as "red flags." Now, as mentioned earlier, we do think it's fair and helpful to allow space in your evaluation criteria for something like "Is there anything else the interviewer deems critical to share with the hiring team?" Managing expectations with the other interviews is therefore critical to ensure that they clearly under-stand what *their* role is, and they complete their role exactly as stated. We realize that this is not always easy to do. Sometimes that critical stakeholder is a more senior leader, and it's unwise to criticize their decision-making process. Navigating this with finesse is critical and we are absolutely rooting for you! In such situations, bringing in a perspective from human resources or employment law may also be helpful.

CONSIDER THIS

Some of this will require interviewer training to help manage expectations, and other parts of this simply require practice. We feel that what matters most is that your interviewers are following a structured and consistent process across all candidates to assess them on what matters most for day one success on the job. If some interviewers provide insight in their evaluation guides that go a little beyond what you're asking of them, that's ok—work to give them feedback, help them grow, and provide continued support for all interviewers through structured interviewer training and regular calibration sessions.

On the opposite end of the spectrum, the additional interviewers may not submit ratings on time. We recommend scheduling a conversation in that case and collecting the ratings from them verbally. To ensure a fully consistent process, it's important for everyone to participate in a structured way, otherwise it can erode all the hard work done to create consistency and reduce cognitive error in the process. Sadly, the higher up in the management chain interviewers are, the less time they have to dedicate to the process and may inadvertently derail the interview without meaning to. Contracting with all your stakeholders in advance, and having them assert their commitment to the structured process can be helpful.

Overall, making decisions about either a single candidate or multiple candidates always involves setting up your criteria and then applying it with consistency to each person.

Part 4 Summary: Key Learnings

This part outlined a step-by-step process to evaluate candidates effectively, from taking interview notes to making a final hiring decision. Here's a summary:

Taking Interview Notes

- **Best practices for note-taking**
  Learn the importance of capturing accurate and relevant information during interviews. Two common methods are:
  o **Verbatim notes:** Detailed, word-for-word accounts of the candidate's responses, ensuring accuracy but requiring more effort.
  o **Summarized notes:** Focused on key points and themes, quicker to take but may miss nuances.

- **Other Considerations:**
  - o Recording interviews can provide additional accuracy but requires legal consent and might affect candidate trust. We don't recommend doing this.
  - o The goal is to collect comprehensive data that informs objective decision-making. We feel you can do this by learning to take thorough interview notes. The easiest way for newer interviewers to learn how to do this is by beginning to capture close-to-verbatim notes.

Building and Using a Rating Scale

- Effective evaluation begins with a clear, well-defined rating scale.
- Rating scales should offer meaningful differentiation while remaining simple to use.
- A 5-point scale is commonly recommended, with levels of performance reflecting proficiency or sophistication.

Evaluation Criteria

- The evaluation process is based on the **Observe and record, Analyze, Decide** framework:
  - o **Observe and record:** Observe data during the interview and capture the notes throughout.
  - o **Analyze:** Linking candidate responses to the KSAs being assessed. Look for patterns and assess performance against the evaluation criteria.
  - o **Decide:** Determine the numerical rating that best aligns with the evidence you have for each KSA you are evaluating and provide supporting data so the hiring team understands the rationale for your ratings.

Scoring Candidates

- We recommend evaluating candidates on a 5-point scale, aligning their responses with the expectations outlined in the rating criteria.
- A well-scored interview relies on objective evaluation, where evidence from notes supports the ratings.

Making a Hiring Decision

- Use a consistent guideline for hire/no-hire decisions, even when hiring a single candidate.
- If hiring multiple candidates, prioritize those who score higher in critical KSAs or demonstrate proficiency in harder-to-learn skills.

Moving Forward

With a clear rating scale, comprehensive notes, and an understanding of the KSAs required for the role, you are now ready to build a job profile and begin interviewing candidates!

This structured approach ensures that your hiring decisions are fair, objective, and data-driven.

Part 4 Key Terms

5-point scale: Most commonly used to evaluate performance in business settings, this has a mid-point of "competence," with higher and lower scores on both sides.

Analyze: Evaluating interview data against the KSAs to identify patterns.

Average rating: Calculating the mean score of a candidate's performance across different KSAs.

Bucket method: Organizing examples of candidate performance into categories to determine the fullness of positive versus negative examples.

Central tendency error: The tendency to rate candidates in the middle of a scale to avoid extremes.

Cognitive error management: Addressing and controlling biases from interviewers to ensure accurate evaluation.

Consumer scale: A rating system commonly used in reviews (e.g. 1–5 stars) but less suited for job evaluations.

Decide: Making hiring decisions based on the analysis of interview data.

Evaluation criteria: Standards or benchmarks used to assess candidates' responses and performance.

Evidence-based rating: Using specific examples and data from the interview to assign scores to candidates.

Hire/no-hire decision: The final choice to either hire a candidate or not based on their ratings.

Interview notes: Summary of what you asked and how the candidate responded in the interview.

Observe and record: Collecting and documenting data from interviews.

Proficiency levels: Descriptions of different levels of skill or competence, ranging from basic to advanced.

Rating scale: Structured system to evaluate and score candidates based on predefined criteria during the interview process.

Scale: A set of levels or points used to rate candidates' performance, such as 3-point or 5-point scales.

Strictness bias: The tendency to underutilize the highest ratings due to a personal opposition to giving top scores.

Summarized notes: Brief notes capturing main themes and relevant points.

Verbatim notes: Detailed, word-for-word records of the interview.

Notes

1 Tripathy, M. (2020) Relevance of Soft Skills in Career Success, *MIER Journal of Educational Studies Trends and Practices*, 10(1), pp. 91–102, https://doi.org/10.52634/mier/2020/v10/i1/1354 (archived at https://perma.cc/V8YW-5BQS)

2 Jensen, K. (2015) Intelligence is overrated: What you really need to succeed, *Forbes*, February 10, www.forbes.com/sites/keldjensen/2015/02/10/intelligence-is-overrated-what-you-really-need-to-succeed-continued/ (archived at https://perma.cc/VV53-WE7S)

3 Noor, N. et al (2023) Bias, halo effect and horn effect: A systematic literature review, *International Journal of Academic Research in Business & Social Sciences*, 13(3), pp. 1116–1140

PART FIVE

Other Considerations

In this section, we offer a comprehensive overview of the laws, regulations, and best practices related to privacy and employment in the United States, Europe, the United Kingdom, India, and China. The section also covers topics such as candidate feedback, adverse impact, job-relatedness, and data protection. Finally, we dive into strategies for mitigating risks and ensuring compliance with relevant laws and regulations. Overall, this section serves as a practical guide for considerations when using the Three-Step Assessment Process.

23

Can Human Bias Be Helped?

Let's start with some important context. We're not attorneys, privacy experts, or labor economists—those fields bring their own invaluable insights and best practices. We often collaborate with professionals from these areas, seeking their feedback and guidance. What we're offering here comes from our expertise as industrial-organizational psychologists. Our work occasionally overlaps with areas like labor law, employment law, and privacy law when designing and implementing client solutions. For example, in the United States, we've documented the fairness of selection processes to support labor attorneys in compliance efforts with the Department of Labor. While we strive to make these intersections of law and psychology easy to understand, we're not lawyers. We strongly recommend consulting a local employment attorney to validate and apply the insights shared here.

Now, an additional disclaimer: Our professional experience is rooted in the United States, even when working with international companies. The guidelines we discuss reflect knowledge gathered through conversations with hiring experts globally, but we do not claim expertise in hiring practices specific to regions like China, India, or Europe. This book is designed to serve as a starting point—offering important considerations and guiding questions to explore with regional experts.

On to the substance. Many training programs addressing bias in hiring leave participants feeling flawed in a way that seems fundamental or unchangeable. While rarely stated outright (because, let's face it, that would be unkind), this message is often implied. These courses tend to focus on reshaping how people think about decisions rather than on what they actually do during the hiring process.

Let's revisit key tenets of psychology: Understand behavior, predict behavior, and change behavior. The third step—changing behavior—is where we focus when we work to change bias. We've found that when mitigating bias in hiring, it's often more practical to start with changes in action or behavior rather than attempting to start by changing thoughts or beliefs.[1] Asking someone to suspend judgment and follow a structured, deliberate interview process is more effective in practice than trying to "change hearts and minds."

This philosophy underpins our work: Focus on tangible steps and create processes that guide better decisions without requiring individuals to overhaul their subconscious biases overnight. Structured processes, like the ones we describe in this book, can make a measurable difference in hiring improvements while empowering hiring teams to act with greater fairness and precision.

The United States has undoubtedly made progress in employment fairness since desegregation in the 1960s.[2] Legal advancements have played a crucial role in creating more opportunities for women, people with disabilities, and underrepresented minorities. These changes highlight the effectiveness of behavior-first strategies—altering actions before attempting to shift deeply held attitudes.

In psychology, since Gordon Allport's work on subtle forms of racism, the focus has been on reducing prejudiced, irrational judgments.[3] However, as the conversation around discrimination has expanded, the terminology has sometimes become less precise. Today, a wide range of behaviors, from unconscious slights to overt discrimination, may be grouped under the single term "racism." While this framing draws attention to issues, it can complicate the path toward solutions in workplace contexts. Broad terms like "racism" risk alienating allies, oversimplifying the complexity of behaviors, and hindering targeted corrective actions.

Microaggressions, for example, are subtle and often unconscious actions that can cause harm but typically offer opportunities for training, education, and growth. Macroaggressions, in contrast, involve deliberate and often systemic actions—such as intentionally excluding people of color from hiring decisions—which are more challenging to address and often require legal or systemic intervention.[4] Recognizing the distinction between these behaviors is critical to fostering accountability and progress while maintaining the potential for individuals to improve.

Thus, we aim to avoid labeling individuals making flawed hiring decisions with terms like "biased," "racist," or "sexist," especially when their actions may stem from lack of awareness, or unconscious or systemic influences. Instead, this book invites you to join us on a shared journey toward equitable hiring. If you're committed to basing hiring decisions on job-related data rather than personal characteristics, then we're aligned in our goals—we're all working together to make better decisions.

Notes

1 Nguyen-Phuong-Mai, M. (2021) What bias management can learn from change management? Utilizing change framework to review and explore bias strategies, *Frontiers in Psychology*, December 15, 12:644145, doi : 10.3389/fpsyg.2021.644145 (archived at https://perma.cc/B3EX-3AKU), PMID: 34975601; PMCID: PMC8714784

2 US Equal Employment Opportunity Commission (2015) African Americans in the American Workforce, www.eeoc.gov /special-report/african-americans-american-workforce (archived at https://perma.cc/2VUP-W8VX)

3 Allport, G. W. (1954) *The Nature of Prejudice*, Addison-Wesley

4 Levchak, C. C. (2018) Microaggressions, macroaggressions, and modern racism. In C. C. Levchack, *Microaggressions and Modern Racism*, Palgrave Macmillan, https://doi.org/10.1007/978-3-319-70332-9_2 (archived at https://perma.cc/5MHA-KBMM)

24

Privacy and Employment Best Practices: United States

Each state in the United States has unique employment laws. We don't have space to cover them all in this handbook, but we'll discuss the common threads that apply across the whole nation.

A Little Bit of Legislation...

When affirmative action was first signed into law by President John F. Kennedy on March 6, 1961, it was openly admitted that equal opportunity cannot exist because of the pervasive power of prior (and continued) oppression and racism.[1] The subsequent implied message was that humans from the powerful and oppressing group are incapable of fairly judging the school and college admissions or job applications of those they oppress. Since then, we've seen a number of revisions to these original laws, with the current laws focused on making illegal any decisions that are directly related to age, ancestry, color, disability, ethnicity, gender, gender identity or expression, genetic information, HIV/AIDS status, military status, national origin, pregnancy, race, religion, sex, sexual orientation, or veteran status, or any other bases under the law. Overall, when it comes to jobs, the US laws boil down to the use of job-related criteria, versus personal criteria. Lawsuits often revolve around how to define what is, and what is not, job related. Emerging over time and continuing into the future, we will see more legislation in the United States targeting the use of automation and AI-based assessments. We advise checking with employment lawyers in your state of hire to ensure that any practices you put in place for testing or assessing candidates are compliant.

We met with experienced employment attorney and I-O psychologist Paige Munro-Delotto, PhD, owner of Munro-Delotto Law Offices, which practices employment law, largely in federal courts in Connecticut, Massachusetts, Rhode Island, and Alabama.

As Paige explains, the Civil Rights laws passed beginning in 1964 "prohibit discrimination on the basis of race, color, religion, sex, or national origin." These were later amended with pregnancy discrimination laws, including not just pregnancy but also pregnancy-related medical conditions. US supreme court cases have also added protections for sexual orientation and gender identity. Lastly, the legislation also includes disability and age protections, which are equally relevant in current employment law claims as anti-discrimination laws from the original 1964 legislation.[2]

Although many hiring managers took the laws seriously and made intentional efforts to ensure their hiring practices were open to a broader group, others did not. The laws passed as a result of overwhelming evidence that interviewers made biased decisions about candidates. Sadly, in some cases, interviewers were creatively and intentionally finding ways to avoid hiring women, people of color, certain religious and national groups, and others who were at a disadvantage. Even as recently as 2024, a study conducted at the University of California by economists found that certain industries tended to favor candidates based on perceived race or gender from a resume.[3]

The problem of discrimination has not gone away.

There Are Many Creative Ways to Discriminate Against Applicants

Let's talk about hair as a source of discrimination. Yes, we refer to hair on the head or facial hair. Hair is a source of discrimination. In some situations, people were denied employment based on having the wrong hairstyle. Paige confirmed that a number of laws in individual US states expressly prohibit discrimination based on hair coverings or traditionally Black hairstyles.[4,5] In other words, a hiring manager made assumptions about someone else's qualifications based on *how they wear their hair*. Specifically, this has landed on people of color repeatedly. Braids, twists, and dreadlocks are all commonly worn hairstyles by Black job candidates. In hiring situations, it has happened too often that someone was not hired or even interviewed because someone thought that these hairstyles were viewed by their clients or by the company as less "professional."

This is a lie. It's a great example of a subtle way to discriminate against Black applicants. Once more… **there is absolutely no job where the ability to perform the job is related to how someone wears their hair.** If you have a client who doesn't like dreads, it's time to get rid of the client. That client is behaving in a discriminatory way, and they will cause your company to have problems and potentially legal challenges.[6] If your company claims that having long hair is also not acceptable, then the company has a discriminatory hiring practice against women. It's clear, plain and simple, and the United States Equal Employment Opportunity Commission (the federal commission against discrimination at work) will take it seriously.

The examples regarding hair are a great way to illustrate the complexity of US employment laws, and hair comes up a lot. Paige weighs in that she has seen several cases where an African American is treated differently due to a head covering or traditional hairstyle:

> Often with these cases, the difficulty is *proving* that is the reason for the adverse job action—which is generally considered to be the "big" acts like failure to hire, termination, and failure to promote/demotion. For example, we have to prove that the adverse job action was "because of" the head covering or hairstyle. That is difficult to prove. Where we *can* prove these cases, we look for similarly situated comparators. Say that an African American with a particular, traditional hairstyle is terminated (which usually happens when there is a new boss or some change in circumstances) because of the "dress code" or a similar excuse. We would research whether Caucasian coworkers who also acted outside of the "dress code" were similarly terminated. Conversely, in a "failure to hire" case we would compare the qualifications of the similarly situated majority group (i.e. Caucasians) and if the African American with the hairstyle was more qualified, we might have a shot at proving it.

She has also seen cases where a person of color was likely believed to be White on the basis of the resume, but when the company leaders (often from a majority group) met the employee and discovered not only the applicant's race, but hairstyle, they then took action to terminate the employee. She continues to explain:

> I have had other cases where the employee is harassed due to their traditionally African American hairstyle. An example would be likening the employee to Whoopie Goldberg as a joke. Clearly race-based harassment, this constitutes a whole separate cause of action for discrimination from the "adverse job action" form of discrimination.

Long and short, Paige makes it clear that this form of harassment/discrimination still happens.

In general, which types of cases are currently most prominently featured in the courts? Paige explains that she and other employment lawyers today

spend a disproportionate amount of time on age, disability and gender identification, sexual orientation, and pregnancy cases. As of 2024, she finds that
age is most prevalent, after cases where employers terminate employees
following a pregnancy disclosure.

What About "Reverse Discrimination?"

Protection for people of color at the expense of White employees is not
acceptable. In a Starbucks lawsuit from 2023, a White female manager was
fired for being accused of "absence of leadership," because one of her team
members had taken what was found to be discriminatory action. The team
member with the discriminatory action accusation was a person of color,
and not fired. As the court interpreted the case, any decisions that are made
about people at work *cannot* be related to personal characteristics, which
include race. They must be related solely to the proven qualities of their job
performance. The White female manager who was fired had a positive
performance track record, which showed that the decision could not have
been made based on her performance. In the subsequent trial, she was
awarded $25 million by a jury.[7,8,9]

Paige comments:

> However, based on my experience, "reverse discrimination claims" (where the
> majority group claims discrimination in favor of the minority group—defined
> as the protected classes) are rarely brought to court. Why? Law firms that bring
> the discrimination claims are generally largely or solely contingency based.
> Simply put, the lawyer does not get paid unless their case is good enough to
> merit settlement or win a jury award. So in practicality, plaintiffs' lawyers do
> not usually feel such cases will play well with the jury, even if the majority
> group (i.e. non-disabled, heterosexual, Caucasian males under 40) complains
> about discrimination. However, that said, there are cases such as the Starbucks
> case. The key to avoiding any issues is simply hiring (and firing) based on merit
> and not because of anything related to a protected class.

Women Can Do the Heavy Lifting

According to the US employment laws, if lifting heavy things is required for
a firefighter, then it's up to the fire department to figure out exactly how
heavy the lifts will be, and then test candidates on that exact weight. Not
more and not less. The fire department may not make the lifts heavier
beyond the job requirements. The lifting requirement discriminates against

women. However, because lifting heavy things is a *necessary job function*, it is not in violation of any anti-discrimination law, including even those focused on disabilities.[10,11]

Similarly, Paige provided an example of actors, where a *necessary job function* may be male or female status (although now that line is getting blurred with acknowledgment of transgender status). A *necessary job function* can be thought of as a part of the job which, if not able to be completed by the employee, means the job is not being done. It most often comes up in the context of disability law. In a case where an employee requests accommodation, they may request a preview of what will be tested before being hired, such as the ability to work on a computer with voice recognition. Under disability law, if a person cannot perform the necessary job functions, they are not a "qualified person with a disability."

Paige explains:

> Although it's technically not considered discrimination to not hire or to terminate someone who cannot perform the necessary job functions, the bar to prove this is quite high (because what are truly the necessary job functions can be ambiguous in a lot of jobs, and thus it can "look" like discrimination and still result in a law suit), but there are very few examples where the bar is met. As an example, consider a nurse in a hospital where their job cannot be done remotely, yet that employee asks for an accommodation to work from home. Although an extreme example, obviously, a nurse (unless part of a web-based treatment system) working from home or remotely in that exact job does not meet the requirements of the job. Often, however, cases are less clear-cut.

Similarly, if the weight requirement to perform the job is known and documented, then it is perfectly legal to not hire someone who cannot meet that requirement. Does that mean that fewer women will make the cut? Yes. Men and women are, on average, physiologically different. However, Paige has counseled female marines who can in fact carry more than 99 percent of the weight of civilian men. As a result, in reality, gender comes into play only occasionally.

Paige also points out that race (which can, as she explained, become apparent through hair discrimination among other methods) is extremely difficult to relate to a *necessary job function*, except possibly in the acting profession: "If a movie company is casting for a Caucasian person, then this is considered a legitimate reason (there are few). The same can be said for casting for an African American and legally excluding Caucasians."

Paige noted that in these types of cases, if the knowledge, skills, and abilities of a job are properly defined, it is not discriminatory to not hire an applicant or even terminate an employee if they cannot perform the necessary job functions.

Correcting Past Wrongs

Knowing that an assessment is causing adverse impact is uncomfortable for all of us. We absolutely hate knowing that certain people—based on their group—are less likely to perform well on coding challenges than the majority groups. It just feels unfair.

Our HR friends point out to their engineering leaders, however, that the unfairness happened before they applied to the particular role. It was unfair that boys in high school received more encouragement and support when learning coding, while girls were subtly (or not so subtly) told to focus on being pretty and watching unboxing make-up videos on social media. It's unfair that differences in education based on economic factors cause some students to do better at math. It's unfair that by the time a young woman attends coding classes in college, she is a minority, and perhaps may get invited to fewer study groups. It's unfair that during her first college internship at a tech company, she worked for a manager who didn't go out of his way to make her feel welcome because he wanted to avoid any favoritism or special treatment… Except that she noticed how out of place she felt *more* than all of the other interns. This pattern continues, and somehow the disadvantaged candidates receive fewer interesting projects at work, and therefore fewer promotions and then 15 years after college, somehow the woman ends up with more than five years' less experience than a guy who graduated from college during her same year. When it's time for both her and the guy to apply for a job, he has risen to one or two levels above her, even though they have the same total years of experience. Perhaps he worked at more prestigious companies. Perhaps he had more, better mentors.[12] However, according to the US employment laws, it is not legal for the employer to help her catch up by getting a job someone else is more qualified for based on experience. It's not our job to fix *this* particular problem in the hiring process with *this* particular hiring decision.

Our HR friends have also weighed in with their experience on this exact phenomenon, something that seems to be, but should not be, a gray area in business. We'd like to make it as clear as possible for your hiring purposes.

As you know, we are not attorneys, but we do train our HR clients in the United States on how the laws apply to the use of assessments and interviews at work.

Paige emphasizes that when hiring, as far as potential lawsuits are concerned, the hiring must be based on merit:

> Unfortunately, due to systematic and systemic issues as to race and gender, there can be advantages for Caucasian males over women and minorities. But that said, what I and other employment lawyers see more often in such cases is majority classes being systematically favored—despite merit. This happens without objective hiring protocols (such as tests and unstructured interview guides), and without those, the cases are much easier to win.

Let's say a company with a strong diversity mandate wishes to hire more women in technical jobs where few qualified candidates are available. The company's leadership team, filled with positive intentions, adds diversity goals for each director. These directors are thus held accountable for hiring 45 percent female engineers across their entire teams in their yearly performance reviews. This is a tough ask in a field where there are simply fewer women applicants in engineering.

As a consequence, in an effort to ensure balanced representation among the higher-level engineering roles, women might then be pushed through the hiring process in a more expedited way. In a few instances, directors may become desperate and make offers to female hires who have lower interview scores than male candidates.

Let's say it bluntly: **This is a violation of the US laws.** We don't advise placing diversity goals at the bottom of the recruiting funnel (the phase during which a hiring decision is made).

Paige's view on this: "If the hire is made for any reason other than merit—whether it is a female or male who is not hired—if the decision is made 'because of gender,' it can be unlawful."

Alternatively, let's say the same company makes offers to all the female candidates who performed less well in the interviews, but at jobs in lower levels, and therefore for lower pay. Later, these women discover that they are working alongside men who were hired with the same number of years' experience, but at higher levels (meaning they were getting paid more, violating legislation on equal pay). The women are confused as to why they have the same years of experience, but make less money. Without knowledge of how they performed in the interview, these women make inquiries into pay equity discrimination. If an analysis shows any patterns in differences between male and female pay for similar jobs, the women may have a case to bring against the company. Such cases have recently settled for as much as $215 million.[13] Even if the investigation finds that the women had poorer scores on their assessments and therefore the leveling decisions were legitimate, the cost of the inquiry, the potential settlement, and the public shame in the media as a company that systematically pays women less than men will do considerable damage.

Paige explains: "Some of the most key elements to pay disparity claims for pay disparity claims include the similarity of the jobs, the employees' skills, and the employees' job tasks; some legal sources frame those examples as follows:

1 The work one employee and another employee performed was completed in similar working conditions.

2 Both were involved in equal work requiring equal skill, responsibility, and effort.

3 One was paid less than the employee of the opposite gender who performed the same type of work."

How do interviewers keep this from happening? By leveraging a structured job profile, MQs, and the specific KSAs required at each level of job performance. If these are clear, then the initial claim is less likely to occur.

Who You Hire

Protected group categories are race (Black, White, Asian, etc.) ethnicity (Hispanic, Arab, Jewish, etc.), gender (Male, Female—some states in the US also include Non-Binary), nationality (Indian, Norwegian, Russian, etc.), religion (Hindu, Catholic, Muslim, etc.) age (over 40 are protected), and disability status (Physical and Mental Disabilities included). In the past, some US states included sexual orientation but now the US Supreme Court has recognized sexual orientation and gender identity are protected under Title VII along with gender and pregnancy status.

As Paige explains to her clients, especially as she is hearing more about prospective clients bringing any kind of cases:

> You can be legally terminated, or not hired, for any reason, or for no reason at all, unless it is *discriminatory* (based on a protected class) or *in retaliation* for reporting discrimination (or similar protected reports such as whistleblowing).

There are a few other protected areas that are industry-specific, and then of course there are broad prohibitions on termination in retaliation for taking Family Medical Leave Act time off, and/or for making wage and hour complaints under the Fair Labor Standards Act.

As to hiring specifically, while it's true that one cannot be denied a job based on a protected class, proving that this happened can be hard. We normally need to catch companies making inappropriate comments related to a protected class applicant made during the hiring process, hence all the emphasis in interviewer training on questions not to ask. For example, I worked at a company before I built my law practice, where my team thought it was funny to hang up notes from interviews where inappropriate comments were written about candidates. For example, in a customer service role, an interviewer wrote, while declining the candidate, that they "talked too ghetto." Needless to say I put an end to that practice—both the inappropriate notes and the sharing of the notes. These days, I see fewer highly overt comments such as these.

In failure to hire cases, therefore, the only other option is to look for the similarly situated comparators who were hired but less qualified (if we have access to that information, say, through a friend who applied or worked at the company). Meaning, if a more qualified minority group member is passed over for a less qualified majority group member (or the reverse), then there is likely a case that can be brought. But getting that proof is not always possible at the outset of taking a case so it is a risk to take a case and hope to find that information in discovery, but these cases will sometimes be taken. Bear in mind, lawyers who do what I do take cases on contingency so we have to choose our cases carefully—the less evidence up front, the less likely even a valid case will be brought.

The dominant group (i.e. White males) is no less protected than the other groups, even if lawyers are less eager to take on such cases. There cannot be any advantage to *any* of the above groups in the job application process. Whether your action rights previous wrongs or is advantageous to vulnerable populations, even if the actions can be immensely helpful toward eradicating future bias or bringing more diversity to an organization that desperately needs it, it's not legal.

Although these words are not written in the document, it is implied that you can legally test people on whatever you want, related or unrelated to the job, as long as the test doesn't have different results for protected versus non-protected groups. For example, you can theoretically ask all your candidates to an ear-wiggling challenge, which will not differentiate any single group from the other and then use the outcomes of that test to hire people, even though it doesn't predict or relate to job performance, according to the law. We don't recommend it, because it's just plain useless.

So how did so many large corporations get away with asking ridiculous, completely non-job-related questions for such a long time? Many of these questions did not appear to have a direct negative impact against certain groups. The law is violated only with an assessment that gives an advantage or disadvantage to a group named in any of the US acts against discrimination. If there is no difference in how a woman, Hispanic, or White man answers a question like "How much should you charge to wash all the windows in Seattle?," then it's harder to win a suit against a large corporation for not getting a job as a result of badly answering that question. They would have needed to track applicant data proactively and it's their burden of proof to show that their questions don't cause a different experience by personal characteristics. These numbers are usually calculated by I-O psychologists and rarely shared across the organization. There are specific requirements for conducting these calculations to make them valid. By the way, many corporations' hiring practices have significantly evolved, and they have ceased to ask such questions.

If your test is easier or harder for some groups to pass than others, you can legally use it, if you prove that it predicts job performance. For example, a test of lifting heavy things for firefighters is generally acceptable. However, ethically, we recommend putting forth every effort possible to find assessments that have no differences by group. In that example, you want to make sure you know the minimum amount someone needs to lift to do the job, and avoid testing them on *more* than that amount.[14,15]

The Complexity With Adverse Impact

The firefighter example is pretty obvious, which is why it makes a great example. In reality, it's not easy to determine whether you caused a negative impact on a certain group's ability to get hired (we call this adverse or disparate impact). If you hire a salesperson for your team, and you want the person to be clean-shaven to make a "certain" impression on customers, is this discriminatory? Are you ready to prove in a court of law that customers are more likely to buy from a clean-shaven person? What if people of color or with certain religious affiliations are less likely to shave their beards? Be cautious in your assumptions.

Paige advises that:

> ... any characteristic that can arguably be linked to a gender, race, age, or person with a disability is a minefield for employers to use as hiring criteria. The key is having clear KSAs based on a quality job analysis, and deriving the hiring characteristics directly from that—and not from anything else. It is also risky for another reason. Say that there is a clean-shaven Caucasian hired over a non-clean-shaven African American. Even if the choice was truly race-free, there can be an appearance or perception of discrimination by those groups such as African Americans and other minority groups (including women) who have suffered such long-standing and overt discrimination. With lawsuits in the United States, sometimes *perception* matters more than facts; one can never truly know the discriminatory bias, or lack thereof, in the heart of the hiring manager. Yet, if a protected class member *perceives* discrimination, there is a sufficient storyline to make it seem plausible, then a costly lawsuit can arise.

Summary: You can't make up any type of assessment that you happen to think is important, and say "This is a job requirement," when it has a negative impact on a certain group.

The Uniform Guidelines describe standards for ensuring fair and non-discriminatory practices in employee selection procedures. The specific recommendations that we provide below are based on the Uniform Guidelines.[16] The guidelines were created as a way to advise US employers on how they could better comply with the US employment laws through their interviewing and assessment policies. The guidelines outline specific ways of proving that whatever you're asking of your candidates is related to the job. Much of this content was written by I-O psychologists. Although it was originally drafted before widespread use of the internet or AI, we still refer to this guide in our everyday work, as do employment lawyers.

Evaluate Risk and Safety-Proof Your Job Profile

Figure 24.1 outlines various hiring strategies and their impact on the diversity of hires. Drawing on our extensive experience with hiring processes across numerous organizations, we've identified key trends summarized in this visual. It serves as a guide to evaluate whether your approach to building diversity on your team may pose potential risks. While the chart highlights a spectrum of hiring practices and their associated risks of discrimination, it is not exhaustive and should be used as a starting point for reflection and refinement of your hiring processes.

FIGURE 24.1 Spectrum of Hiring Practices: Balancing Fairness, Legality, and Job-Related Rigor

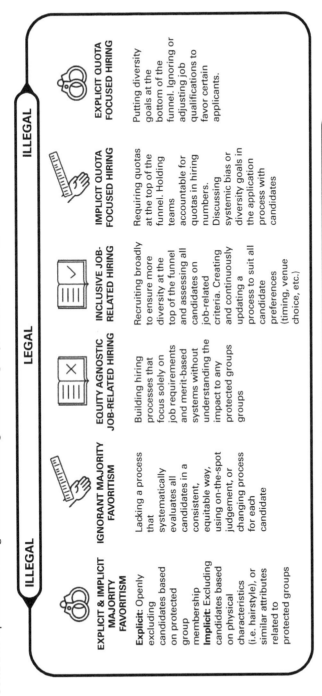

<table>
<tr><th colspan="2">ILLEGAL</th><th colspan="2">LEGAL</th><th colspan="2">ILLEGAL</th></tr>
<tr><th>EXPLICIT & IMPLICIT MAJORITY FAVORITISM</th><th>IGNORANT MAJORITY FAVORITISM</th><th>EQUITY AGNOSTIC JOB-RELATED HIRING</th><th>INCLUSIVE JOB-RELATED HIRING</th><th>IMPLICT QUOTA FOCUSED HIRING</th><th>EXPLICIT QUOTA FOCUSED HIRING</th></tr>
<tr>
<td>**Explicit:** Openly excluding candidates based on protected group membership
Implicit: Excluding candidates based on physical characteristics (i.e. hairstyle), or similar attributes related to protected groups</td>
<td>Lacking a process that systematically evaluates all candidates in a consistent, equitable way, using on-the-spot judgement, or changing process for each candidate</td>
<td>Building hiring processes that focus solely on job requirements and merit-based systems without understanding the impact to any protected groups groups</td>
<td>Recruiting broadly to ensure more diversity at the top of the funnel and assessing all candidates on job-related criteria. Creating and continuously updating a process to suit all candidate preferences (timing, venue choice, etc.)</td>
<td>Requiring quotas at the top of the funnel. Holding teams accountable for quotas in hiring numbers. Discussing systemic bias or diversity goals in the application process with candidates</td>
<td>Putting diversity goals at the bottom of the funnel. Ignoring or adjusting job qualifications to favor certain applicants.</td>
</tr>
</table>

MINORITY DISCRIMINATION   MAJORITY DISCRIMINATION

The spectrum of hiring practices ranges from overtly discriminatory to inclusively equitable, with significant legal and ethical implications at each stage. Understanding these approaches will help you to design fair, effective hiring systems while avoiding the pitfalls of systemic bias or unlawful practices. By breaking down these practices, the framework emphasizes the balance between equity, legality, and maintaining job-related rigor in hiring processes. We advocate for thoughtful, inclusive practices that expand opportunities without compromising fairness or process integrity.

At the far left of the spectrum lies more traditional **explicit and implicit majority favoritism**. With **explicit majority favoritism**, organizations or hiring managers intentionally exclude candidates based on their membership in a protected group. This could include racial, gender, age, disability, or other forms of discrimination. Examples include the study finding that certain retail organizations still systematically and intentionally ignored applications from people of color.[17] This is unequivocally illegal and represents the most blatant form of discrimination. **Implicit majority favoritism** involves indirect exclusion based on characteristics tied to protected groups, like rejecting candidates for wearing hairstyles associated with certain cultures or disqualifying individuals with accents. Though subtler than explicit favoritism, these practices are often discriminatory and can lead to legal challenges.

Further along is **ignorant majority favoritism**, which results from the absence of a structured and consistent hiring process. Without clear guidelines, hiring decisions are left to personal judgment, increasing the risk of unconscious bias and inconsistent criteria. While not always illegal, such processes fail to guarantee job-related decisions and risk unintentional discrimination.

Next is **equity agnostic job-related hiring**, which prioritizes job qualifications without acknowledging systemic biases that may disadvantage underrepresented groups. For instance, requiring multiple technical screens for a role might unintentionally exclude highly capable candidates who excel in softer skills. While this approach is generally legal, it can perpetuate inequities by ignoring broader contextual factors.

Inclusive job-related hiring is exactly this—using a job-related process to assess candidates and ensuring that the process minimizes risk of excluding certain candidates. This approach addresses these limitations by creating equitable, job-focused processes designed to reduce barriers for underrepresented groups. This might include offering flexible interview timing, recruiting from institutions with diverse talent pools, or building evaluation criteria upfront to assess skills that minority candidates may bring. This approach ensures fairness while expanding opportunities for a broader range of candidates. If your target population includes neurodivergent applicants, focusing on traits like friendliness during collaboration assessments may inadvertently exclude qualified candidates. Instead, prioritize evaluating the quality of their ideas and how they align with the KSAs critical for the role. For underserved college undergraduates, consider recruiting through campus organizations or clubs that support these populations. Additionally, monitor how different groups perform during the interview process. Use these insights to refine and improve your hiring practices, ensuring they remain equitable and inclusive. The overarching goal is to build a hiring process that not only adheres to job-related criteria but also reduces systemic barriers, resulting in a diverse and qualified slate of candidates.

At the riskier end of the spectrum, **implicit quota-focused hiring** introduces diversity quotas, particularly at the early stages of recruitment. While this can help diversify the candidate pool, it risks shifting focus away from job-related criteria. Similarly, **explicit quota-focused hiring** prioritizes diversity goals at the final decision stage. Adjusting qualifications or favoring certain groups over others risks legal challenges if decisions are made based on non-job-related factors. For instance, consider a situation where two candidates meet the basic qualifications for a job. One is from a majority group and the other is from a minority group. Hiring based on the minority status alone could be problematic. However, no two candidates are entirely equal; one might have more relevant experience or expertise. The decision should always tie back to the job profile, focusing on which candidate aligns better with the role's requirements. Pressure to meet quotas can lead leaders to prioritize non-job-related factors, increasing legal risks.

This framework underscores the importance of balancing legal compliance, inclusivity, and job-related rigor in hiring practices. Organizations should strive to create processes that are both fair and effective, ensuring that hiring decisions are driven by merit while actively reducing barriers for underrepresented groups.

In the United States, if your employment law team approaches you with a challenge to a selection process or a selection decision, they will need you to demonstrate to the US Equal Employment Opportunity Commission that your selection method was job-related.[18] Per Paige, common claims of the past revolved around whether or not a candidate was offered a job, a promotion, or entrance to a training that could lead to a promotion. Today, claims may be less about an offer/no offer decision and more related to which level you assigned to a candidate, resulting in drastic pay differences on the job, per the pay equity and engineer example. Post-hire, an employee may suddenly realize that they were leveled lower than equally qualified candidates based on the assessment process, and therefore given reduced pay and career advancement. In other cases, a candidate may feel that the level they were offered was unfair before they were even hired. We've seen hiring committees use the "lower-level offer" as a way to avoid rejecting a candidate outright, knowing that they would not accept a job at the lower level. If you are hiring for a role that has complexity in leveling, and it's challenging to clearly define differences in interview performance by level, then we don't advise creating the assessment process on your own.

You may be wondering how much of a risk you actually take when building and implementing your hiring process. We can't answer that without talking with you directly. But we have found, in our experience, that our clients who follow these guidelines reduce the risk in a number of ways. First, they are less likely to cause alarm or suspicion to candidates, because generally, candidates appreciate a process that feels structured and job-related. That means they will be less likely to even bring forth a claim. Second, their decision criteria should have been based on evidence and job-related data, not personal data about the candidate. If they can prove this, then a claim is not likely to go far.

In fact, Paige explains:

> ... in lawsuits, we must allege that the person could or did adequately perform the *job* to properly plead many cases of discrimination under all of the federal anti-discrimination laws, including the Civil Rights Act, the ADA, and the Age Discrimination in Employment Act (as well as under all state analog laws which track, and in some states even expand, what is covered for anti-discrimination federally). Unfortunately, most companies we see do *not* conduct proper job analysis—even informally—to be able to understand the status of (and legally defend) an adverse job action (non-hiring, firing, failure to promote, etc.) based on a personal characteristic, like the firefighter strength example related to a protected class of gender.

In short, there are very few human and personal characteristics legitimately linked to the protected classes, which could be found to be defensible means to not hire (or to fire) someone using the *necessary job function* defense. If you do spend the time to properly analyze and understand the KSAs for a job, it is wholly defensible to not hire/promote a person who does not have the ability to do a *necessary job function*.

Proving Job Relatedness

There are two ways to prove job relatedness. The first test of job relatedness is something that usually feels intuitive to people. We often are asked, "How do we know that candidates who do well on our tests are also doing well on the job?" One of our clients leveraged a comprehensive culture interview on four broad cultural factors. Intuitively, they could tell that they hired more people who exhibited collaboration, enthusiasm for new and different ways of working, as well as a zest for community building. But how can we actually prove that we found these traits and differentiated them among candidates in our interviews?

In work that Paige has done in this area, she finds:

> ... the key is a good job analysis to determine the KSAs (which are also often called the *necessary job functions*, in legal terms) and then ensure the interview guide taps into these traits and has good behaviorally anchored rating scales. That takes much of the bias out of the process. But at minimum, as a lawyer, it is very hard to prove bias if these are in place. In fact, it is nearly impossible to do so, and lawyers like me may not be willing to take on a case litigating a case against an employer (which is time consuming and costly to the plaintiff's lawyer) for an employee where the company did everything right and had the correct procedures (such as objective hiring methods).

The job profile you build is the first point of evidence of the validity of the assessment. This means that the content of the assessment you use matches the job content. If we create a coding challenge to hire a software engineer, the code in the test should look like the code on the job. If you are using the assessment for many hundreds of candidates, it's not always enough to have a job profile in case you get challenged. You'll want to ensure you collected evidence that experts agree that these are in fact critical components of job performance. The Uniform Guidelines advise that you get some sort of evidence from about 10 percent of the people on the job. In order to validate a knowledge test, you need that number of experts to agree on the content of the assessment. In the tech companies we consulted with, invariably, engineers just dive right into writing test questions. But as we talked about initially, that is not the first step, it's the second-to-last step. For a sizable role (more than 20 employees with the same or similar job), make sure you hand evidence to HR or your employment law team in the form of a document that shows the following points:

1 Company name, address, and HR person responsible for this role-hiring process.

2 Who contributed to the job profile (names, job titles, tenure in years, and brief description of their expertise), including recruiters.

3 The job profile.

4 The assessments or interviews.

Make sure that both HR and the employment law team save a copy of the document. Ideally, it is never needed.

Candidate Feedback in the United States

Many employment law and HR teams request that managers do not give any feedback to candidates after the interview beyond the status of their future employment. This applies especially those who will not move forward in the process. The intention is to avoid triggering candidates to question the employment decision or argue with the decision. Why is that? There are a couple of reasons. Practically speaking, it's really time consuming. Recruiters hiring in high-volume roles don't have the bandwidth to explain a decision to each candidate. But separately, there is a real risk of providing feedback in a way that makes a candidate question the validity of the whole process. Even if an employment case is hard to win, the time and effort of responding to an inquiry is exhaustive. Therefore, it is often safer to give too little information versus too much.

Paige advises that:

> ... as stated above, with employment discrimination claims, since one can never know for sure if there was discriminatory animus in the heart and mind of the hiring manager, it is often about perception. Any additional information you provide a candidate, whether minority or majority class, can trigger a *belief* that a person was discriminated against. It is not advisable to give any information because getting a job or not getting a job can be very emotional, and human perception tends to be flawed. A candidate could take any reason given and in their mind, consider this discriminatory. Then, as an employment lawyer, if we can link that reason to any protected class, then we have "evidence" that there was a comment or statement made which was (or was perceived to be)

discriminatory. We, the lawyers, then have to weed through the information provided knowing that we're only hearing it from the employee side. If a reason is given such as "you did not interview as well as other candidates" and the candidate, for example, had a stroke and spoke with a slur (even if otherwise qualified), we're off to the races on a disability claim since this comment would seem directly related to the disability, even if the hiring manager had no knowledge of the disability or stroke event, or if the manager knew about it but truly did not consider these characteristics in making the statement that the person did not "interview as well as other candidates."

With executives, however, it's a little different. We've often provided detailed feedback to executive candidates after a thorough selection process, even when they didn't get the job. The same principles apply as above. In that situation, we may be looking at just two or three candidates. Also, to put it plainly, executive candidates don't launch lawsuits for not being hired very often. On the other hand, the reputational risk for the company is greater with a candidate at a higher level. It's not unheard of for a leader to go through a selection process with a company, be rejected, to come back a couple of years later and get that job or a different job. This is less common for non-managers.

In California, however, privacy laws dictate that a candidate has the right to review any data you collect about them.[19] That means that a candidate may request feedback on any data that was collected during the interview. If you interview candidates in California, ensure that you feel comfortable presenting any evidence and notes that you collected on that candidate back to the candidate. That's one of the main reasons we are often concerned when we see weird notes in a company applicant tracking system (ATS) making inappropriate or personal comments about candidates.

In Europe, many companies have taken proactive measures to give feedback.[20] Since California privacy laws are newer, as of 2024, most companies do not have a process for this. We've known of situations where candidates have directly requested feedback in writing, and still heard nothing back. Most of the time they simply give up or go to a lawyer to receive the feedback as part of a claim. That doesn't mean that the risk is lower. It means that California companies are finding it difficult to track and submit their data in an acceptable format. This could change at any time, and we recommend being ready for that change when it happens. Once the privacy regulations in California become fully buttoned up with regard to marketing and credit reporting, employers may be fast follows.

A Few More Thoughts About Best Practices

To boil it down in plain language, the US laws state two important things: Your selection process and assessment must be job-related, and if there is any negative impact to one of the protected groups, including those added to certain states like California, then you must prove that the assessment is job-related.[21,22] Although all the regions we cover in this book have laws preventing discrimination, the United States sees far more lawsuits than any other nation. That means making an error in your hiring process can be more expensive in the United States. As we wrote in Part 1, the cost of a claim or settlement can include more than just the claim amount for wronged employees. If it's not clearly job related, then don't ask the question.

Notes

1   Kennedy, J. F. (1961) Executive Order 10925, Federal Register, 26(50), pp. 1977–78, www.eeoc.gov/special-report/african-americans-american-workforce (archived at https://perma.cc/6X7K-ELFQ)

2   Civil Rights Act of 1964, Pub. L. 88-352, 78 Stat. 241 (1964), www.govinfo. gov/app/details/STATUTE-78/STATUTE-78-Pg241 (archived at https://perma.cc/ BRZ3-84DE)

3   Miller, C. C. and Katz, J. (2024) Berkeley economists among a group of researchers that found bias against Black job applicants, *The New York Times*, April 9, https://ls.berkeley.edu/news/berkeley-economists-among-group-researchers-found-bias-against-black-job-applicants (archived at https://perma. cc/F99K-7BBD)

4   Burton, L. S. and Howe, L. (2022) Massachusetts CROWN Act goes into effect on October 24, 2022. Ogletree Deakins, https://ogletree.com/insights-resources/ blog-posts/massachusetts-crown-act-goes-into-effect-on-october-24-2022/ (archived at https://perma.cc/ZH26-83JC)

5   Rosseau, S. and Webster, F. (2019) US: California employers can't discriminate based on hair, Mercer, July 11, www.mercer.com/insights/law-and-policy/us-california-employers-cant-discriminate-based-on-hair/ (archived at https:// perma.cc/GN45-2MQG)

6 California State Legislature (2019) SB 188: Create a Respectful and Open Workplace for Natural Hair (CROWN) Act, https://leginfo.legislature.ca.gov/faces/billNavClient.xhtml?bill_id=201920200SB188 (archived at https://perma.cc/CG7G-VDZA)

7 Petri, A. (2023) Starbucks manager says she was fired because she is white, jury agrees, *Los Angeles Times*, June 14, www.latimes.com/world-nation/story/2023-06-14/starbucks-manager-says-fired-because-white-jury-agreed (archived at https://perma.cc/QJ9Q-BMLD)

8 Zahn, M. (2023) Starbucks discrimination lawsuit awarded white employee $25 million, ABC News, June 16, https://abcnews.go.com/Business/starbucks-discrimination-lawsuit-awarded-white-employee-25-million/story?id=100104620 (archived at https://perma.cc/K6UW-GFEX)

9 Wiener-Bronner, D. and Sgueglia, K. (2023) Starbucks manager claims she was fired for promoting racial diversity, CNN Business, June 14

10 U.S. Equal Employment Opportunity Commission (n.d.) CM-625 Bona Fide Occupational Qualifications, www.eeoc.gov/laws/guidance/cm-625-bona-fide-occupational-qualifications (archived at https://perma.cc/LNP6-DUVB)

11 Hollar, D. E. (2000) Physical ability tests and Title VII, *The University of Chicago Law Review*, 67(3), pp. 777–803, https://doi.org/10.2307/1600340 (archived at https://perma.cc/8ZT2-FFE5)

12 Vanterpool, L. (2024) Where are all the female engineers? Let's hear what one has to say, The Sterling Choice, www.thesterlingchoice.com/blog/where-are-all-the-female-engineers-lets-hear-what-one-has-to-say/#:~:text=Research%20has%20shown%20that%20women,lack%20of%20mentorship%20and%20sponsorship (archived at https://perma.cc/K9FR-2W69)

13 de la Merced, M. J. (2023) Goldman Sachs to pay $215 million to settle gender bias suit, *The New York Times*, May 9, www.nytimes.com/2023/05/09/business/dealbook/goldman-sachs-discrimination-lawsuit.html (archived at https://perma.cc/5A8U-3YEE)

14 Courtright, S. H. et al (2013) A meta-analysis of sex differences in physical ability: Revised estimates and strategies for reducing differences in selection contexts, *The Journal of Applied Psychology*, 98(4), pp. 623–41, https://doi.org/10.1037/a0033144 (archived at https://perma.cc/92KG-4LWF)

15 US Equal Employment Opportunity Commission, Department of Labor, Department of Justice, Civil Service Commission (1978) Uniform Guidelines on Employee Selection Procedures. Federal Register, 43(165), pp. 38295–312

16 Ibid

17 Miller, C. C. and Katz, J. (2024) Berkeley economists among a group of researchers that found bias against Black job applicants, *The New York Times*, April 9, https://ls.berkeley.edu/news/berkeley-economists-among-group-researchers-found-bias-against-black-job-applicants (archived at https://perma.cc/97WC-XPY3)

18 Civil Rights Act of 1964, Pub. L. 88-352, 78 Stat. 241 (1964), www.govinfo.gov/app/details/STATUTE-78/STATUTE-78-Pg241 (archived at https://perma.cc/967K-2GZH)

19 California Office of the Attorney General (2024) California Consumer Privacy Act (CCPA), https://oag.ca.gov/privacy/ccpa (archived at https://perma.cc/DJ7E-9PLQ)

20 GDPR.eu (2024) Issues on Personal Data, https://gdpr-info.eu/issues/personal-data/ (archived at https://perma.cc/V3ED-HTHG)

21 US Equal Employment Opportunity Commission (2024) Title VII of the Civil Rights Act of 1964, www.eeoc.gov/statutes/title-vii-civil-rights-act-1964 (archived at https://perma.cc/NSV6-DLZZ)

22 US Equal Employment Opportunity Commission (2024) Employment Tests and Selection Procedures, www.eeoc.gov/laws/guidance/employment-tests-and-selection-procedures#:~:text=Title%20VII%20prohibits%20employment%20discrimination,or%20national%20origin.%E2%80%9D%2042%20U.S.C (archived at https://perma.cc/DKT3-3CZN)

25

Privacy and Employment Best Practices: Europe and the UK

To explore how Europe generally handles laws involving employees, we met with an experienced psychologist with expertise advising clients on large assessment programs, James Bywater. James is Senior Client Partner at Korn Ferry, a global organizational consulting firm focused on the design of optimal organization structures, roles, and responsibilities. With close to 30 years of experience, he is also a Fellow of the British Psychological Society.

Similar to the United States, although to a much greater extreme, laws in Europe may differ significantly depending on your location. Therefore, you must seek the counsel of an experienced employment lawyer and/or privacy lawyer in your local country. However, we provide a brief overview of one of the significant laws impacting European employees.

General Data Protection Regulation (GDPR)

The legislation that undoubtedly impacts hiring in Europe is the personal data law GDPR, a law applied differently in each European country but containing some common tenets.[1] As James explained, the spirit of GDPR remains highly consistent, and he also notes that the costs of getting this wrong have become severe, especially for large companies. An example of this is the case of the European Parliament where applicants' passport information, addresses, and other similar information had been leaked.[2]

In terms of defining "data," James explains that personal data is "… any information which is related to an identified or identifiable natural person." Interview notes and interview summaries count as personal data. Anytime that you, representing the employer, hold such personal data, the data collection and storage must comply with broad data protection principles; it should be kept for a reasonable purpose, it should be securely stored, and be accurate/up to date. These are derived from the Seven Principles of GDPR: Lawfulness, fairness, and transparency; Purpose limitation; Data minimization; Accuracy; Storage limitation; Integrity and confidentiality; and Accountability. Companies should have a policy on how long data is kept and have an appointed officer in charge of compliance.

Purpose

For those of us conducting interviews, interview notes are clearly an appropriate use, but it's critical to only use those interview notes for the purpose for which they were originally intended (making employment decisions). Furthermore, James noted that we should state (on the interview form) the purpose of the interview and why the data was collected.

Accurate and Up to Date

Data security may not always be clear cut. Ideally, the data should be deleted when it's no longer needed. If you have a requisition that took three months to fill, then it would be reasonable to hold on to the data for three months. If it took a week, then it's more reasonable to hold on to the data for less than a month. Generally, James has found that most clients keep the data for a minimum of six months. He noted that the UK tends to keep data longer, while the Netherlands and Scandinavian countries may keep data for less time. In some cases, companies may hold data for up to seven years, such as if the job continues to be open for a longer time or is under a lot of scrutiny by Regulators (e.g. Financial Services). Again, each company should consult with a legal expert for guidance on their specific requirements.

Secure

Whatever amount of time you hold on to the data, it should be kept in a secure and encrypted location with passwords (or physical notes are kept in a locked file).

Candidate Feedback

One of the GDPR requirements involves meaningful feedback. For anyone accustomed to hiring in the United States, this may sound surprising, since US employment lawyers often advise against giving substantive or performance-related feedback following an assessment or interview process. Why? Because the feedback could go badly, and thus could potentially cause a candidate to question the process and initiate a claim. In essence, the avoidance of sharing this valuable information has more to do with potential individual error versus the principle of providing feedback. Meaningful feedback on data held about them should be given on request to the data subject within a reasonable period of time. This covers test scores, interview scores, credit scores, or similar information. This also forces employment lawyers and HR to provide clearer guidelines to their hiring managers and recruiters. In EMEA (and in California as well), candidates have a right to do subject access requests and examine the data the company collects on them.[3]

In EMEA (and in California as well), candidates have a right to do subject access requests and examine any data the company collects. If the data is not "meaningful," such as scores on an interview without the accompanying rating scale or skills lists, they have the right to understand what that data means.

James has found that many organizations proactively offer feedback in a systemic fashion. Others may be more guarded and only respond after being contacted. Often, for particularly high-volume roles (i.e. post-graduate professional roles), in which a large group are competing for a small number of roles, companies usually offer a "do no harm report." These reports may list out the areas required for the role, and a couple of paragraphs of narrative summary of how the candidate performed.

We are personally not against providing very careful, curated feedback to all candidates, provided that your interview is based on an excellent job analysis and your selection criteria are fair to all candidates. In our experience, candidates are grateful for feedback, and well-delivered feedback can improve the candidate experience and build loyalty to your company.

When you provide feedback, use only narrative/verbal feedback, and avoid giving them scores.[4] Here is a quick example of feedback that may be helpful to a candidate:

Dear Candidate,

I hope this message finds you well. I wanted to take a moment to express our gratitude for your time and participation in the interview process for the [Job Title] position at [Company Name].

Your interview showcased several remarkable strengths, particularly in the area of influence and negotiation. Your ability to navigate [mention a specific situation or example where influence and negotiation skills were demonstrated during the interview, e.g. convincing stakeholders or handling a hypothetical negotiation scenario] was impressive and aligned exceptionally well with the requirements of the role.

Furthermore, your proficiency in [mention any other notable skills observed during the interview, e.g. communication, strategic thinking, or problem-solving abilities] also stood out prominently. Your experiences and insights demonstrated a solid foundation that resonates deeply with our company's values and objectives.

While your performance in influence and negotiation, as well as other skills, was commendable, we ended up selecting a candidate who had particularly strong experience with managing difficult global collaborations.

We appreciate your interest in joining our team and value the effort you invested in the interview process, and we wish you success in your future endeavors.

Thank you once again for your interest in [Company Name]. Should you have any questions or require further feedback, please don't hesitate to reach out.

Another form of candidate feedback may happen during the interview. You may find it helpful to provide some verbal feedback based on the examples that the candidate provides in answer to your questions. For example, if the candidate did not provide an example that helped illustrate their skills in a particular area you're interested in, you may let them know that the job specifically requires this, so you can ask how they might plan to improve in this area should they be hired. This approach provides some important feedback to the candidate on their development opportunities but also gives them a chance to propose how they could fix it.

Ultimately, your HR team (with guidance from employment lawyers) will guide the feedback process.

Final Thoughts for EMEA

We found that James's advice generally followed the same principles we would recommend for anyone making hiring decisions... anywhere. He closed our discussion with: "Analyze and consider the unique and important aspects of the role, ask your candidate relevant questions consistently, write your stuff down, keep it for a reasonable time, explain to candidates what's happening, and then delete it at an appropriate point."

In addition, like with the United States, check on changes to GDPR as they may relate to the use of automation and AI in assessments.

Notes

1 GDPR.eu (2024) Issues on Personal Data, https://gdpr-info.eu/issues/personal-data/ (archived at https://perma.cc/WFC8-L6GK)

2 Armangau, R. (2024) European Parliament under scrutiny after data breach complaints, Euronews, www.euronews.com/next/2024/08/22/european-parliament-under-scrutiny-after-data-breach-complaints (archived at https://perma.cc/WUQ9-R96M)

3 Information Commissioner's Office (2024) A guide to the data protection principles, https://ico.org.uk/for-organisations/uk-gdpr-guidance-and-resources/data-protection-principles/a-guide-to-the-data-protection-principles/ (archived at https://perma.cc/8SJ2-L4NW)

4 McCrary-Ruiz-Esparza, E. (2024) Why employers are stingy with job interview feedback BBC, www.bbc.com/worklife/article/20240123-why-employers-are-stingy-with-job-interview-feedback (archived at https://perma.cc/P49A-LAVF)

26

Privacy and Employment Best Practices: India and China

India

To learn about another important and massive global business region, we met with Ankur Tailang, VP and Global Head of Talent Acquisition for RateGain, to discuss employment law in India.

Ankur has extensive experience leading talent acquisition teams in global companies such as Airbnb and Amazon. A series of employment laws have been in place for over 50 years, and they address issues ranging from:

1 Equality and lack of discrimination on grounds of religion, race, caste, sex, disability status, or place of birth
2 Equality of opportunity in matters of public employment
3 Equal pay
4 Transparency in hiring
5 Affirmative action for underrepresented groups

As with EMEA and the US, the laws listed above are general across India. Laws may be expanded or differ in each state, so ensure that you check with a legal representative knowledgeable about your particular region.

Accountability for complying with these laws in India can be complex. Because of the lack of a singular governing body taking responsibility for enforcement of discrimination rights and the variation in how the laws are set from one state to the next, it's not always simple to know where to go with a complaint. In an example provided by a law firm posting guidance on the topic, the POSH Act stipulates that an employee can go to either an internal committee or the jurisdictional court. If these claims are successful, then a claim could be settled by employers, but an alternate dispute resolution mechanism could also be leveraged to avoid government involvement. Typically, an employer will offer compensation and reinstatement to the role should the claim be successful. Under the POSH Act, the successful claimant may be provided compensation, which can become expensive for employers. In some cases, the government can levy statutes, sanctions, and penalties, doing further harm to the overall business.[1,2]

China

Like many other parts of the world, the Chinese government provides a set of guidelines on employment and hiring that address safety, pay, equity, and discrimination. Similar to India, our experts in China informed us that the legal system is rarely used to enforce those laws. We met with Louis Yang, an experienced HR consultant who worked in local and global firms advising his clients on employment best practices.

He explained that the law clearly states that discrimination against anyone based on age, gender, or socioeconomic status is illegal. As a summary, Chinese labor laws revolve around working hours, wages, and health and safety.[3]

Companies are required to provide employment contracts that include a job description, work location, and salary. The laws do not allow discrimination based on ethnicity, race, gender, religious belief, disability, or pregnancy status. China's Personal Information Protection Law requires any use of data to have a clear purpose, minimize harm to individuals, and avoid unfair automated decisions (for example, discriminatory pricing). The law also holds large online platforms accountable to implement data protection systems, release regular reports, and undergo public oversight.[4,5,6]

What are some violations typically taking place in China, and things to ensure you avoid doing when hiring in the region? Louis provided examples of companies indicating that a certain position is restricted to certain levels of education, but without an accompanying performance standard or reasons for the needed degree. In other cases, companies refuse to hire anyone older than 35 years old. Why only 35, we asked Louis? Since the retirement age was only 60 for men, and going up to 63, employers worry about not getting enough employment time for older workers. Even more, employers worry that workers older than 35 have families to care for, which could cut into their work time. A phenomenon known as "996" emerged in the world of Chinese tech industry employment, in which companies would demand workers work from 9 am to 9 pm, six days per week. Not allowed per employment regulations, the expectation had become unspoken. Employees who don't have responsibility to care for others are more likely to comply with the unspoken mandate. Louis explained that the companies are willing to compensate well for such work, but such demands are not legal.

The Ministry of Human Resources and Social Security (MOHRSS) does not necessarily hold individual companies accountable to lack of discrimination in each instance of a violation, however. Instead, employees who have experienced behavior in violation of these laws may post their experiences on social media platforms (such as WeChat or Weibo), and should enough others find the post and follow, the government may follow up to investigate a substantiated or persistent issue.[7]

Louis explained the difficulty in tracking and enforcing such decisions, since the companies would not often post such decisions publicly. Therefore, reliance on individual whistle-blowers to post complaints becomes more critical for fair employment. On the other hand, repercussions for violations can be detrimental to companies. In one particular case, involving a company called Baidu, a VP made inappropriate comments to employees. She was subsequently fired for negatively representing the organization.[8]

Louis provided some tips for those who plan to hire in China.

Positive Candidate Experience

During all communications in the recruitment process, he recommends being alert, respectful, and showing empathy for candidates. This includes ensuring they are given attention and time during interviews, and the company is represented positively. Louis mentioned that he's heard of situations where a manager fell asleep during the interview with a candidate! The hiring team should be trained for structured interviewing. Providing feedback at the end of the process is also important, even when a candidate is not offered a role. At minimum, Louis recommends sending a thank you letter to every candidate at the conclusion of the interview.

Know the Relevant Laws

Obtaining a labor relations qualification certificate, occupational assessment skills certificates, and any ability and personality testing and behavioral interviewing skills are helpful in gaining knowledge of the laws. There are trainings available for non-HR people as well. He recommends avoiding asking questions that are clearly illegal, such as whether a woman plans to have children in the next two years. Just like other regions, the idea is to use good tools and methodologies to hire people without evaluation of personal characteristics.

Protect Information Security

In the recruiting process, collect only the necessary information, and in a legally compliant way (meaning, don't hire private investigators without consent or ask for references that were not provided by the candidate), and protect personal information. For example, some standard recruiting forms may include an emergency contact person, but do not need to include marital status. Informed consent is important for any candidate data collection, and ensures that the recruiting company explains the reasons for collecting this information.

Give Voice to Issues

All organizations should establish an effective complaint and feedback mechanism. This can be as simple as an employee suggestion box in a physical office space or website. Then, if or when complaints arise, investigate and deal with these in a timely manner. Ensure there is a formal review process in place. Gain consent from the complainant. After a regular interval of time, perform audits of the process to ensure the right information was gathered and actions were taken to retrain hiring managers.

Learning Circles

Louis also discussed that companies who established task forces or learning circles were less prone to violations. The groups meet on a regular basis, discuss and learn about recruiting best practices, accumulate case experience, and often use social media (i.e. WeChat) to advise one another and share experiences.

Build a Pool of Diverse Candidates

Louis recommended finding ways to build a diverse talent pool before a hiring need even emerges. For example, these could be sourced from previous inquiries or applicant tracking databases.

Notes

1 Human Rights Watch (1999) Broken people: Caste violence against India's "Untouchables," www.hrw.org/reports/1999/india/India994-15.htm (archived at https://perma.cc/R4KK-9DEF)

2 ICLG (2024) Employment and Labour Laws and Regulations: India, https://iclg.com/practice-areas/employment-and-labour-laws-and-regulations/india (archived at https://perma.cc/5EPB-97CL)

3 China Labour Bulletin (2023) Workers' rights and labour relations in China, https://clb.org.hk/en/content/workers%E2%80%99-rights-and-labour-relations-china (archived at https://perma.cc/CHJ8-HQ9Z)

4 Personal Information Protection Law of the People's Republic of China (2024) https://personalinformationprotectionlaw.com/ (archived at https://perma.cc/G6CN-L9TF)

5 Dai, K. (Jianmin) and Deng, J. (Zhisong) (2022) China Personal Information Protection Law (PIPL) FAQs, Bloomberg Law, https://pro.bloomberglaw.com/insights/privacy/china-personal-information-protection-law-pipl-faqs/ (archived at https://perma.cc/RQ3C-XSDY)

6 Yip, W. (2021) China steps in to regulate brutal "996" work culture, BBC News, www.bbc.com /news/world-asia-china-58381538 (archived at https://perma.cc/2DEE-N3UJ)

7 Yin Weimin (2024) Ministry of Human Resources and Social Security, *Global Times*, www.globaltimes.cn/db/government/14.shtml (archived at https://perma.cc/46FQ-2NPT)

8 Long, Z. (2024) Baidu VP resigns amid backlash over controversial remarks, SHINE News, www.shine.cn/biz/company/2405094737/ (archived at https://perma.cc/P8WH-P7WD)

27

Cheating, Leakage, and Lying

In the world of testing knowledge, cheating and item leakage pose a significant risk to the integrity of your process. Our philosophy is to find ways to make cheating useless to candidates.

What does that mean? In practice, it means that we want to create a way of testing for knowledge or skills that is so transparent that any amount of data someone might get about the questions in advance still won't help them unless they actually learn and practice the thing we want to test them on.

First, let's define *cheating* versus *leakage*. Cheating on an assessment is when someone copies the answers from another person, after being told that they are supposed to generate the answers independently. It is also cheating to have another person take an assessment in their place. Both of these situations have commonly occurred worldwide, and occur increasingly when the situation is highly competitive (meaning, there are few spots but lots of applicants, or the result of the assessment will bring tremendous professional value). Because these are ethics violations, we recommend that you build and document a no-tolerance policy around cheating. First, during any sort of knowledge test, state to the candidates that you expect them to generate their own response without AI, Google, other people, etc. Next, create a list for the interviewers and scorers of ways to determine if someone was at risk of cheating.

Consider the example coding challenges for software engineers. We encourage engineering interviewers to not just develop a challenge and its correct answer, but to also offer a few alternative paths of coding challenge offshoots. These test how well a candidate can adapt their approach to changes or new problems.

In one situation, Kasey was alerted to a pattern of suspicious interview behavior amongst candidates for a software engineering role. The interviewer was certain that the software engineer was pasting the question into a chatbot, copying the answer, and pasting this back into the coding app. The reason? The answers were coming too quickly. Whenever the interviewer asked a new question, the answers came so quickly, there was no chance that the candidate was writing all this code. Kasey asked: Had the candidates been told that chatbots were not allowed during the interview (no). Could we really call this cheating? (no). Instead, could we call it an unreliable measure of their skill? (yes). The company had not defined their policy, therefore it was challenging to fairly enforce it. They had to provide a retest opportunity, with proper guidance, and also with additional guidance to interviewers on how to detect cheating. One of the primary means to suspect cheating was unrealistically rapid generation of responses.

In the end, the candidate declined to return for a second interview. It's likely they were simply hired somewhere else with an interviewer who was less concerned about cheating.

How should you handle a situation where you suspect cheating? Should a candidate produce the answer too quickly, the interviewer will ask a series of "if this had been (different)..." type questions, related to the same problem. If the candidate shows that they can adapt their approach in the moment, their experience is more likely to be legitimate. If they quickly solve the core problem, but can't solve deviations, then it indicates either potential cheating (or having seen the question in advance), or that they don't fundamentally understand the construct behind the problem enough to solve the variations.

Leakage, on the other hand, is when the assessment or interview contents are made publicly available ("leaked"), making it easy for candidates to study. We don't like to accuse them of cheating as much as simply being resourceful or prepared in that situation, and the direct implication to ethical behavior is less. If you have a job with questions that are prone to leakage, the first option is to make the leakage less helpful. Trying to control the dissemination of information if you work for a popular firm is a losing battle. Realistically, for example, rather than stop all the hackers, we just try to avoid falling into their traps. Dealing with leakage is similar.

Let's say your interview questions ended up online. Perhaps you found them yourself, or someone else alerted you. If you then meet with a candidate who seems incredibly well prepared and you suspect they did research beforehand to improve their performance, does this mean that the candidate is not qualified? In the end, if they were successful in answering the question, perhaps they are still proving their knowledge.

Stretching and Lying

On the other hand, let's say that a candidate researched your job posting for a medical device representative, and wanted to present themselves as having sold similar devices. Using information online, the candidate fabricated examples of experiences that they didn't actually have. If the candidate does so, but does not have the experience, then they are lying.

Lying is an ethical violation, which most of us can agree on, and is grounds for termination and candidate rejection. When a candidate lies, they are trying to present themselves as having knowledge, experience, or capabilities that they don't have.

How is that different from the software engineer who found a leaked problem, learned how to solve it, and performed well on the coding interview? The candidate who used the leaked question actually practiced that skill and showed that they could use it. The sales rep who claimed to have sold a medical device similar to yours cannot really prove that they understand how to relate to physicians in an actual conversation about this device, or answer questions that could come up in a real setting. Similarly, a candidate for a project management role who claims successful outcomes on projects that were not successful is misrepresenting their experience and actual capabilities. We are not interested in knowing that they *could* gain these experiences; what's important is that they are entering a job contract with false information.

Sometimes candidates exaggerate or stretch the truth. How do you distinguish between these? Take a look at Table 27.1 for some examples of the spectrum between truth, stretches, and lies. The zones on the left side are acceptable in many jobs, but the zones on the right are not.

TABLE 27.1 Fact vs. Fiction: Detecting Candidate Misrepresentation

Total honesty		Stretching...		Lying
I don't like working with spreadsheets and I am terrible at it	I have experimented with and navigated through spreadsheets	I feel relatively comfortable opening, navigating, and building spreadsheets	I have a number of hours of experience creating spreadsheets for different purposes	I am an expert in spreadsheets and can build any functionality you need

(continued)

TABLE 27.1 (Continued)

Total honesty		Stretching...		Lying
I lost three customers in a month due to not responding quickly enough	I am always working to improve my response time to customers	I generally respond in a timely fashion to customers	I have a track record of responding to customers on time	I have never lost a customer due to lack of response
I have never been alone in a room with a senior leader	I don't often interact with senior leadership, but I do prepare information that will be forwarded to them	I commonly put together recommendations and slides to be shared with our senior leadership	I run many forecasting analyses for the senior leadership team	I am the person in charge of all information and analyses that we bring to senior leadership

All in all, the best cure for all of these ailments revolves around great probes. When it comes to behavioral interviews, we are less worried about "cheating." If someone has job experience, they will describe a detailed scenario during the "tell me about a time when…" questions. As we have previously discussed, it's difficult to lie with the needed amount of details. Eventually, with good probes, you'll figure out that someone is fabricating their experience. We certainly advise becoming proficient at probing to detect and avoid these situations.

28

Continuous Improvement

If Malcolm Gladwell is correct in stating that once you've practiced doing something for 10,000 hours, you become an expert, after a certain amount of job profiles built and/or interviews conducted, you will become an expert at job profiling and interviewing.[1,2] When you reach that milestone, allow us to give our sincerest congratulations! We are genuinely excited for you. The clock starts ticking from the time you implement structured job profiling and interviews into your process.

We estimate that we've exceeded 10,000 hours a few times over. Have we improved over time? Yes! Do we still make mistakes? Absolutely! It's an unfortunate truth about this line of work. We have observed even the most experienced assessors make mistakes. We are in favor of taking steps to get a second opinion or rethink any analysis, and we talk to one another often. I-O psychologists are a collaborative, chatty group of people who always seek to improve themselves. Some of the mistakes that we see over time even amongst the most advanced practitioners have been referenced throughout previous sections and are listed below. In the spirit of continuous improvement, we're going to overview some of these topics in greater detail below. In every "acceptable" mistake scenario, the interviewer was missing information they needed to make an accurate assessment of the candidate.

Ensuring You Gather Relevant Data

Keeping Interviews on Track

If you run out of time in an interview before covering all the areas you need, it likely points to one of these issues:

1 **Too many KSAs were included** for a single interview and should be divided across two interviews or given more time.

2 **The candidate spent time on irrelevant details,** requiring redirection.

3 **The candidate provided useful information but took too long,** focusing too much on one topic at the expense of others.

Handling Missing Information

If time runs out:

- If you decide to schedule a follow-up call, be prepared to adjust the process for all candidates to maintain fairness. While granting one candidate additional time introduces inconsistency, making decisions with incomplete data is riskier. However, offering follow-up interviews to every candidate can be impractical, especially for high-volume roles or when several candidates have already completed interviews without additional time. In such cases, we recommend avoiding this option and instead refining the interview process to prevent time management issues in the future.

- If follow-up isn't an option, score the candidate based on available data and note the gaps in your evaluation.

- As a last resort, assess the candidate with incomplete information and document the missing elements.

Avoiding Future Issues

If **too many KSAs** were included, to improve the structure of this interview in the future, evaluate whether the number of KSAs covered matches the allotted time. For a 45-minute interview, especially with less experienced interviewers, we recommend focusing on three to four KSAs. If the list of KSAs is too long, consider splitting them across two interviews to allow sufficient depth of discussion for each. Alternatively, revisit the job profile to ensure all included KSAs are truly essential for day-one success, refining the scope as needed.

If the **candidate dominates the interview** with off-topic or overly detailed responses, be proactive in managing the conversation. Politely interrupt and redirect as needed. For instance:

> "This is helpful, but I want to ensure we cover all the topics. Can you briefly summarize this point?"

> "Let's circle back to this later. For now, I'd like to focus on [specific topic]."

Taking Control of the Interview

Candidates often enjoy elaborating on their experiences but may lack brevity. If they go off-topic or provide overly complex answers, you may need to interrupt mid-sentence to keep the interview on track. Interruptions can be uncomfortable but are necessary to maintain focus and gather all required information.

> "Hey, I apologize for interrupting. The example you are giving me is interesting, but for the sake of time, we're going to need to move on to the next question. Do you want to take just a moment to complete your thought (or not!), and then I'll ask the next question?"

> "Excuse me, but I'm going to need to cut this question short. While the information is interesting, I am worried we won't get to the rest of the questions in the time we have. Are you comfortable if we move on?"

> "Thanks so much for this explanation. I have gotten the answer I needed for this topic. For the sake of ensuring we get to all the questions, we need to move on to the next question."

These phrases all convey an important message. For them to do well in the interview, and for you to fully understand their experience, you need a chance to lead and guide them through all the questions you need to ask. We also find it helpful to address them by name, which tends to get someone's attention more quickly.

Not Probing Deeply Enough

At the end of an interview, the candidate has left, and you are left with pages of notes and a scoring sheet. You look at "negotiation" with the intent to write out the evidence for your score. However, somehow, there just isn't enough information to make a good score on this topic, even though you asked the candidate a question about negotiation. Why? How? Often, the candidate gave a vague answer to your question. When you get a vague answer that doesn't allow you to fully understand what the candidate did, or how they did it, it's up to you to follow up with probes. We talked about standard probes in the previous section, but during an interview with a candidate who struggles to provide specifics, it feels like pulling teeth to keep asking over and over again for real, specific examples. Your mission in this situation is to ensure that the candidate's issue is not poor communication, but lack of experience. You won't know the difference until you keep asking them to provide more details. Here's an example:

Kasey: "Can you describe a time when you engaged in a tough negotiation? What was the topic, and the outcome?"

Candidate: "All my negotiations are tough, and I do them all the time."

Kasey: "Pick one from the last week."

Candidate: "It was a mediation session. My client insisted on certain conditions in this merger contract we were working on, but the buying company refused. So, we had to make a couple of concessions, and a few changes to the conditions, but I would say the client got 85 percent of what she needed from the deal."

The candidate is done, ready for the next question. In the next example, Kasey needs to guide the candidate through the scenario, piece by piece, as if putting together a play.

Kasey: "How did you present your clients' conditions to the company?"

Candidate: "I read them from the contract revision."

Kasey: "What was the response?"

Candidate: "Full refusal."

Kasey: "What happened next?"

Perhaps now the candidate sighs loudly, finally realizing that they do need to give a blow-by-blow account of what happened for this annoying interviewer. The interviewer doesn't mind being annoying, because they know it's the best way to give this candidate a full chance to showcase their best selves.

Candidate: "Yeah, so I said the deal's off without the conditions. But my client asked for a break, during which she said the deal can't be off. So I said to her, 'Pick which one of these three you absolutely need,' and she did. Then we went back in, and I still played the 'deal's off' card, but we both sat there, open to the opposing lawyer and listening. They figured we would be willing to talk, so they offered up two of the three conditions. They were the right ones, so we accepted."

This gives enough information about the candidate's approach to show that the candidate is willing to go all out for their client, but also knows how to bluff the other party, and understands when it's time to take the deal and move on based on client feedback. Ultimately, the candidate successfully showcased their negotiation skills, but only after significant probing.

We've realized with our own experience, in almost every case, it's our fault that we didn't collect enough data. Just like how auto insurance companies refer to "accidents" as "collisions," because defensive driving can almost always prevent an accident, as the interviewer, it always falls upon **you** to get all the information you need. It's up to you to guide them in answering all your questions.

What Can I Do to Increase Diversity?

If you, like us, would like to see more diversity at work, we recommend finding legally appropriate ways to impact individuals who may be at a disadvantage early in their careers. Mentor high school or college students in your field. Create or join an internship program in your own company and spend extra time understanding the unique challenges non-traditional employees have and will face and help them navigate and overcome these. These programs make a tremendous impact on individuals, who often "pay it forward" and draw more nontraditional workers along with them. It may not change overnight, but the landscape will look different in as few as 10 years if we all put forth effort. In our own field of I-O psychology, traditionally a White, male-dominated field, we have seen a two-fold increase in female and minority members.[3]

Notes

1 Gladwell M. (2008) *Outliers: The story of success*, Little, Brown and Company; San Francisco, CA

2 Kahneman, D. (2011) *Thinking, Fast and Slow*, New York: Farrar, Straus and Giroux

3 Gardner, D. M., Ryan, A. M., and Snoeyink, M. (2018) How are we doing? An examination of gender representation in industrial and organizational (I-O) psychology, *Industrial and Organizational Psychology*, 11(3), pp. 369–88, doi:10.1017/iop.2018.4 (archived at https://perma.cc/L5EU-Q3DZ)

29

GenAI: General Tips

Although the exciting world of AI technology (in particular the use of GenAI and chatbots) has hit the media just recently, the use of automation for decision-making for job candidates has already existed for over 30 years. For example, Kasey has built formulas that used candidate survey results to project their skill scores, and then these would combine to create an overall recommendation score. In other instances, Kasey and her colleagues built a series of narrative texts that were selected and displayed on candidate reports based on their survey responses. These are examples of simple automation and natural language processing that enables high volumes of reporting or scoring without human intervention.

In Part 3, we discussed some of the differences on the spectrum from automation to artificial intelligence. We might put it this way:

AI is an umbrella term that encompasses technology that is designed to have machines perform tasks like humans. Machine learning (ML), sometimes used interchangeably with AI, is a subset of technologies within AI that allow machines to learn from data and make decisions based on this data. For example, we might build formulas that use candidate survey results to project their skill scores, and then these would combine into an algorithm that generates an overall recommendation score. In simple terms, NLP is searching for and interpreting certain words or phrases, but does not take actions that are not human-programmed in the algorithm.

Table 29.1 provides a quick reference to differentiate the spectrum from automation to machine learning, as it applies to assessing candidates.[1]

In a pivotal example, consulting firms we knew leveraged trained models for candidate recommendations as far back as 2010, but many had to stop the process due to excessive bias and random outcomes. In the end, it's because the models were trained by humans, who have a tendency toward bias. We don't have a way to not train the models as humans, so

TABLE 29.1 Understanding the Spectrum of Technology Used in Candidate Assessment

Automation	Natural language processing	Machine learning	GenAI
Automating a task that was previously done by a human based on written rules or guidelines (often in the form of an algorithm). Rules remain exactly the same as the human programmed.	Using human language/words to "read" text (or audio or video) and moves them into categories. Analyzes sentiments, translates languages, or provides interpretations.	Building algorithms that use information from NLP (for example) to add to and improve the algorithm.	Generated content based on prompts into a system such as ChatGPT or others. As opposed to a custom machine learning application, this uses information from all over the web to generate content.
Example: An algorithm that adds up all the scores on given criteria (such as skills or abilities), and creates an average for use as an overall score. OR, an algorithm generates certain statements based on specific scores to provide narrative evaluation from numerical scores.	**Example:** An algorithm "reads" interview text from interview notes and suggests strengths or development areas based on key words determined in advance.	**Example:** A video-interview scoring system gathers data from inputs on future candidate performance on the job to assess additional characteristics which were not taken into account in the first iteration.	**Example:** Placing interview or other candidate assessment content into a chatbot and prompting the chatbot to provide a score based on certain skills and a rating scale.
Pros: Transparency and easy to understand how the results were generated. Works much faster than a human.	**Pros:** Flexibility to determine exact criteria and guidelines for analysis. Works much faster than a human.	**Pros:** May develop creative and/or more accurate interpretations of the data. Works much faster than a human.	**Pros:** May develop creative and/or more accurate interpretations of the data. Works much faster than a human.
Cons: Does not adapt, take into account a wider range of potential information, or become better at the prediction on account of collecting data.	**Cons:** Accounting for all the possible ways someone's skills and abilities can be assessed is extremely challenging. NLP often misses important interpretations, and other times over-interprets information that is not important.	**Cons:** It may not be clear how the results were determined or how the machine "learned," therefore it lacks transparency. In some cases, the machine learned based on something that was not accurate or useful and went down a wrong path, making all the results useless.	**Cons:** We have no clue how the decisions were derived or which source of data was used for scoring outside of our inputs. In some cases, even inputs added are ignored if the server becomes overwhelmed.

that problem will persist. The best way to manage this, as we discussed in Part 3, is to monitor how the algorithms affect the results and ensure it's not discriminating.[2,3,4,5,6]

If you plan to implement any systemic algorithms for selection decisions, we advise that you don't do it without a psychologist or trained data scientist who has a solid understanding of social sciences.

Tips for Using AI Effectively

Right now, those of us in consulting firms who need to generate content for clients have found interesting ways to use chatbots for analyzing data and creating content. Specifically, at APTMetrics, for example, where Kasey works, we create custom, secure chatbots for some clients and compare jobs in their company with our databases of similar jobs. Understanding how a job overlaps with others is a good way to start the job analysis process, but a chatbot compares a job to other jobs much faster than a human can.

Alternatively, we might also ask a chatbot to write a first draft of interview questions, skills definitions, or instructions for an interviewer. You can also use a chatbot to generate interview questions by prompting something like: "... write three behavioral interview questions for each of these skills: Collaboration, Results Drive, and Influence." The chatbot will give you more than you ever asked for in much less time than you can type it out, even if you already know what you want to write.

Examples of where we recommend chatbots for generating content are:

1 writing your interview questions
2 suggestions for how to evaluate great and not-great responses to those questions
3 names for skills
4 generation of technical questions and answers
5 benchmarks with other similar jobs in the industry or field of work
6 drafting candidate communications
7 draft feedback for candidates

Others will continue to be formed as the chatbots become more sophisticated. Whatever you do, it's never harmful to have another brain help you out with a first draft of something.

Some Caution

Although we're excited for the latest wave of accessibility of these tools, and the ability to teach a machine how to build something for us, we have some recommendations to share to ensure you're using GenAI for its strengths while recognizing some of the significant deficits when compared to human judgment.

While a chatbot can theoretically make a good decision or judgments based on access to far more data, the question is always "What data actually goes into that decision?" Meaning, where did the questions come from? You can ask a browser to do the same thing, but instead of just sending you a list of interview questions, the browser will point you to websites where interview questions exist. The browser will also probably try to connect you to consulting firms who can create interview guides for you. Although there is some commercial motive behind the order in which the search results appear (since companies pay browsers for higher rankings), you can see where they came from and evaluate the validity of the responses in a browser. For example, we may be more inclined to grab interview questions from a site that is a government office than from a blog post or social media. When a chatbot generates your interview questions, however, they could come from one single blog written by someone with zero interviewing experience who got annoyed about a bad job interview and wanted to write better questions. Or, it could come from a parents' group that recommends how to interview housekeepers. Is this the data you want? Maybe, or maybe not. For that reason, everything being returned should be fully audited. Even worse, what if you decide to research employment laws in your country, and the chatbot similarly pulls information from a random and incorrect blog rather than an official government website?

As of 2024, we, your authors, still feel more confident about our interview skills than we do our friendly chatbots.

As we discussed in Part 3, the chatbots do not return details on how the information was retrieved or where it came from. As of 2024, we also noticed that chatbots sometimes add random references for information (or complete nonsense). Other studies have found that chatbots often truncate the amount of data analyzed when the system is overloaded without informing you that the data was truncated.[7,8,9]

Nevertheless, as a first draft, chatbots can save a lot of time in coming up with the content you need. Just make sure to evaluate and edit what you find. Therefore, only use this approach if you have the knowledge to verify the information. As an example, you can compare this list to other lists of skills for the same job, such as at O*NET online. Always ensure your output is comprehensive and make a note to document the analysis and research that you conducted.

Notes

1 Morelli, N. (n.d.) SIOP White Paper Series Artificial Intelligence in Talent Assessment and Selection, www.siop.org/wp-content/uploads/2024/12/Artificial-Intelligence-in-Talent-Assessment-and-Selection.pdf (archived at https://perma. cc/4Q9J-QQFT)

2 Hao, K. (2021) Auditors are testing hiring algorithms for bias, but there's no easy fix, *MIT Technology Review*, February 11, www.technologyreview.com/2021/ 02/11/1017955/auditors-testing-ai-hiring-algorithms-bias-big-questions-remain/ (archived at https://perma.cc/5GQD-68KT)

3 Deloitte Insights (2020) AI model bias can damage trust more than you may know. But it doesn't have to, www2.deloitte.com/us/en/insights/focus/cognitive-technologies/ai-model-bias.html (archived at https://perma.cc/PE6Q-W2YN)

4 Willner, K. and Saba Murphy, C. (2022) Class action targeting video interview technology reminds employers of testing risks, Paul Hastings LLP, www. paulhastings.com/insights/client-alerts/class-action-targeting-video-interview-technology-reminds-employers-of (archived at https://perma.cc/84AX-YNV5)

5 Williams, K. Z., Schaffer, M. M., and Ellis, L. E. (2013) Legal risk in selection: An analysis of processes and tools, *Journal of Business Psychology*, 28, pp. 401–10, https://doi.org/10.1007/s10869-013-9299-4 (archived at https:// perma.cc/2R8G-98UM)

6 Dastin, J. (2018) Insight – Amazon scraps secret AI recruiting tool that showed bias against women, Reuters, www.reuters.com/article/world/insight-amazon-scraps-secret-ai-recruiting-tool-that-showed-bias-against-women-idUSKCN1MK0AG/ (archived at https://perma.cc/DKZ8-7S57)

7 Jones, N. (2024) Bigger AI chatbots more inclined to spew nonsense—and people don't always realize, *Nature*, www.nature.com/articles/d41586-024-03137-3 (archived at https://perma.cc/UW3G-WQS9)

8 Magette, L. (2023) Chatbot overload: How to keep your Chat GPT running smoothly during high traffic, Medium, https://medium.com/@nardo626364/ chatbot-overload-how-to-keep-your-chat-gpt-running-smoothly-during-high-traffic-8b04ad6e72cc (archived at https://perma.cc/79M8-6N26)

9 Zuckerman Institute (2023) Verbal nonsense reveals limitations of AI chatbots, https://zuckermaninstitute.columbia.edu/verbal-nonsense-reveals-limitations-ai-chatbots (archived at https://perma.cc/WG3P-ZH9T)

30

When the Standard Hiring Process Doesn't Fit

Job Profiles Versus Demographics

One of our HR friends headed People Operations at a trucking facility based in a rural area about an hour outside of Sacramento. She asked Kasey if her company should use a structured assessment for hiring. She explained that retention was an issue. She struggled not only with constant turnover, but frequent no-shows for her trucking roles. A consulting contact suggested that she could use more structure in their interviews to screen for the risk. However, she explained that often, candidates did not even show up for their job interview.

Actually, it turned out, the best predictor of tenure was the distance from home to the facility. Simply put, the closer someone lived to the workplace, the longer the likely tenure. She found the same to be true in a variety of other towns around the country who hired for manufacturing or processing facilities. As the HR leader went into more detail, it occurred to Kasey that anything gleaned in an interview was not terribly predictive, beyond just showing up to be interviewed. The data revealed that actually people like to work among others in their community, they want to be close to home while working, and they may want to socialize with the same people at work as in their communities. More research is needed to confirm this on a larger scale. In other work for a client—a large pharmaceutical facility—Kasey found that employees who lived closer had tenure averages of close to 30 years, significantly higher than those who did not live close by.

While proximity to work location seems like a good way to select candidates, in the United States we are not legally allowed to ask employees how far away they live or base an employment decision on their address. Our friend may not use this information as an assessment criterion. Even asking about someone's commute could be taken to be invasive about their status as a home-owner or other economic, non-job-related characteristics. Instead, she focused recruiting efforts more intentionally within the community through sponsoring events and visiting high schools or the community college. She did what she could to ensure structure existed in the interview process, but she also kept the candidate experience positive, concise, and job-related.

In the case described above, the HR team went through the process of creating a standard job profile, using the job profile to build interview questions, and asking each candidate the list of questions. They kept the interview short and also offered telephone interviews as a first step. This way, they reduced their time commitment on the process until candidates basically self-selected into the role. The probationary and training period was used to screen for safety and compliance behaviors on the job.

There are additional situations where your job profile may not be the best predictor of job performance. When we work with personality assessments, we attempt to find correlations between eventual job performance and how they performed on certain aspects of the assessment. Although we set up a hypothesis and prediction in advance of actually doing the study, we are occasionally wrong. Here's an example:

One of our consulting firms was tasked with predicting which physicians would be more likely to pass and then leverage training on a specific laparoscopic tool for surgeries. The company producing the tool had poured tremendous resources into the development and curation of the training, so they asked us to build a custom assessment that would prioritize training for those physicians who met the profile. Before we started our analysis, the talent manager let us know that she suspected the typical "doctor" profile was not going to be as predictive of eventual use as we would think.

What is a typical "doctor" profile? We imagined this to contain skills and qualities such as attention to detail, empathy, problem solving, or critical thinking, resilience, adaptability, ethics, time management, and maybe even a passion for medicine. We began our research with interviews with some of the doctors who were already known to use the new technology frequently. They confirmed that these skills were likely the most critical. Thus, we approached the study with this hypothesis.

This kind of research study we describe is how people in our field "prove" that an assessment is likely to actually predict higher job performance. It's called a *Concurrent Validation Study*.[1] We identified a list of doctors who had completed the client's training. Then, we asked the doctors to take an assessment in exchange for receiving a comprehensive report of their results. The assessment looked at a detailed list of personality traits in areas related to how they work with people, how they make decisions, and their typical energy level around work. We then gathered further data on the doctors regarding their typical use of the laparoscopic tool from the client (who had kept accurate records). Next, we calculated correlations to see which scales on the assessment were correlated with doctors using the tool. To our surprise, the strongest correlations were not the ones we hypothesized. These were also helpful, but we found that the strongest predictors were actually willingness to take risk, energy towards learning, innovation, and a healthy degree of "disruptive" thinking. It appeared that the profile of a physician who was prepared to actually change how they did surgery with new technology was agile, risk-taking, and open to change. Had we not performed this study, we would have significantly reduced the number of successes post-training.

In essence, even the subject matter experts, the doctors we interviewed, were unaware of what actually drove their own job performance. For some more complex roles, it is increasingly difficult for a person to understand what makes even themselves good at a job. In some cases, we still question the validity of the job profiles we built for common roles like software engineer, because we suspect that there are more personality traits at play than what is recognized by the technical focus placed in the interviews. If you suspect that more is happening "below the surface" in predicting job performance, we recommend reaching out to either of us through social media. You can also identify a test publishing firm to learn more. A qualified professional will help in setting up the research, running the statistical analyses, and ensuring that the results are accurate.

Job Profiles Versus Safety

In general, while this book aims to provide comprehensive guidance on conducting job analyses independently, it is important to note that certain roles may involve health or safety implications that require a more rigorous and specialized approach. Hiring managers and recruiters should exercise due diligence in such cases and ensure they follow appropriate procedures beyond the scope of this book. For positions where the well-being of individuals or the public is at stake, we recommend it essential to engage with experts or consulting firms well versed in health and safety considerations to conduct a more thorough job analysis. The responsibility for adhering to legal and regulatory requirements lies with the reader, so you will want to seek professional advice as necessary to meet all applicable standards. This book only purports to cover some aspects of conducting a job analysis for such roles where health and safety are key considerations for hiring practices (e.g. air traffic control, police officers, healthcare workers, etc.). The good news is that our field has conducted hundreds of research studies to guide assessments for these kinds of jobs. You are encouraged to prioritize safety and well-being for those use cases and the like.

Note

1 Irwing, P., Booth, T., and Hughes, D. J. (Eds.) (2018) *The Wiley Handbook of Psychometric Testing: A multidisciplinary reference on survey, scale and test development*, John Wiley & Sons

31

Concluding Thoughts

After conducting thousands of interviews for employee selection and development across all job levels and industries, we've been struck by how much wisdom and inspiration we've gained from our interviewees. We will leave you with some of these thoughts and some of our most powerful messages gained from candidates and interviewees throughout the years.

False Negatives—What Are We Missing?

We both interviewed with the same engineering leader for one of our consulting jobs. The leader, a thoughtful man with intense eye contact and a passion for assessment, wanted to understand precisely what we could do to eliminate the "false negatives" from the hiring process at the company. Meaning, how do we ensure that we don't incorrectly eliminate candidates from our hiring process?

We absolutely loved his question! And surprisingly, this question is rarely asked of us. Most of our discussions tend to focus on the false positives, in which people were hired who should not have been hired. Even this book focuses far more on false positives than false negatives as primary means to inspire the use of a structured process. Yet, the main impetus for many of us who do this work each and every day is to eliminate the false negatives—those people who were qualified but did not make it to hire.

Our client's question was backed with a crucial insight. He was convinced that if his company could rethink their approach, particularly with technical roles, they would gain valuable thought leadership, innovation, and competitiveness. As we went on to explore how interviews were conducted, we found interviewers constantly finding ways to reject candidates, instead of finding ways to include them.

Realizing that we've presented a number of scary scenarios of bad hires, once you have implemented solid structure in your process, shifting your mindset from *exclusion* to *inclusion* is massively important to your success as an assessor. Part of this shift involves training yourself to ask the question: "How can I learn about all the great things this candidate has to offer, as they apply to my job?" With our engineering leaders' support, we were able to work with the technical teams to craft an empowering communication that always focused on curiosity, probing, and openness to candidates, thereby increasing the company brand, candidate trust, and ultimately the quality of hires.

Finding Purpose in Any Job

After interviewing our fair share of business analysts, security managers, and network engineers, we're excited to report that even those jobs that seem straightforward or "mundane" can offer deep purpose and meaning. It turns out that saving lives is not the only thing that inspires purpose. One of our intentions in our work is to find a way to make every single job feel meaningful and fulfilling.

Here's an example:

A few years ago, Kasey consulted with a company that grew starter plants for agriculture systems throughout the US West. The client asked for a leadership development assessment for their Chief Science Officer (CSO), an engineer with 30 years' experience in sprinkler technology. She headed into the three-hour interview with a sense of dread. She readied herself to discuss center pivot, drip, and fixed spray systems, associated costs and the advantages and disadvantages of each. Instead, however, the CSO surprised her by asking the first question:

"Do you like raspberries?" Of course! (Who doesn't?) And thus began three of the most interesting hours she had ever spent. The CSO described, while answering questions about his approach to solving technology, economic, and people problems, the lifecycle of a berry from seed to farm production, giving insight to the environmental and even political factors faced in farming. World-wide food shortages, minimum wage policies, and corporate monopolies were all important considerations in this leader's job. Rising to the challenge, he had thoughtfully weighed the strategic impact of water usage throughout the farming process from the start of his career, reflecting on past mistakes and how to correct them. He had worked in the fields while taking classes at the local community college and continued to gain experience that led him to the eventual role of CSO. She felt like she was watching a documentary describing the history of agriculture in the West, told through the eyes of a deep expert. Three hours passed by far too quickly, and Kasey walked away believing that there is no such thing as a "tedious" or "boring" job. Instead, we are inspired by those employees who have the ability to make a job their own; growing something seemingly small into a much bigger impact.

Several years ago, Mollie interviewed a mid-level manager at a tech startup who was transitioning from a completely different industry: Education. On paper, she wasn't sure if they had all the technical qualifications listed in the job description, so she dug deeper. When she asked about their proudest professional achievement, they spoke about creating an after-school program for underprivileged students that ended up becoming a district-wide initiative. The candidate detailed how they convinced local businesses to sponsor laptops, navigated district bureaucracy, and built trust within the community. It became clear that this candidate had an extraordinary knack for building coalitions, a skill often more valuable than technical expertise in a fast-paced startup environment. They were offered the job and went on to launch a groundbreaking mentorship program that significantly reduced employee turnover in the company. The candidate stayed in touch with Mollie post-hire, sharing his ongoing achievements. He subsequently hired Mollie for leadership coaching and development when he was promoted a few years after the interview. This candidate reminded Mollie that it's important to go through your "checklist" and requirements, but you can't lose sight of the unique value each individual can bring to an organization.

A few years after that, Mollie interviewed another candidate, for a municipal recycling coordinator role, who left a lasting impact on her. It's the kind of job most people might overlook—handling logistics for waste management and ensuring compliance with recycling guidelines doesn't sound particularly thrilling. But as they spoke, she quickly realized how transformative this work could be in the right hands. The candidate shared a story about their time in a similar role in a small town. Faced with low participation rates and widespread apathy toward recycling, they made it their mission to change attitudes, not just policies. They organized community education campaigns, visited schools to engage young minds, and even spearheaded an initiative to showcase art installations made from recycled materials. The result wasn't just higher compliance with recycling guidelines, it was a cultural shift. Residents began seeing recycling as a point of pride, and businesses started collaborating to reduce waste. The town became a model for sustainable living in the region, earning awards and media recognition. What struck Mollie most was how the candidate approached a seemingly routine job with creativity, passion, and commitment to impact. By the end of the interview, she realized this wasn't just someone who managed recycling logistics; this was a changemaker who saw the potential for something bigger in every role they took on. Their story continues to inspire Mollie to see the possibilities for impact in every role.

We've been profoundly inspired by the candidates we've encountered over the years. Our interactions with them often transcend the typical application process, revealing something far richer. Each candidate represents a distinct journey filled with unique experiences, challenges, determination, and aspirations. Their stories—whether marked by triumphs or setbacks—remind us of our shared ability to persevere, grow, and achieve.

As we evaluate qualifications, we see more than skills and experience; we see the potential for transformation. These candidates are not just individuals seeking roles—they are future change-makers within their organizations, embodying possibility and progress. Their journeys continually inspire us to pursue excellence, foster empathy, and champion inclusivity in all we do.

Part 5 Summary: Key Learnings

In this part, we touched on the legal guidelines that can guide how we make decisions about interviews and candidates. We learned about the Civil Rights Act, the Uniform Guidelines, and potential pitfalls that could increase risk for yourself and your company.

We discussed best practices for ensuring compliance in hiring. We feel that it's easier to change your behavior (by using a structured process) than to try to change inherent biases.

We reviewed the historical context of anti-discrimination laws, like the Civil Rights Act and affirmative action in the United States, and privacy laws in Europe and California, and how laws impact hiring in large regions such as India and China. Regardless of where you hire, job-related data should guide hiring decisions, not personal characteristics.

We also covered ways you can continuously improve how you interview, and what to do if you suspect that a candidate has cheated on the interview.

We talked about GenAI, and ended with a few examples of how we've been personally inspired during interviews.

We also discussed candidate feedback post-interview, noting that while some HR teams avoid giving feedback to prevent disputes, privacy laws in places like Europe require transparency. Proper feedback, tailored to fair job criteria, can enhance the candidate experience and loyalty.

Part 5 Key Terms

Adverse impact: Occurs when a hiring practice disproportionately affects members of a protected group.

Affirmative action: Policies aimed at increasing opportunities for historically disadvantaged groups.

Behavioral interviews: Interviews where candidates describe past experiences to demonstrate their skills.

Candidate feedback: Information provided to job candidates after an interview about their performance.

Cheating: The act of deceitfully gaining an advantage in testing or assessments.

Civil Rights Act: Created in 1964, Title VII of the Civil Rights Act outlines rules about how you can assess and test people for jobs. US legislation prohibiting discrimination based on race, color, religion, sex, or national origin.

Continuous improvement: The ongoing effort to enhance job profiling and interviewing practices.

Diversity goals: Targets set to ensure a diverse workforce, which should not compromise job performance standards.

False negatives: Candidates who are wrongly excluded from hiring despite being qualified.

False positives: Candidates who are wrongly included in hiring despite being unqualified.

Generative AI (GenAI): AI tools used to create content, such as interview questions or feedback drafts.

Hairstyle discrimination: Discrimination based on hairstyles associated with race or ethnicity.

Job-related: A requirement or assessment that directly relates to job performance.

Job-related data: Information about a candidate's abilities relevant to the job, not personal characteristics.

Leakage: When interview questions are made public to prospective candidates

Microaggression: Subtle, often unintentional, discrimination against marginalized groups.

Privacy laws: Regulations that mandate candidates' rights to receive feedback about data collected during interviews.

Protected groups: Categories of individuals safeguarded from discrimination, including race, ethnicity, gender, nationality, religion, age, and disability status.

Structured job profile: A detailed outline of required qualifications, skills, and abilities for a specific job to guide fair hiring decisions.

The Uniform Guidelines: The Equal Employment Opportunity Commission's published guidelines on how to legally assess candidates for a job.

Uniform guidelines: Standards that ensure fair and non-discriminatory employment practices, guiding the validation of selection procedures.

Validation: The process of demonstrating that a test or assessment accurately measures job performance.

On April 23 2025 an Executive Order was issued directing federal agencies to eliminate the use of disparate impact liability "to the maximum degree possible." This directive stands in contrast to longstanding federal civil rights law, including Title VII of the Civil Rights Act of 1964 and judicial precedent established in Griggs v. Duke Power Co., 401 U.S. 424 (1971), which recognized disparate impact as a legitimate basis for identifying employment discrimination. While the order may influence short-term enforcement priorities for the agencies under the executive branch, it does not override statutes enacted by Congress or binding Supreme Court rulings and is expected to face significant legal and political challenges.

INDEX

NB: page numbers in *italic* indicate figures or tables

"996" 279–80

ad-hoc questions 127
adverse impact, defining 190, 305
affinity bias *131*
affirmative action 252
    defining 305
Age Discrimination in Employment Act 266
Airbnb 186–87
Allport, Gordon 250
Amazon 16, 113
    bias in recruitment 118
    rating scales 207
Americans with Disabilities Act (ADA) 266
analyze, defining 244
anchoring bias *131*
Apple 16, 113
applicant, defining 34
applicant tracking systems (ATS) 30, 31, 59
    defining 100, 190
    interview notes, storing 195, 203, 269
artificial intelligence (AI) 4, 95
    "AI Utopia," the 116, 119
    "black box," the 118
    generative artificial intelligence
        (GenAI) 6, 292–96
        caution with 295–96
        cheating, in interviews 145, 164
        to generate a rating scale 211
        to generate interview questions 129,
            135, 136, 294
        to generate skills 48, 52–53, 60, 294
        other applications 294
    impact on job profiles 95–98, *96*
    machine learning 292, *293*
    natural language processing (NLP),
        using 116–17, 292, *293*
    screening with
        bias, risks of 118
        "noise" 115–16
assessment, defining 34
automation 4, 6, 31, 292, *293*
    and legal liability 252
average rating, defining 244

Baidu 280

basic proficiency scale 80–81, *84*
"beer test," the 32, 105–07
Behavioral Anchored Rating Scales
        (BARS) 81–83, *82–83*, *85*, 160
behavioral interviews 134–37, *140*, 141
    defining 190, 305
    see also interviews
benchmarking 59–60
bias, avoiding 3, 4, 5, 7, 11, 32, 249–51
    AI, using 118, 292, 294
    cognitive errors 129–30, *131*, 244
    and diversity 11–12
    how to 12–13
    interview guide, the 155
    and legal liability 12
    multiple interviewers, using 183
    "necessary job functions" 267
    unstructured interviews, risks of
        124, 129
biographical interviews 137–38, *140*, 142
    defining 190
"black box," the 118
"Blitzscaling" 17
body language 165, 201
Boeing 22–23, 129–30
bucket method, defining 244
burnout 18
Bywater, James 273, 274, 275, 276

California Consumer Privacy Act
        (CCPA) 195
candidate, defining 34
candidate feedback
    defining 305
    in Europe and the UK 274–76
    in the US 268–70
centralized HR functions 29
central tendency error, defining 244
chatbots *see* generative artificial intelligence
        (GenAI)
cheating, in interviews 6, 283–84
    coding interviews 145, 164, 283–84
    defining 305
    preparing candidates 163–65
    versus leakage 284
Cisco 113

Civil Rights Act 266
    defining 305
Cochran, Ruth 177
coding interviews 145, 164, 283–84
cognitive errors 129–30, *131*, 244
competencies, defining 34
Concurrent Validation Study 298–99
confirmation bias *131*, 156
consistency, ensuring 3, 5
consultants, using 123
consumer scale, defining 244
continuous improvement, defining 305
contrast effect *131*
Covid-19 pandemic 16–17
C.R. Bard 22
cross-functional roles, interviewing for
        60, 178

data encryption 274
data minimization 198
data protection 198–99
Davol 22
decentralized HR teams 29–30
decision, making a
    defining 244
    multiple interviewers, using 240–42
    passing criteria 236–37
    qualified candidates
        too few 238–40
        too many 238
    "red flags" 236
Department of Labor 52, 249
desegregation, in the US 250
Dimon, Jamie 95
discrimination 249, 250
    in China 279
    hairstyles 253–54, 264, 305
    majority favoritism 264
    pay equity 22, 258–59
    perceived 262, 268
    protected groups 259, 306
    reverse discrimination 255
    in the US 252, 253–57, 259, 261, 262
diversity, encouraging 257–59, 260, 262,
        263, 291
    defining 305

Eichinger, Bob 53
equity agnostic job-related hiring 264
evidence-based rating, defining 244
evidence, writing up 199–203
exaggeration, in interviews 285–86, *285–86*

existing job data, researching *61*, 64–65, 66
expansion, rapid 17–18
explicit majority favoritism 264

FAANG companies (Facebook, Amazon,
        Apple, Netflix, Google) 113
Facebook (Meta) 16, 113
"false negatives" 301–02
    defining 305
first impressions bias *131*
focus groups, using *61*, 62–63, *62–63*, 66
follow-up questions 127–28
"free work," asking for 145–46

gender pay equity 22, 258–59
General Data Protection Regulation
        (GDPR) *195*, 198–99, 273–76
generative artificial intelligence (GenAI)
        6, 292–96
    caution with 295–96
    cheating, in interviews 145, 164
    defining 305
    to generate a rating scale 211
    to generate interview questions 129, 135,
        136, 294
    to generate skills 48, 52–53, 60, 294
    other applications 294
Gladwell, Malcolm 287
Goldman Sachs 22, 55
Google (Alphabet) 16, 113
    Google Forms 31, 187
    "Googleyness" 54–55
gratitude, showing 166

halo effect *131*, 156
hire/no hire decision, defining 245
hiring manager, the 30
    hiring manager-driven job analysis,
        using *61*, 65–66
    screening 178, 179
horns effect *131*, 156
HR, collaboration with 29–30

ignorant majority favoritism 264
implicit majority favoritism 264
inclusive job-related hiring 264–65
Indeed 31, 60, 119
Industrial-Organizational (I-O)
        psychology 7–8, 13, 14
Instacart 16
interrupting 166–67, 174, 175, 288, 289
interviewer time, cost of 19–21, 27

interviews
    behavioral interviews 134–37, *140*, 141
    bias, avoiding 129–30, *131*
    biographical interviews 137–38,
        140, 142
    body language 165, 201
    cognitive overload 175, 176
    confidentiality 146
    consultants, using 123
    control, taking 289
    evaluation of 227–33
    following up afterwards 288
    follow-up questions 127–28
    "free work," asking for 145–46
    gratitude, showing 166
    interrupting 166–67, 174, 175, 288, 289
    interview guide, the 154–62
    interview program, designing a 186–88
    multiple interviewers, using
        bias, avoiding 183
        cross-functional roles, interviewing
            for 60, 178
        decision, making a 240–42
        leading the team 181–82
        numbers, choosing 183–85
        roles, defining 182
    note-taking
        defining 245
        and legal liability 195, 198–99, 203
        recording, taking a 197–99
        summarized notes 196–97, 245
        transcription (verbatim notes)
            196, 245
    presentations 149–50, *150*
    probing questions 127–28, 171–77, 191,
        289–91
    question banks 123
    questions, writing 152–53
    "robotic," being 125–26, 165
    role plays 146–49, 191
    sequence, the 132
    shared situations, assessing 168–69
    situational interviews 138–39, *140*, 142
    STAR framework (Situation, Task,
        Action, Result) 140, 157,
        169–71, 172
        defining 191
        STAR + Why/How 175
    take-home exercises 151
    technical questions 143–46, 191
    training, importance of 141, 180,
        241–42

    trust, building 163–67
    unstructured interviews, risks of
        124–25, *125*
    vague responses 164
Isaac, Mike 43–44

job activities 49, *49*
job analysis
    activities 49, *49*, 74, *75*
    components of 70–71
    defining 34, 45–48, 100
    documenting 99
    effort required 86–88, *87*, *88*
    example activities and KSAs 75–77, *78*
    KSAs 35, 50–57, *78*
    methods for 59–67, *61*, *62–63*
    minimum qualifications 57–58, 101
    preferred qualifications 58, 101
    preparing for 69
    topics and sample questions 72–74
job description 91–92
    defining 34, 89, 101
job expert, defining 101
job profile 90–91, 99–100
    ad-hoc questions 127
    defining 34–35, 89, 101
    impact of AI on 95–98, *96*
    and legal liability 267
    reviewing 95
Jobs, Steve 106

KSAs
    abilities 55–57
    critical versus secondary 239
    defining 35, 50–57
    evaluation of 79–86, 190, 215–21, 244
        basic proficiency scale 80–81, *84*
        Behavioral Anchored Rating Scales
            (BARS) 81–83, *82–83*, *85*
        light and universal scale 79–80, *84*
    evidence, writing up 199–203
    "hard to teach" 238
    impact of AI on 97–98
    interview guide, the 154–62
    knowledge 50–51
    skills 52, 51–55
    weighting of 93–94, 101, 238

Law of Conservation of Mass 53
layoffs, impact of 17–18
"leakage," of interview questions 284, 285
    defining 306

learning circles 281
legal liability 5, 12, 22, 23
    in China 279–81
    discrimination 249, 250
        hairstyles 253–54, 264, 305
        in China 279
        majority favoritism 264
        pay equity 22, 258–59
        perceived 262, 268
        protected groups 259, 306
        reverse discrimination 255
        in the US 252, 253–57, 259, 261, 262
    in Europe and the UK
        AI, using 276
        candidate feedback 274–76
        data encryption 274
        interview notes 274
        subject access requests 275
    in India 278–79
    interview notes 195, 198–99, 203
    interview questions 124, 136
    in the US
        adverse impact 261
        AI, using 252
        candidate feedback 268–70
        diversity, encouraging 257–59, 260,
            262, 263
        job-related hiring 264–65
        majority favoritism 264
        "necessary job functions" 255–57,
            266–67
        quota-focused hiring 265
        retaliation 259
leniency bias 131
light and universal scale 79–80, 84
LinkedIn 31, 60, 89, 112, 119
Lion Air 129–30
lying, in interviews 285–86, 285–86

macroaggessions 250
Merck 22
microaggressions 250
    defining 306
Microsoft 16, 113
    Microsoft Forms 187
minimum qualifications (MQs) 111
    defining 57–58, 101
Ministry of Human Resources and Social
        Security (MOHRSS) 280
Moneyball 13
Munro-Delotto, Paige 253, 257, 258,
        259–60, 262, 265, 267, 268–69

natural language processing (NLP),
        using 116–17, 292, 293

"necessary job functions" 267
Neiman Marcus 13
Netflix 113
network, using your 31
newly-created roles, interviewing for 60
note-taking
    defining 245
    and legal liability 195, 198–99, 203
    recording, taking a 197–99
    summarized notes 196–97, 245
    transcription (verbatim notes) 196, 245

O*NET 52, 53, 55, 56, 59–60, 87, 296
observe and record, defining 245
online assessment 4
Oracle 22, 131

passing criteria 236–37
past behavior interviews 134–37, 140, 141
pay equity 22, 258–59
Peloton 17
Pennington, David 18–19, 21, 41, 105
Personal Information Protection Law 279
Polypropylene Hernia Mesh Products
        Liability Litigation 22
POSH Act (Sexual Harassment of Women
        at Workplace (Prevention,
        Prohibition and Redressal) Act,
        2013) 278
preferred qualifications (PQs)
    defining 58, 101
presentations 149–50, 150
privacy laws 269–70
    defining 306
probing questions 127–28, 171–77
    defining 191
proficiency levels, defining 245
protected groups 259, 306

question banks 123
questionnaires, using 61, 64, 66
quota-focused hiring 265

rating scale, choosing your 79–86, 207–13
    AI, using 211
    basic proficiency scale 80–81, 84
    Behavioral Anchored Rating Scales
        (BARS) 81–83, 82–83, 85
    defining 245
    light and universal scale 79–80, 84
    number of points 209, 209–10
recency bias 131
recruitment funnel, the 27–28, 28, 33, 36,
        109–10, 110
"red flags" 236

retaliation 259
reverse discrimination 255
Robert Half 22
"robotic," being 125–26, 165
role plays 146–49
    defining 191
Rotolo, Christopher 9

Salesforce 16
scenario-based interviews 138–39, *140*, 142
screening
    AI, using 115–19
        bias, risks of 118
        "black box," the 118
        natural language processing (NLP),
            using 116–17
        "noise" 115–16
    evaluation of 221–27
    interviews 119–21, 191
    manually 112–15
    methods for 110
    pilot studies, using 112
severity bias *131*
Shopify 17
Silzer, Rob and Jeanerette, Richard 3
similarity bias *131*, 156
situational interviews 138–39, *140*, 142
    defining 191
small businesses, hiring in 30–32
Starbucks 255
STAR framework (Situation, Task, Action,
        Result) 141, 157, 169–71, 172
    defining 191
    STAR + Why/How 175
Sterling Jewelers 22
Stixrud, Jora 115, 119
stress 23
stretching the truth, in interviews 285–86,
        285–86
strictness bias 233–34
    defining 245
Stripe 17
structured interviewing, defining 3, 35, 129
subject access requests 275
subject matter experts (SMEs) 31, 36

Super Pumped: The battle for Uber 43
surveys, using *61*, 64, 66

Tailang, Ankur 278
take-home exercises 151
technical roles, interviewing for
        143–46, 191
    AI, using 145, 164
    confidentiality 146
    "free work," asking for 145–46
training, cost of 23
TripAdvisor 207
trust, candidate 163–67
    body language 165, 201
    defining 190
    gratitude, showing 166
    interrupting 166–67, 174, 175, 288, 289
    preparing candidates 163–65
turnover, reducing 5

Uber 43–44
Uniform Guidelines 262, 267
    defining 306
unstructured interviews, risks of
        124–25, *125*
US Equal Employment Opportunity
        Commission (EEOC) 8, 86,
        254, 265
    EEOC guidelines, defining 100

validation, defining 306
Vioxx Products Liability Litigation 22

Walmart 16, 113
"war for talent" 18, 42
WeChat 280, 281
Weibo 280
weighting 93–94, 101, 238
Why/How technique 175
workload, increased 18, 23

Yang, Louis 279, 280–81
Yelp.com 207, 208

Zoom 16

Looking for another book?

Explore our award-winning
books from global business
experts in Human Resources,
Learning and Development

Scan the code to browse

www.koganpage.com/hr-learning-
development

More from Kogan Page

Kristin Saling

DATA-DRIVEN TALENT MANAGEMENT

Using analytics to improve employee experience

ISBN: 9781398615786

Kevin Wheeler **and** Bas van de Haterd

TALENT ACQUISITION EXCELLENCE

Using digital capabilities and analytics to improve recruitment

Foreword by Dave Ulrich

ISBN: 9781398614161

www.koganpage.com

EU Representative (GPSR)

Authorised Rep Compliance Ltd, Ground Floor, 71 Lower Baggot Street, Dublin, D02 P593, Ireland

www.arccompliance.com